The City in Roman Palestine

The City in Roman Palestine

Daniel Sperber

New York Oxford
OXFORD UNIVERSITY PRESS
1998

Oxford University Press

Oxford New York
Athens Auckland Bangkok Bogotá Buenos Aires
Calcutta Cape Town Chennai Dar es Salaam
Delhi Florence Hong Kong Istanbul Karachi
Kuala Lumpur Madrid Melbourne
Mexico City Mumbai Nairobi Paris São Paulo
Singapore Taipei Tokyo Toronto Warsaw

and associated companies in
Berlin Ibadan

Published by Oxford University Press, Inc.
198 Madison Avenue, New York, New York 10016

Library of Congress Cataloging-in-Publication Data
Sperber, Daniel.
The city in Roman Palestine / Daniel Sperber
p. cm.
Includes bibliographical references and index.
ISBN 0-19-509882-X
1. Cities and towns. Ancient—Palestine. 2. Palestine—Civilization—History—To 1500. 3. Jews—History—70-638
4. Rabbinical literature—History and criticism.
5. Palestine—Antiquities. I. Title
DS111.1.S74 1999
933'.009732—dc21 98-28559

1 3 5 7 9 8 6 4 2
Printed in the United States of America
on acid-free paper

Contents

Acknowledgments, vi

Abbreviations, vii

Introduction, 3

1. The Market: Physical Aspects, 9
2. Administration and Organization of the Market, 26
3. Market Control, 32
4. Pubs, Drunkards, and Licensing Laws, 48
5. On the Bathhouse, 58
6. Public Buildings, 73
7. Roads and Backstreets, 103
8. City Walls, 117
9. Water Supply, Sewage, and Drainage, 128
10. Archeology and the City, 149

Appendix 1: Unidentified "Public" Buildings, 188

Appendix 2: Urban Synagogues, 190

Index, 195

Acknowledgments

I should like to express my heartfelt thanks to my parents-in-law, Philip and Clare Magnus, for their never-ending help, to Mrs. Blanca Wintner for establishing in memory of her dear husband the Milan Roven Chair in Talmudic Research at Bar-Ilan University, of which I am the incumbent, and that over the years has greatly facilitated my ability to carry out my research. I thank my ten dear children for their encouragement, each in his or her own manner. Lastly, but most of all my thanks to my beloved wife, Chana, without whom none of this could have been.

Abbreviations

AJA	*American Journal of Archeology*
B	Bavli (Babylonian Talmud)
BA	*Biblical Archeology*
BASOR	*Bulletin of the American Society of Oriental Research*
BB	Baba Batra
BGU	*Berliner griechische Urkunden,* Berlin 1895–
BK	Baba Kama
BM	Baba Meẓia
Cant.	Canticles
CIG	*Corpus Inscriptionum Graecarum,* Berlin 1828–77
CIL	*Corpus Inscriptionum Latinarum,* Berlin 1862
Cod. Just.	Codex Justinianus
Eccles.	Ecclesiastes
ed.	editor, edition
EHHA	Ha-Encyclopedia ha-Ḥadashah le-Ḥafirot Archiolo giot be-Eretz-Israel
HA	*Ḥadshot Archiologiot*
HUCA	*Hebrew Union College Annual*
IEJ	*Israel Exploration Journal*
JESHO	*Journal of the Economic and Social History of the Orient*
JHS	*Journal of Hellenic Studies*
JJS	*Journal of Jewish Studies*
JQR	*Jewish Quarterly Review* (OS, Old Series; NS, New Series)
JSJ	*Jewish for the Study of Judaism*
JSS	*Journal of Semitic Studies*
Lev.	Leviticus
LSJ	Liddell, Scott and Jones, *A Greek–English Lexicon,* 9th ed., Oxford 1940–

M	Mishna
MGWJ	*Monatsschrift für Geschichte und Wissenschaft des Judentums*
Or	Oration
P	Papyrus
PWRE	Pauly-Wissowa Real-Encyclopädia
QDAP	*Quarterly of the Department of Antiquities for Palestine*
SEG	*Supplementum Epigraphicum Graecum,* ed. J. J. E. Hondius, Leyden 1923–
SEHHW	M. Rostovtzeff, *The Social and Economic History of the Hellenistic World,* Oxford, 1966
SEHRE	M. Rostovtzeff, *The Social and Economic History of the Roman Empire,* 2nd ed., Oxford, 1957
R.	Rabbi, Rav
REJ	*Revue des Etudes Juives*
T	Tosefta
Tert	Tertulian
VL	Variae Lectiones
Y	Yerushalmi (Palestinian Talmud)
ZDMG	*Zeitschrift der deutschen morgenländische Gesellschaft*

The City in Roman Palestine

Introduction

At the end of the introduction to my book *Roman Palestine, 200–400, the Land: Crisis and Change in Agrarian Society as Reflected in Rabbinic Sources* (1978), I wrote: "Finally, developments in the rural community cannot be divorced from those of the urban community. The two communities are mutually interdependent, their interactions significant for each as for both. This I hope will be shown in a future volume dealing with the conditions of urban life during the same centuries" (p. 2). Some fifteen years have passed, and I have still not fulfilled that hope. This volume only satisfies my promise of a supplementary volume in a partial manner. Whereas the two former volumes, *Roman Palestine, 200–400, Money and Prices* (1974; 2nd edition, 1991) and the volume quoted above, presented a socioeconomic historical thesis, the present volume does not.[1] Hence its chronological parameters have been broadened to encompass much of the Tannaitic period, and it covers a period of some three hundred years, from ca. 100 to 400 C.E.

Unlike the present-day studies of ancient urban history, it does not deal with a specific city—for example, Tiberias, Sepphoris, Caesarea, or Lod—and is thus unlike the excellent studies of Lee I. Levine on Caesarea, Joshua J. Schwartz on Lod, Stuart S. Miller on Sepphoris, Gustav Hermansen on Ostia, and more recently, Donald W. Engels on Roman Corinth.[2] My book synthesizes what is known of urban life in Talmudic Palestine and hence deals with a theoretical, nonexistent, "synthetic" city."[3] The reader will readily see that I have been greatly influenced by Jerome Carcopino's seminal work on everyday life in Roman times, the classic *Daily Life in Ancient Rome*, which to a great extent set the tone for this genre of writing. However, he was writing about a specific town. In a sense, my narrative is closer in character to A. H. M. Jones's paradigmatic *The Greek City from Alexander to Justinian.* I have also been somewhat influenced by W. A. Becker's *Gallus, or Roman Scenes of the Time of Augustus*, although from a literary point of view, his work is closer to historical fiction.[4]

This volume does not attempt to cover all aspects of Palestinian urban life; only key subjects have been selected in accordance with the evidence and my own understanding of it. Thus, I have described the physical aspects of the city,[5] its markets, pubs, streets, bathhouses, and so on, more than I have its inhabitants. Hence, I have not discussed

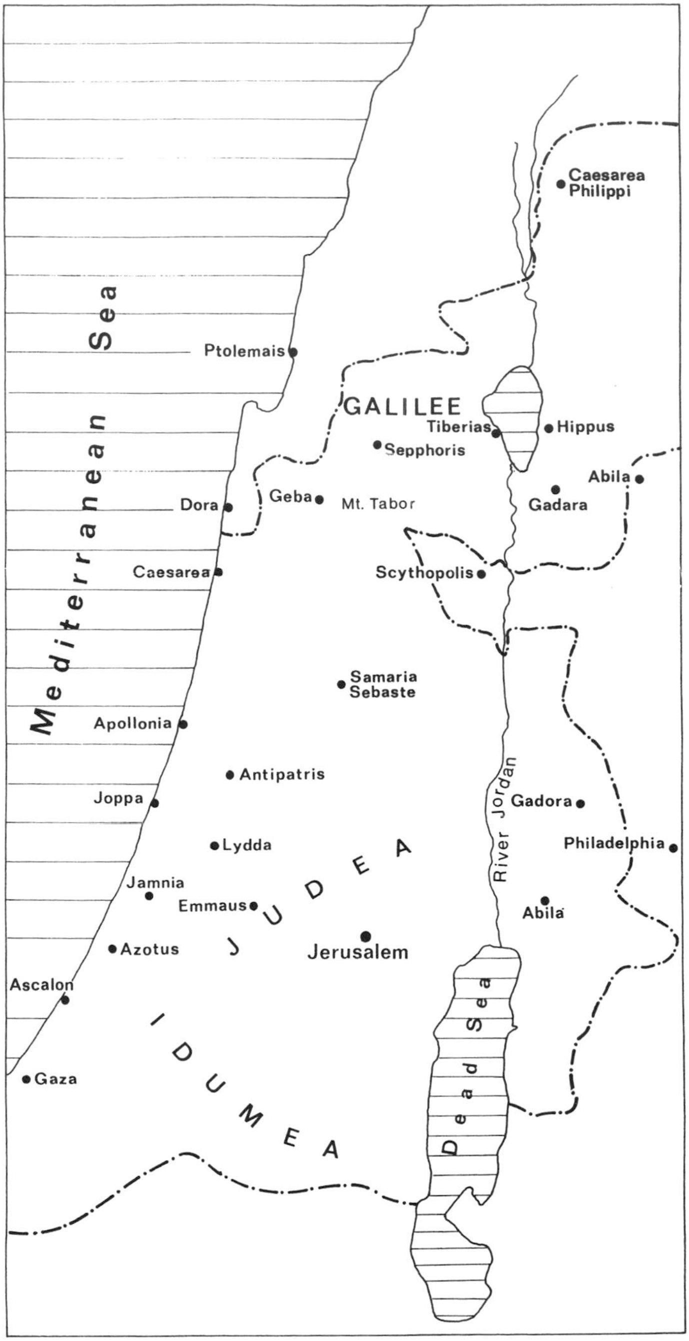

Figure 1. Major cities in the land of Israel with archeological remains during the Roman period.

urban trade, crafts, and family life. This volume is selective in subject matter, partial in description, and synthetic in conception.

A fine start was already made in this direction in 1910 by Samuel Krauss, the pioneer of Talmudic archeology, in his invaluable *Talmudische Archäologie*, albeit within a different structural presentation and in a more organized fashion than in his Hebrew version of 1924, entitled *Kadmoniyyot-ha-Talmud*.[6] However, his work is marred by several methodological flaws, the most serious of which is a lack of clear distinction between Palestinian and Babylonian material.[7] Furthermore, in the intervening seventy-odd years a great deal of new material has become available, most especially in the area of archeological evidence, enabling us to move forward very considerably in this field.[8]

As I've indicated, the literary sources are readily available and the archeological evidence is sufficiently rich and well analyzed to enable an attempt at such an overall view. And even if we jump about from Judaea to the Galilee, from maritime port towns to inland cities perched on hilltops, and from the first to the fourth centuries, I believe the conclusions and the resulting descriptions are legitimate, valid, and generally reflect the historical truth. I therefore trust that the reader, ever aware of the conceptual framework of this volume, will gain greater insight into the life and times of the towns of Roman Palestine; those who study the Talmud regularly will also gain a deeper understanding of the *sugyot* and the real-life background of their legalistic discussions.[9]

With my conceptual plans formulated, my literary agenda crystallized, and most of the manuscript completed, I became ever more aware of the fact that I could not, in good conscience, present the public with my "synthesized" conclusions without giving some kind of survey of the scope of the archeological evidence. I therefore turned to my good friend and colleague Joshua J. Schwartz, a well-known authority in the field of the historical geography of Roman Palestine, and asked him if he would be willing to contribute a brief chapter or appendix reviewing this material. He readily acceded to my request, and the results exceeded all my expectations. Rather than the thumbnail sketch that I had anticipated, he rendered the subject in a deep and comprehensive manner, demonstrating his full control of the material in the context of this period. I wish here to express my heartfelt gratitude to him for his effort in enriching this book.

With his contribution in hand, I then had to consider whether to attempt to integrate the body of evidence into my own writing or to leave it intact. The latter was not merely the easier and more convenient alternative but also the more satisfactory one: We see both the complementary nature of the two bodies of evidence and the occasional lack of correspondence between them. The fact that the archeological findings do not always bear out what the literary sources seem to suggest may be explained in a number of different ways: the basically different nature of the two sets of evidence, the "happenstance" element in the survival of archeological artifacts as well as literary records, the extent to which a Rabbinic halachic or homiletic source reflects current reality as opposed to an archaic (scripture-based?) situation or a nonreal legalistic construction. I suspect that in every case of such a divergency, a careful analysis of the possible causes by a Talmudist and by an archeologist would lead to different results. Hence, leaving the two bodies of evidence as discrete entities will demonstrate their complementary character as well as their occasionally contradictory nature. The juxtaposition of these two sections may thus solve some problems while posing others, opening the way to further areas of study, research, and analysis.

Notes

1. The two former volumes were both published by Bar-Ilan University Press (Ramat-Gan, Israel).

2. L. Levine, *Caesarea under Roman Rule* (Leiden, 1975); J. Schwartz, *Lod (Lydda), Israel: From Its Origins through the Byzantine Period, 5600 B.C.E.–640 C.E.* (Oxford, 1991); S. Miller, *Studies in the History and Traditions of Sepphoris* (Leiden, 1984); G. Hermansen, *Ostia: Aspects of Roman City Life* (Edmonton, 1982); and D. W. Engels, *Roman Corinth: An Alternative Model for the Classical City* (Chicago, 1990). See also Y. Ne'aman, *Sepphoris in the Period of the Second Temple: The Mishna and the Talmud* (Jerusalem, 1993) [in Hebrew].

3. Here I should like to call attention to the fascinating book by Xavier Hernáandez, illustrated by Jordi Ballonga, entitled *Barmi: A Mediterranean City through the Ages* (1st American ed.; Boston, 1990) that describes with words and pictures the historical evolution of a fictional city which did not exist but which "could exist . . . almost anywhere in the Mediterranean coastal zone . . . [and] is a composite of these southern European cities to which Western civilization owes so much" (inside cover). It should be noted that I have not attempted clearly to define the differences between village, town, and city. I use the terms *town* and *city* interchangeably. For the methodological problems involved in such distinctions, see F. Abbott and A. Johnson, *Municipal Administration in the Roman Empire* (1926; reprint, New York, 1968), p. 24.

4. See J. Carcopino, *Daily Life in Ancient Rome* (Harmondsworth, 1956); A. H. M. Jones, *The Greek City from Alexander to Justinian* (Oxford, 1940); and W. A. Becker, *Gallus, or Roman Scenes of the Time of Augustus*,[2] trans. F. Metcalfe (London, New York, Bombay, and Calcutta, 1907).

5. Although I have not dealt with Palestinian-Roman town planning systematically, I am assuming a basic knowledge of the main principles in the field. The standard works are H. Haverfield, *Ancient Town Planning* (Oxford, 1913); R. Martin, *L'Urbanisme dans la Grèce Antique* (Paris, 1974); F. Castagnoli, *Orthogonal Town Planning in Antiquity* (Cambridge, Mass.: 1971); J. B. Ward-Perkins, *Cities of Ancient Greece and Italy: Planning in Antiquity* (London, 1974); and, most recently, the fine synthetic study by E. J. Owens, *The City in the Greek and Roman World* (London, 1992), which contains a full bibliography and which may now readily be used as a standard introductory textbook. Attention should also be given to Lewis Mumford's seminal work *The City in History* (London, 1966).

6. S. Krauss, *Talmudische Archäologie*, 3 vols. (Leipzig, 1910–12); reprint, (Hildesheim, 1966); Krauss, *Kadmoniyyot ha-Talmud*, vol. 1, part 1 (Berlin and Vienna, 1924). Actually this first volume was originally published in Odessa (Moriah) in 1914 (see introductory note in 1924 edition, vol. 2, part 1) and is now quite rare. *Kadmoniyyot ha-Talmud* is not a translation of the earlier German version but a complete reworking, and the section on the town is new. The first edition contains a short but valuable introduction, which was omitted in the second edition.

7. For a detailed analysis of the failings of this work, see the introduction to my *Material Culture in Eretz-Yisrael during the Talmudic Period* (Jerusalem, 1993) [in Hebrew]. Krauss, in his introduction to *Kadmoniyyot* (first edition, see note 6 above), addressed this issue, showing his awareness of the problematic nature of his methodology and nonetheless justifying it. However, his arguments are not convincing.

8. I should also like to refer the reader to the excellent study of Yaron Dan, *The City in Ereẓ-Yisrael during the Late Roman and Byzantine Periods* (Jerusalem, 1984) [in Hebrew], with its fine analysis of municipal administration and commercial activity. Its most significant contribution is its analysis of the Byzantine period.

9. Here I should like to make a further methodological observation. One may readily assume that there was a considerable difference between the physical organization of villages and that of towns. Villages tended to be less planned and more the result of "disorganized" growth. Towns, in contrast, were usually better laid out and had impressive public buildings, broad commercial areas, and better roads. In Rabbinic sources, it is often difficult to know whether a text is referring to a town or a village. Town side streets were probably wider than village alleyways, for example. A fine analysis of a village in Samaria from the Mishnaic period (first and second centuries C.E.) is the work by S. Dar, Z. Safrai, and Y. Tepper, *Um Rihan: A Village of the Mishnah* (Israel, 1986) [in Hebrew]. Here Rabbinic sources were utilized to interpret the archeological findings. The sources referred to—presumably this was Safrai's contribution—were assumed to reflect the village scene. In some cases I have used the same sources, interpreting them somewhat differently because my assumption was that they reflect the city scene. Scholars will have to judge which is the more convincing interpretation.

1

The Market: Physical Aspects

The Forum Market Type

One of the most distinctive features of the urban landscape in antiquity was undoubtedly the marketplace or, more exactly, the market area. In Roman Palestine this at times was organized around a large open space surrounded by colonnades with buildings containing shops and stalls or booths between the columns, much as in a Roman forum. Here people came from villages to sell their wares,[1] perhaps bringing them on a donkey laden with panniers,[2] while the locals sat comfortably in their permanent locations and plied their trades. This seems to have been the case in Caesarea. In Y. Baba Kama 2.5,3c we read of a man who brought his קלטירא *[sic]*, chair (בפורא) into the forum,[3] and a muleteer (חמר) passed by and broke it. The case came before Rabbi Isaac bar Tavlai (flr. ca. 280–320 C.E.) who ruled that the muleteer did not have to pay any damages because the forum is a public area (and anyone who places an object in a public area assumes the risk of its being damaged). Lieberman[4] has demonstrated that this text refers to Caesarea, a center of the Palestinian Roman administration, and hence the use of the Latin term *forum* rather than its Greek equivalent *agora*.[5] This kind of open space market area may be what is frequently referred to as סרטיא ופלטיא—*strata* and *platea* (πλατεῖα),[6] suggesting wide streets (*strata*) or crossroads opening onto a broad open area (*platea*).[7] Through these streets passed not only muleteers but also fully laden camels, carriages, and other heavy traffic.[8]

Street Lined with Shops Type of Market

In other places the market was not in an entirely open area, and was not an agora in the full Greek sense, but was rather more like a street lined with shops and booths, apparently with residential units actually within the market area[9] (fig. 1.1). This seems to have been the case in Lod (Lydda),[10] as we may derive from a text in Y. Moed Katan 3, 81d:

> One time [Rabbi Eliezer, late first century C.E.] was passing through the market and saw a woman sweeping (refuse out of her) house, and she threw it [out] and it fell on his head.

Figure 1.1. Palladius Street: street and adjacent buildings, looking west. In center (from left to right), *propylaeum*, row of shops and west portico, *exedra*, and remains of Odeon; behind them, bathhouse; below, east portico and lower shops. (From *Excavations and Surveys in Israel*, vol. 2, The Bet Shean Excavation Project (1989–1991) (Jerusalem, 1993), p. vii, fig. F. Used with permission.).

Multistory Buildings Next to the Marketplace

Clearly, the woman's house was close to the market and most probably inside it. Apparently, she lived on the second floor, on top of one of the shops of the petty craftsmen and retailers, and threw the refuse down into the unroofed center of the street.[11] We are reminded of Juvenal (died 130 C.E.) Satires 3.269–72, who, writing on the dangers of living in Rome and walking the streets at night, cautions us thus: "You should therefore pray and carry with you this pitiable wish: that people may be content to empty over you, from their windows, only an open basin (i.e., a basin of dirty water or food slops, and not a chamber pot)."[12] Indeed the *Digesta* has many passages referring to such incidents, and Ulpian (died 228 C.E.) clarifies the various clues by which it might be possible to trace the culprit of such unacceptable behavior.[13]

Lack of Water in Upper Stories

Jerome Carcopino in his classic, *Daily Life in Ancient Rome*, justifies such irresponsible actions when describing the situation in Rome:

> The tenants of the upper *cenacula* had to go and draw their water from the nearest fountain. The higher the flat was perched, the harder the task of carrying water to scrub the floors and walls of those crowded *contig-*

> *nationes*. It must be confessed that the lack of plentiful water for washing invited the tenants of many Roman *cenacula* to allow filth to accumulate, and it was inevitable that many succumbed to the temptation for lack of a water system such as never existed save in the imagination of two optimistic archeologists. . . . There were other poor devils who found their stairs too steep and the road to the dung pits too long, and to save themselves further trouble would empty the contents of their chamber pots from their heights into the streets. So much the worse for the passer-by who happened to intercept the unwelcome gift.[14]

In this context we may, perhaps, understand the Mishna in Baba Kama 3.2, which rules that "he who pours out water in a public place, and someone was damaged by it, he [who poured it] is liable for the damages." Perhaps a more auspicious arrangement was one in which the ground story was used for a shop and the upper story served as a storage space.[15]

The Colonnades

As I've mentioned, the shops were often to be found under the colonnades, or *stoa* (איסטיב).[16] In the case of two-story buildings facing onto the colonnaded area, the Tosefta rules:[17] "Shops opening onto the *stoa*, the bottom one pays [expenses] for the ceiling (תקרא) [above him], and the upper one pays for the roof (מעזיבה)."[18] The ground floor shops opened onto the *stoa*, which in turn faced the *platea*, as described in Tosefta Shabbat: "He who throws [something] from a shop via the *stoa* into the *platea* . . . ."[19] It would appear that in some cases there was also a double row of columns supporting the colonnade, with the columns not placed opposite one another (see B. Shabbat 7a). The columns themselves had, on occasions, ornate capitals, which protruded well beyond the breadth of the base.[20]

Tradesmen's Guilds

Leading off from the broad open *platea* were the smaller alleyways (מבואות) that were usually also filled with shops and booths.[21] These *mevo'ot* (also called *shuka*) often had a concentration of specialized traders and craftsmen, perhaps organized in some kind of guild framework (*collegia*). Thus, in Tiberias we find markets for potters and basket weavers, for the manufacture of sacks, and for the production of wooden planks.[22] Indeed, in Y. Moed Katan 2, 81b we read of the following incident:[23]

> The guild of flax traders (חנוותא דכיתנאי)[24] held a meeting,[25] and there was [among their members] a man by the name of Bar Ḥubaz who did not attend. They said: What shall we eat today? One replied: Ḥubaz (i.e., cheese). The official said: Let Bar Ḥubaz be summoned. R. Yoḥanan said: This man made a hidden denunciation.

We find then that the shops (חנוותא) are organized into guilds (*collegia*) according to trade and specialty.[26]

There was also the low-life area, with its brothel (שוקא דזונות), mentioned specifically in B. Pesaḥim 13b. But the main market in Tiberias, called the אסרטיון (*strateion*) or דרמוס (δρόμος),[27] was the key area, because the market prices were fixed there.[28]

Display of Wares

As I mentioned before, the marketplace was often surrounded by colonnades, with stalls placed between the columns, and the city drew a handsome revenue from the rental of these sites.[29] Some merchants had permanent places in the market—perhaps like the one who placed his chair there. Merchants locked up their stores at night, either raising a shutter and locking it at the top or inserting a shutter into slots and locking it.[30] The poor merchants sought out a spot on which to hang their box of paltry wares on a hook fixed into one of the columns.[31] So would the merchant hawk his wares, loudly crying out to advertise his stock.[32] Often the salesman moved his products out of the private shop area or out of the covered stalls into the public areas. In those places where the side streets were so narrow as to allow no more than a single carriage to pass by, the rising tide of outspread merchandise blocked the passage of traffic.[33] This practice continued until Domitian (81–96 C.E.) intervened with an edict forbidding the display of wares in the street. His edict is commemorated in the epigram: "Thanks to you Germanus, no pillar[34] is now girt with drained flagons, . . . nor do the grimy cook-shops monopolize the public way. Barber, tavern-keeper, cook and butcher keep within their own threshold. Now Rome exists, which so recently was one vast shop."[35] The situation in Roman Palestine was not so critical, and as we have already seen, the columns of the colonnaded *stoa* were still being used to display wares in the early third century. Wares were exhibited outside the actual confines of the shops, as we learn from a passage in Genesis Rabba 19.5, ed. Theodor p. 175, where Rabbi Berechia in the name of Rabbi Akiva (died ca. 135) tells of a blind man (עירוני)[36] who was passing by a glass-vendor's shop. In front of him, on the street, was a box[37] containing glasses and *diatreta*, cut or engraved glass vessels. The blind man swung his stick (הפשיל במקלו) and inadvertently broke the glassware. The vendor caught hold of him and said to him: "I know I can't get anything (payment of damages) out of you (דלית אנא מהני מינך כלום), but come, let me [at least] show you how much valuable merchandise you have destroyed." Furthermore, the Talmud (B. Baba Kama 27b, Y. Bama Kama 3.1) tell of cases in which a potter obstructs the public thoroughfare with his jars (בממלא את כל רשות הרבים), and at times passersby had to break their way through with a staff or trample their way across (Y. Baba Kama 3.1; אלא יטול המקל וישברנה או יעבור עליה). This, then, was common practice, and the vendor sold his wares at his own risk.[38]

Awnings

Presumably when the wares were spread out in the street outside the shop and perhaps even outside the colonnades, they would have to be shielded from the burning summer sun or from the winter downpours. To this end, the shopkeepers put up flimsy awnings of plaited wickerwork and the like, which extended into the public area;[39] at times they would even sleep under these temporary shelters.[40]

Lighting and Fire Hazards

It appears that there was relatively little public lighting in the markets and streets.[41] Indeed, Rabbinic literature is replete with references to "dark alleys" (מבואות אפלות).[42] Both in the narrow alleyways, as well as in those shops situated within the covered portico area, natural light would be dim by day and gloomy in the evening and had to be augmented by candlelight, either simple lamps[43] or more elaborate fixtures.[44] For this reason the danger of fire[45] was always imminent, especially in the upper stories, which often served as storage areas, were less accessible to water and generally had wooden-beamed roofs.[46] Hence, the well-known Rabbinic phrase: נשרפו חטיך בעליה—Your grain has been burned up in the loft.[47] Or, in the words of Juvenal: "Smoke is pouring out of your third-floor[48] attic; but you know nothing of it; if the alarm begins on the second floor, the last man to burn will be he who has nothing to shelter him from the rain but the tiles, where the gentle doves lay their eggs."[49] Indeed, the same poet writes: "No, no, I must live where there is no fire, and the night is free from alarms."[50] Small wonder the Sages ruled (M. Baba Meẓia 2.3) that one must not open a bakery (חנות של נחתומין) or a place for dyeing fabrics under a neighbor's storage area (אוצרו של חברו). Here again, the storehouse is on the second floor, and a business such as a bakery would endanger the safety of the stocks in storage.[51]

Lack of Fire Brigades

In Rome, where never a day passed without several outbreaks of fire,[52] there was a special fire-fighting corps, called *vigiles*, and the *praefectus vigilum*, captain of the fire brigades, reminded the commandant of the Roman firemen that it was his duty to warn tenants always to have water ready in their rooms to check an outbreak.[53]

Although there is, to the best of my knowledge, no mention in Rabbinic sources of the *vigiles*, there may be a reference to an official police unit, which also served occasionally as a fire-fighting unit. In T. Shabbat 13.9, ed. Lieberman p. 60, the following is thus related:

> It once happened that a fire broke out not in the courtyard of Joseph ben Simai of Shiḥin, and the men of the *castra* of Sepphoris came to

> extinguish it. But he did not permit them [to do so]. A cloud descended and extinguished [the fire]. But the Sages said: He did not have to [prevent them from extinguishing it]. Nonetheless, on the night following the Sabbath he (Joseph) sent to each of them (the men of the *castra*) a *sela* (= 4 *denarii*) and to the prefect (הפרכוס) [he sent] fifty *dinarin* (= *denarii*).

This text has been studied in great depth and detail by Stuart E. Miller,[54] who dates it to the late first or early second century C.E. After a long and careful discussion, he accepts Lieberman's suggestion[55] that הפרכוס here is a *hipparchos*, a kind of "chief of police" who had a force of mounted constables (διωγμῖται), a small detachment of which that served to extinguish the blaze on Joseph ben Simai's property.[56] However, we cannot by any means conclude from this example that there were in major Palestinian cities during the Roman period well-organized fire-fighting units, as was the case in Italy, where they were known as *collegia dendrophororum et centonariorum*.[57] And just as the *vigiles* do not figure in Rabbinic literature, neither do the *centonarii*. However, this absence should not surprise us. A. H. M. Jones has already noted:

> Precautions against fires were as a rule most inadequate. Nicomedia in Trajan's reign had no apparatus and no brigade; and though Pliny (Ep. 10.33–34) saw to it that in the future hoses and hooks (for pulling down adjacent buildings and thus isolating the outbreak) should be available, he was unable to persuade the emperor to allow him to establish a volunteer fire-brigade, such as existed in many Italian cities.[58] The reasons which Trajan gave for his refusal were based on local circumstances; Bythnia, and Nicomedia in particular, was a hotbed of factions, and any association would inevitably be turned to political ends. But a story in the life of Polycarp (Vita Polycarpi 28, 29) reveals that in Smyrna also at this date, though apparatus was provided, the general public was expected to turn out to extinguish fires. This suggests that the imperial government, at this time at any rate, uniformly forbade the formation of fire-brigades in eastern cities; there is no evidence that it later changed its policy.[59]

This surely explains the absence of a reference to *vigiles* or *centonarii* in (Palestinian) Rabbinic literature.

Running Water in Public Places

In many Palestinian towns there was running water in the streets and public areas and probably most particularly in the market area, where animals had to be watered and the street vendors spending long hours in the heat had to refresh themselves with drink. T. Eruvin 7.3, ed. Lieberman p. 127, speaks of a water canal (אמת מים) running through the public area (רשות הרבים), and in T. Eruvin 6.26, ed. Lieberman p. 126, we read of such a canal running through Sepphoris. Similarly, there were public wells (M. Eruvin 10.14; T. Eruvin 8.22, ed. Lieberman p. 138) and piping systems that ran through the city (סילונות שבכרכים) (T. Eruvin 6.18, ed. Lieberman p. 123; T. Avoda Zara 5.6, ed. Zuckermandel p. 469). In addition, there were public fountains fashioned in the shape of "faces" that spat forth water (פרצופות המטילין מים) (T. Avoda Zara 5.6, ed. Zuckermandel p. 469), perhaps part of the *nympheion* (Tanḥuma Exodus, Mishpatim 8,108a).[60]

Positioned at certain key points in the market area were blocks of stone upon which the porters (*saccarii*) could place their heavy burdens when lifting them on or taking them off their backs.[61] They were similar to the βάθρα, blocks of stone, set up in the ἐμπόριον of Smyrna for the φορτηγοί, porters, called the Ἀσκληπιασταί, which according to an early second century inscription,[62] were used for sitting while waiting for customers and for resting loads in passing.[63] Porters using these stones were a familiar sight; each carried a bag, *sacculum*, over his shoulder.[64]

Shops, Brothels, and Prostitutes

I have already mentioned the "market of prostitutes," which apparently was an overt "red-light" district. In addition, there were other less obvious institutions that afforded similar services. They "fronted" as taverns, food shops, pubs, and so forth, but a patron entering one of these might well find himself entrapped in "a house of pleasure." This emerges from a careful reading of Sifrei Numbers sec. 131, ed. Horowitz pp. 170–71.[65] The text is an exposition on the Biblical verses in Numbers 25:1–2:

> And the people of Israel abode in Shittim, and the people began to commit whoredom with the daughters of Moab. And they called the people unto the sacrifices of their gods, and the people did eat and bowed down to their gods.

On this the Sifrei has the following aggadic elaboration:

> At that hour the Amonites and the Moabites came and built themselves מקולין—*macellum*,[66] a food market, and placed in them women selling all kinds of sweetmeats (כסנין), and [the children of] Israel would eat and drink. Then a[n Israelite] man would take a stroll in the marketplace and wish to purchase something from an old woman, and she would sell it for its [market] price,[67] whilst a young [girl] would call out to him from inside [the shop saying]: Come [in], and purchase it for less. And he would buy from her on the first and the second day. And on the third [day] she would say to him: Won't you come in and choose for yourself? Are you not a good friend (בן בית)? And he would enter and next to her was a [stone] pitcher (צרצור)[68] full of "Amonite wine. . . . Would you like to drink [some] wine?" she says to him, and he drinks. And the wine would burn within him.[69] And he says: Give yourself to me. And she takes out from beneath her breastband (פסיקיא, *fascia*) a cast (דפוס) of [the idol] Peor, and says to him: Rabbi (or my master), you wish me to give myself unto you? Bow down

> before this [idol, and I will do so]. And he retorts: "Would I bow down before an idol! And she replies: What difference does it make to you? Just bare yourself before him. . . .

The details of this Midrash are, of course, determined (in part) by the Biblical narrative, which mentions eating, idolatry, and prostitution. These elements are picked up by our homilist and worked into his Midrash, which stresses the two evils, idolatry and prostitution. But the basic picture emerging from this text (in its various versions) is one of a marketplace with stalls or shops selling a variety of products. Some of these shops front for brothels. The old hag, the "procuress" who sits outside, reminds us of the "old prostitute" (זונה זקינה—παλαιὰ πόρνη) mentioned in Leviticus Rabba 33.6.[70] It is she who cunningly traps the robust young man into the charms of the youthful and comely maiden waiting inside. Indeed, markets were notorious as places of prostitution, and we can find many references to them. In B. Shabbat 33b we find Rabbi Simeon ben Yohai (mid-second century C.E.) accusing the Romans of building marketplaces only to be able to establish houses of prostitution. And in B. Pesaḥim 113b we read of Rabbi Ḥiyya and Rabbi Oshaya, two early third-century authorities, working as cobblers in the שוקא דזונות, the market of prostitutes (probably Tiberias),[71] and making shoes for the prostitutes without actually looking at them.

Business establishments serving as fronts for prostitution is, of course, a fairly universal phenomenon, and it is not therefore surprising to find this reflected in our sources. An interesting parallel occurred in Rome, where gambling constituted a major problem and was forbidden by law. Again Carcopino's classic, *Daily Life in Ancient Rome*, provides an illustration:

> . . . There is no doubt that the idler had but to make a slight detour in his daily walk to find an opportunity of secretly indulging the vice to which the emperor thought he had given sufficient reign in the circus and the amphitheatre. Not infrequently the inns (*cauponae*) and taverns (*pininae and thermopolia*), whose front counter served cooking draughts or hot wine, concealed in their back premises gambling areas. . . . With . . . relative impunity, the keeper was all the more tempted to equip his shop for seductive, forbidden parties, and by installing prostitutes as barmaids to convert his gambling den into a bawdy house.[72]

Thus, whereas studies of Rome show that shops and taverns fronted for prostitution and gambling, which were forbidden by Roman law, our Rabbinic text indicates that shops fronted not only for gambling but also for prostitution and idolatry, which are forbidden by Jewish law.[73]

Taverns and Prostitution

The main places of prostitution were the taverns.[74] An amusing inscription from Aesernia in Campania, not far from Pompeii, the tombstone of Lucius Calidus Eroticus and his wife Faunia Voluptas, shows a traveler settling his bill, supplementing it with a brief dialogue that seems to be the innkeeper's joke:

> Innkeeper, let's figure the bill.
> You have—wine 1/6 as, bread 1 as, main dish 2 asses
> All right.
> The girl is 8 asses.
> That's all right too.
> Hay for the mule, 2 asses.
> The mule is going to break me.[75]

Indeed, in the *Digesta* (23.2.43.9) we read of such "a woman who conducts a tavern and keeps others in it who prostitute themselves, *as many are accustomed to do* under the pretext of employing women for the service of the house . . . ." The same seems to have been true in Talmudic Palestine, for in the Palestinian Targumin (the Aramaic translations of the Bible), the Hebrew זונה, prostitute, is translated by the Aramaic פונדקאית, mistress of the πανδοχεῖον, the tavern.[76]

Market Competition

The markets served as trading outlets for the immediate area.[77] People normally marketed their produce—certainly the perishable products[78]—close to home, that is, less than a day's journey from their farms.[79] There was a good deal of competition between the merchants to be the first to arrive and to be able to capture the market. An amusing episode describing this situation is related in Midrash Psalms 12.1, ed. Buber pp. 104–105:

> It once happened that a certain town had no salt, and there was a band (= guild) of caravaneers (literally: donkey-drivers) who said: We will go to such and such a place and buy salt, and sell it before others come. Now, they had a leader, [and] they said to him: Let us go this place. . . . He answered them: I have to plough tomorrow, so wait till I have done my ploughing, and afterwards we will go. They said to him: All right. . . . What did he do? He loaded a sack on his ass and went off alone, while his friends slept till morning, [till] they called (her) [him] (i.e., to join them). The neighbours asked: Whom do you want? So and so (i.e., their leader) already went off last night. So they set off in the morning and found him on his way back. They said to him: Why did you act so? He replied to them: Do you not know why? Had we all gone together, the [price] would immediately have fallen to a low level. Now I have brought [salt, and] until you get there mine will have been sold out, so that when you get [there] you can sell yours at a good price.

Clearly the traders and transporters were sensitive to questions of supply and demand, had their own "grape vines," and rushed in to satisfy the local demand. Our street-wise guild master was not averse to tricking his own companions to made a quick profit.[80]

Swindling and Robbery

Trading in the marketplace was a cutthroat business. The markets had their quota of swindlers who would mix wine with water or frankincense with donkey milk or manipulate the scales.[81] Besides swindlers, there were thieves,[82] as evidenced by this message painted on a wall in Pompeii:[83]

> A copper pot is missing from this shop. I offer a reward of 65 sesterces for its return and a reward of 20 sesterces for information leading to its return.[84]

For these reasons, there was a strict market control.

Notice Boards

There also seems to have been a kind of "notice board" in the marketplace on which proclamations were posted. It was situated in a public place, probably somewhere in the market's forum area. This we may derive from Leviticus Rabba 1.10, ed. Margulies p. 25, in the name of Rabbi Eleazar (flr. ca. 260–280 C.E.):

> Like an edict (דיוטגמא—διάταγμα),[85] which has been written and sealed and brought to the city, but in respect where the inhabitants of the city were not punishable until it had been promulgated (עד שתתפרש; literally: stretched out, displayed) to them in the public place (דימוסיא—δημόσια) of the city.[86]

An Incident in the Market Related by Apuleius

The main purpose of the market was, of course, to make available basic needs—food, clothing, and any other purchasable product—to the public. And, indeed, a major part of the market's daily activity involved the sale of foodstuffs. Apuleius (died 123 C.E.), in his *Golden Ass* (1.24.25), gives us a lively description of buying food in the market:

> I went to the marketplace to buy something for dinner. The fish store was well stocked with fish for sale. I asked the price; the clerk said twenty-five denarii; we haggled, and I bought them for twenty denarii. Just as I was leaving, Pythias, who had been a fellow student with me in Athens, bumped into me. After some hesitation, he recognized me and affectionately threw his arms around me. He embraced me and kissed me in a friendly manner and said, "Dear, dear Lucius, it's been a long time since last I saw you, in fact not, by Hercules, since we finished our schooling with Vestius. What's the reason for this trip of yours?"
>
> "I'll tell you about it tomorrow," I said. "But what about you? I'm glad you have achieved success. I see, for example, that you have attendants and *fasces* (a bundle of rods carried by the men who attended a magistrate, thus symbolizing the magistrate's authority), and clothing which befits a magistrate."

> "Yes," he said, "I'm in charge of the market here; I hold the position of *aedile* (superintendent of markets), and if you want to buy something for dinner, I'll be happy to help you."
>
> I declined his help since I had already bought enough fish for dinner. However, when Pythias saw my shopping basket, he shook it a bit so he could have a closer look at the fish. "And how much," he asked, "did you pay for this garbage?"
>
> "With some difficulty, I convinced the fish seller to sell them for only twenty denarii," I said.
>
> When he heard this, he quickly grasped my hand and led me back into the *Forum*. "From which person," he asked, "did you buy this trash?"
>
> I pointed out the old man who was sitting in a corner. Pythias immediately went into action as *aedile* and lashed out at him in a very gruff voice. "All right, all right," he said. "You won't even deal fairly with my friends and with guests in our fair town. With your extortionate prices for food you are going to reduce this town, which is the flower of Thessaly, to a barren piece of rock! But I won't let you get away with this. You are going to learn how you riff-raff will be punished as long as I am *aedile*." Then he dumped the fish out of my basket and ordered one of his flunkeys to jump up and down on them until he crushed them all. Satisfied that he had exhibited the proper severity, my good friend Pythias suggested that I leave. "I've shamed the old man quite enough," he said, "with this harsh treatment." I was astonished and dumbfounded by what had happened, but went off to the baths,[87] having lost both my money and my dinner because of the stern punishment exacted by my quick-witted fellow student.[88]

This passage leads us, naturally, to an examination of the office of the *agoranomos*, the market inspector, in Rabbinic Palestine. Before we do so, we must first investigate certain aspects of the administrative organization of the market.

Notes

1. On the architectural form of Roman markets in general, see W. L. MacDonald, *The Architecture of the Roman Empires: An Urban Appraisal*, vol. 2 (New Haven and London, 1986), pp. 118–19, and cf. pp. 51–66. On the spread of the Italian mecellum type of layout, see J. B. Ward-Perkins, *Roman Imperial Architecture*[2] (London, 1981), p. 395. The village, on the other hand, usually had no market area. Villagers marketed their produce in the nearest town. See M. Megilah 1.1 and S. Dar, Z. Safrai, and Y. Tepper, *Um Rihan: A Village of the Mishnah* (Israel, 1986) [in Hebrew], passim. On the forum area see M. Megila 1.1, and Y. Megila 1.1, and B. Megila 2b; S. Lieberman, *Tosefta ki-fshuṭah*, vol. 5 (New York, 1962), pp. 1126–27 in reference to T. Megila 1.2; and S. Krauss, *Kadmoniyyot ha-Talmud* (Berlin and Vienna, 1924), pp. 74–76. On the centrality of the forum in Roman town planning, see E. J. Owens, *The City in the Greek and Roman World*[2] (London and New York, 1992), pp. 121–48, 154; and R. Martin, "Agora et Forum," *MEFRA* 89 (1972): 903–33.

2. See M. Rostovtzeff, *Social and Economic History of the Roman Empire*[2] *[SEHRE*[2]*]* (Oxford, 1956), pl. XLVIII, no. 2, opposite p. 264; Genesis

Rabba 8.2, ed. Theodor p. 57, a parable by Rabbi Ḥama b. Rabbi Ḥanina, second half of the third century C.E., concerning a city that was dependent for its provisions on a caravan of donkeys (חמרים); and D. Adan-Bayewitz, "Ha-Rochel be-Ereẓ Yisrael," in *Yehudim be-Kalkalah*, ed. N. Gross (Jerusalem, 1985), pp. 69–85, on itinerant peddlers and their function within the markets.

3. See also S. Lieberman, *Talmuda shel Kisrin* (Jerusalem, 1931), pp. 12–13. The word may also appear in M. Tohorot 6.9, פרן; so Krauss, *Kadmoniyyot ha-Talmud* vol. 1, part 2 p. 426, rejecting his earlier interpretation in *Griechische und Lateinische Lehnwörter im Talmud, Midrasch, und Targum*, vol. 2 [*LW*2] (Berlin, 1899, reprint, Hildesheim 1964), p. 491a s.v. פרן II: φάρος—lighthouse. However, on further analysis it would seem that his earlier interpretation is correct because it is difficult to envisage a forum that is a לשבת רשות היחיד, that is, a private area but see chapter 6, note 12.

4. Liebeman, *Talmuda*, pp. 12–13.

5. For ἀγορά in Rabbinic literature, see Krauss, *LW*2, p. 9a s.v. אגורא. An additional reference to a chair placed in a public place is to be found in Y. Shabbat 1.1, 2d: a תרכוס which stands in a public area. . . . This should be corrected to תרנוס—θρόνος—a chair, as noted by many authorities. See S. Lieberman, *Hayerushalmi Kiphshuto* (Jerusalem, 1934), p. 13.

6. See Krauss, *LW*2, p. 413b s.v. סרטיא, pp. 456b–57a s.v. פלטיא.

7. Hence: אין פרזים אלא פלטיות in Avot de-Rabbi Nathan 2, chap. 38, ed. Schechter p. 99.

8. See T. Baba Kama 6.28, ed. Zuckermandel p. 357, on camels and B. Shabbat 5a on carriages. In Sepphoris the paving on one of the main streets, which was recently excavated, still shows the ruts from the carriage wheels.

9. Examples of streets of this nature, with shops opening out onto colonnaded walks, may be found in Beit Shean (see Y. Tsafrir and G. Foerster, *Cathedra* 64 [1992]: 15), in Bostra (Y. Tsafrir, *Ereẓ-Yisrael from the Destruction of the Second Temple to the Muslim Conquest: Archeology and Art* [Jerusalem, 1984] [in Hebrew], pp. 81, 138), and also in Sepphoris and Tiberias.

10. See J. J. Schwartz, *Lod (Lydda), Israel from Its Origins through the Byzantine Period, 5600 B.C.E.–640 C.E.* (Oxford, 1991), p. 93.

11. Ibid., p. 156, n. 50–51, further refers us to Shiqmona, *Ḥadashot Archeologiyyot* 67 no 8 (1978): 24–25, which reported a two-story building found at Shiqmona. The excavators assumed that the bottom floor was a store and the top floor a residence. Schwartz also refers us to Y. Hirschfeld, *Ereẓ-Yisrael* 17 (1984): 173, 179, n. 43–44, for combined stores and residences and for market streets and colonnaded streets in Palestine. See also Y. Hirschfeld, *Beit ha-Megurim ha-Ereẓ-Yisraeli* (Jerusalem, 1987), pp. 49–50. On multistory buildings, see Krauss, *Kadmoniyyot ha-Talmud*, vol. 1, part 1, pp. 319–23.

12. See J.-A. Shelton, *As the Romans Did* (Oxford, 1988), p. 70.

13. Digesta 9.3.5.7, 1–2.

14. J. Carcopino, *Daily Life in Ancient Rome* (Harmondsworth, 1956), pp. 51, 54.

15. See M. Baba Batra 2.3.

16. See Y. Baba Batra 2.3, where the later third century Rabbi Yaakov bar Aḥa moves a confectionary store (חליטר) from one *stoa* to another, and also note 9 above. The subject of colonnades was discussed in detail by Krauss in *Kadmoniyyot ha-Talmud*, vol. 1, part 2, pp. 422–27. The term is complex and must be distinguished from another similar one deriving from στιβάς (?). See

J. N. Epstein, "Le-Ketovot Khorazim," *Tarbiẓ* vol. 1, part 2 (1930): 135, n. 1–2 (and further in chapter 7, note 15, and chapter 2, note 16). See also Yalkut Shimoni Ḥukkat (from Midrash Yelamdenu) sec. 763: that when Rabbi Joshua died, the *stoa* of Tiberias collapsed. This is parallel to Y. Avoda Zara 3.1.42c: that when Rabbi Hoshaya (second century C.E.) died, the קלון—*Kalon*—of Tiberias collapsed. Lieberman, in his *Studies in Palestinian Talmudic Literature* (Jerusalem, 1991), pp. 171–73, has emended קלון to קלונס = כלונס = columnae, the columns (i.e., supporting the *stoa*).

17. T. Baba Meẓia 11.3, ed. Zuckermandel p. 394.

18. Cf. B. Moed Katan 13b.

19. T. Shabbat 10(11).1, ed. Lieberman p. 41; ed. Zuckermandel p. 123, and Lieberman, *Tosefta*, vol. 3, p. 152.

20. This is what emerges from the halachic discussion in Y. Shabbat 1.1,2d on פירחי העמודים, the capitals of the columns. See Liebermann, *Hayerushalmi*, pp. 16–17, for the correct reading of the passage. See Vitruvius 4.1.11 on the proportions of the Corinthian capital.

21. See B. Shabbat 6a: a large *strata* and *platea* from which lead off many alleyways, מבואות המפולשים. See Krauss, *Kadmoniyyot* ha-Talmud, vol. 1, part 2, pp. 59–60, and cf. Lamentations Rabba 1.2 for a somewhat imaginatively exaggerated description of Jerusalem's markets during the Second Temple period, which no doubt reflects in part first century townscapes.

22. See S. Klein, *Ereẓ-ha-Galil* (Jerusalem, 1967), pp. 97–98, with the relevant sources. On the market in Sepphoris, see most recently Y. Ne'eman, *Sepphoris in the Period of the Second Temple, the Mishnah and the Talmud* (Jerusalem, 1993) [in Hebrew], p. 86.

23. See discussion of this text in S. Lieberman, "Palestine in the Third and Fourth Centuries," *JQR NS* 36 (1946) 347–48.

24. Ibid., p. 347 n. 131. Lieberman writes: This (guild) is apparently the meaning of חנוותא. However, the literal meaning is "shops."

25. Ibid., n. 132. הוא לון צומות means to collect or assemble and seems to have been a technical term for meetings of the *collegia*, probably for the purpose of distributing the *leitourgiai*. For the broader context of this passage, see my *Roman Palestine 200–400: The Land* (Ramat-Gan, 1978), chap. 5, p. 102 et seq. and especially p. 106.

26. See further Y. Dan, *Ḥayyei ha-Ir be-Eretz-Yisrael be-Shilhei ha-Eit ha-Atika* (Jerusalem, 1984), pp. 193–99, on guilds in Byzantine Palestine and my remarks in *Roman Palestine 200–400*: *The Land*, pp. 106–107, 167.

27. B. Baba Meẓia 72b; Klein, *Ereẓ-ha-Galil*, p. 98; Krauss *LW*², p. 175b s.v. דורמוס; and cf. my note in *Glotta* 56 no. 3–4 (1978): 221–22.

28. See Y. Baba Meẓia 5.8,10c and cf. T. Baba Meẓia 6.5, ed. Zuckermandel p. 383.

29. Libanius, Oration 11.254, SEG 4,539–40; and A. H. M. Jones, *The Greek City from Alexander to Justinian* (Oxford, 1940), pp. 245, 349–50, n. 10, p. 388 n. 64.

30. See M. Beẓa 1.5, B. Beẓa. 11b, Y. Beẓa. 1.5, on the shop shutters, תריסי חנויות.

31. See n. 16 above.

32. Genesis Rabba 40.3, ed. Theodor-Albeck p. 383, a statement of Rabbi Ḥiyya, fl. ca. 220–40 C.E. cf. B. Pesaḥim, 50b: תגרי סימטא, hawkers of the *semita*. On peddlers, see Adan-Bayewitz, *Yehudim*, pp. 69–85. On the street

criers, see Y. Yevamot 12.1,12d, Leviticus Rabba 17.2, ed. Margulies pp. 349–54; Adan-Bayewitz, *Yehudim*, pp. 81–82; and H. H. Tanzer, *The Common People of Pompeii: A Study of the Graffiti* (Baltimore, 1939), pp. 56–57.

33. See Carcopino, *Daily Life*, p. 58, and cf. my discussion of road breadths in *JSS* 20 no. 1–4 (1969): 81–86, and in chapter 7.

34. For a discussion on the columns of Rome, see Genesis Rabba 33.1, ed. Theodor, pp. 300–301, a statement by Rabbi Joshua b. Levi, third quarter of the third century C.E.

35. Martial (died 102 C.E.) 7.61. Cf. Carcopino, *Daily Life*, p. 59.

36. Ibid. See editor's discussion on p. 175 to line 4.

37. On the peddler's box קופת רוכלין see Adan-Bayewitz, *Yehudim*, pp. 76–77.

38. The Talmudic *sugya* (unit of argumentation) is basically Babylonian, but these items of information are in the Palestinian stratum, too.

39. See T. Eruvin 11.12, ed. Lieberman, p. 13J: מחצלות הפרוסות על פתחי חנויות ברשות הרבום. For a discussion of Roman law on awnings which block out neighbor's light, see G. Hermandzen, *Ostia: Aspects of Roman City Life* (Edmonton, 1982), p. 94.

40. See Y. Sukka 2.2, late third century C.E.

41. See R. J. Forbes, *Studies in Ancient Technology*, vol. 6 (Leiden, 1966), pp. 169–70, 193, n. 179. He writes (basing himself on Libanius and St. Jerome) that the first city to light its streets properly was Antioch, ca. 350 C.E. Nonetheless, there was street lighting much earlier, as he shows clearly from the evidence of Pompeii.

42. See Y. Pesaḥim 1.1, 27a ad inf., Y. Sota 1.2, 16a: לפלטיא בלילה, לחורבה ביום ולמבואות ביום, to the *platea* by night, to a ruin by day, and to a dark alleyway by day. See also L. Mumford, *The City in History* (Harmondsworth, 1966), pp. 247–48.

43. T. Terumot 10.9, ed. Lieberman p. 161, and T. Baba Kama 6.28, ed. Zuckermandel p. 357, in which we read of a camel laden with flax that passes through the street. When the flax enters a shop, it catches fire from a candle in the shop. Subsequently, the whole shop catches fire, and the question is who is responsible for the damages.

44. Y. Berachot 8.6, early fourth century, C.E., במעשן לפני חנותו עששית, and Y. Shabbat 1.1, 2d, on a מנורה—lamp standing in a public place. For a discussion on this term, see J. Krauss, *Talmudische Archäologie* vol. 1 (Leipzig, 1910), pp. 409–10, n. 262–63.

45. T. Baba Kama 6.26,28. The subject of fire hazards has been reexamined by Hermansen, *Ostia*, pp. 208–25. See also Mumford, *City*, pp. 256–57.

46. See Y. Hirschfeld, *Dwelling Houses in Roman and Byzantine Palestine* (Jerusalem, 1987) [in Hebrew], pp. 143–56; S. Krauss, *Kadmoniyyot ha-Talmud* vol. 1, part 2, p. 305 et seq. Vitruvius (2.9.16) calls attention to the dangers of fires in the roof structures, because the roof beams are exposed at the eaves and liable to catch fire from the neighboring houses. See Hermansen's discussion in *Ostia*, pp. 214–15, 227. For a discussion on of fire exposure due to beams jutting out over the walls, see Krauss, *Kadmoniyyot ha-Talmud*, vol. 1, part 2, pp. 302, 307, and see B. Tanit 25a. Here it is in order to cite the (anonymous but probably fourth century C.E.) passage in Midrash Psalms 68.2, ed. Buber p. 315: It is like unto a king whose servants live in his palace, and he lives in the upper story (פלטור העליון) and they in the lower story. And they make smoke, so that

the smoke may rise up [and trouble the king]. . . . On the use of the term *king* (מלך) in Rabbinic parables, see David Stern's fine analysis in his *Parables in Midrash: Narrative and Exegesis in Rabbinic Literature* (Cambridge, 1991), pp. 19–21, 93–97. The king's palace is also commonplace in Rabbinic parables (Stern, *Parables*, pp. 226–27, 231–32). However, despite all these stereotypic motifs, and their deeper homiletic meanings, the simple fact that emerges is how the smoke rises from one floor to the next. Presumably, the fire itself could also do so.

47. B. Eruvin 81b, Kiddushin 28b, Baba Meẓia 46b, 47ab, 49b, Gittin 52b, Ḥullin 83a, statement of Rabbi Yoḥanan, fl. Palestine ca. 250–79 C.E.

48. For multistory buildings in Roman Palestine see T. Eruvin 8.6, ed. Lieberman p. 148 (three stories); T. Eruvin 8.11, ed. Lieberman p. 148 (five stories connected by a אילקטי, winding staircase); and (Jastrow, p. 736 s.v. אילקטי).

49. Juvenal 3.198–202.

50. Juvenal 3:197–98.

51. The lower story would have to be very massively constructed to support the weight of the grain stored in the upper story. See Hermansen, *Ostia*, p. 227 et seq. A. Rickman analyzed the subject of storage houses in Roman antiquity quite competently in his standard work *Roman Granaries and Store Buildings* (Cambridge, 1971). The subject of (urban) store houses in Rabbinic Palestine has been discussed by R. Yankelevich in his article "Granaries and Store Buildings in Eretz Israel," in *Milet*, vol. 1 (Tel-Aviv, 1983) [in Hebrew], pp. 107–19. See also Krauss, *Kadmoniyyot ha-Talmud*, vol. 1, part 2, p. 399, and the section on the basilica in chapter 6. This subject needs further investigation.

52. Ulpian, *Digesta* 1.15.2: plurimis uno die incendi exortis.

53. *Digesta* 1.15.3.5: ut aquam unusquisque inquilinus in cenaculo habeat iubetur admonere. See Carcopino, *Daily Life*, p. 50; P. K. Baillae-Reynolds, *The Vigiles of Imperial Rome* (Oxford, 1926); and L. Homs, *Rome Impériale et l'urbanisme dans l'antiquité* (Paris, 1951), pp. 172–98.

54. S. E. Miller, *Studies in the History and Traditions of Sepphoris* (Leiden, 1984), pp. 31–45.

55. Lieberman, *Tosfefta*, vol. 3, p. 213.

56. Miller, *Studies*, pp. 44–45.

57. See Rostovtzeff, *SEHRE*^{2}, p. 637, n. 57, on the inscription of the *centonarii* from 205 C.E.

58. On five brigades see Jones, *The Later Roman Empire*, vol. 2 (Oxford, 1964), pp. 695, 859; vol. 3, p. 215, n. 16, and J. E. Stambaugh, *The Ancient Roman City* (Baltimore and London, 1988), pp. 128, 348. (Cf. with n. 43 above).

59. Jones, *Greek City*, p. 215.

60. For an example of "faces" that spit forth water, see Tsafrir, *Ereẓ-Yisrael*, p. 196 (from J. M. Iliffe *QDAP* 3 (1934): pl. LXVI), head of Pan from Askalon, part of a fountain, out of whose mouth water gushed forth. See also Lieberman, *Studies*, p. 381, n. 6, who suggests that these "busts"—פרצופות—were usually lions' heads. For contrast see the Judean Fountainhead, illustrated in W. H. Stephens, *The New Testament World in Pictures* (Cambridge, 1987), p. 96, fig. 197. For an example of a *nymphaeum*, see the one on the main street in Beit Shean and see Tsafrir, *Eretz Israel*, pp. 76–79; for Gerasa, see Tsafrir and Foerster, *Ereẓ-Yisrael*, pp. 22–23, and Schwartz's discussion below in chapter 10. For a comprehensive discussion, see O. Irshai, apud *The Aquaeducts of Ancient*

Palestine: Collected Essays, ed. D. Amit, Y. Hirschfeld, and J. Patrich (Jerusalem, 1989), pp. 47–55. The water distribution system will be discussed in chap. 9. Note that the forum of Herculaneum (the Decumanus Maximus), which was lined on the front side with private houses and *tabernae*, had a well at the central crosspoint where the main north-south street, Cardo IV, met with the Decumanus Maximus.

61. See B. Shabbat 8a: עמוד תשעה ברשות הרבים ורבים מכתבין עליו, and the discussion in my *Material Culture in Ereẓ-Yisrael during the Talmudic Period* (Jerusalem, 1993) [in Hebrew], pp. 25–28 (first published in *Sinai* 97 [1983], 39–42). The text is from the late third or early fourth century C.E.

62. See Rostovtzeff, *SEHRE*^{2}, p. 619, n. 43, IGRR IV 1414.

63. For more incidental information about porters, see Y. Shabbat 1.1, 3c; expert porters used to handling particularly heavy loads: כתפייא אומניא. On the forms of payment to porters, see B. Baba Meẓia 51b, based on Baba Meẓia 3.23, ed. Zuckermandel p. 378, and B. Baba Meẓia 68b, 115a.

64. Tanzer, *Common People*, p. 59, referring to C164, 274, 497, 2040, 5019.

65. Parallels in Y. Sanhedrin 10.2.28d; B. Sanhedrin 106a; Tanḥuma Buber Numbers, Balak sec. 27, p. 147; Tanḥuma Buber Numbers, Balak sec. 11, Numbers Rabba 20.23; Yalkut Hosea sec. 526; Pirkei de-Rabbi. Eliezer chap. 47, p. 112b. There are slight variations in these different versions, some of which will be noted below. See Z. Safrai's comments in "Fairs in the Land of Israel in the Mishna and Talmud Period," *Zion* 49, no. 2 (1984): 145–46.

66. Y. Sanhedrin has them building a קנקלין, a latticed enclosure from the Greek κιγκλίς; Tanḥuma has קלעין, tent-like enclosures; Yalkut Hosea has קלעים, tents (at fairs) = קליעין in B. Sanhedrin, while Pirkei de-Rabbi Eliezer has חנויות, shops. See Krauss, *LW*^{2}, p. 349b s.v. מקולין. The sense of all the variants is a shopping area. On the *macellum*, see N. Naber, "The Architectural Variations of the *Macellum*," *AJA* 72 (1968): 169 et seq.

67. Y. Sanhedrin has: They saw an old woman outside and a young maiden (נערה) within. . . . Tanḥuma Buber adds: The old woman would say to him: Surely you wish to buy linen from Beit Shean (a famous brand), and she would show [some] to him. The old woman would ask him for more [than the market price], and the young maiden for less . . . and the young maiden would come out perfumed and bedecked with ornaments, and would seduce him. . . . There are later elaborations of the basic text.

68. Perhaps there is a play on צרור in Numbers 25:17. Note also כזבי בת צור in Numbers 25:15.

69. Y. Sanhedrin reads: Amonite wine which is strong, and which tempts the body to debauchery, and whose fragrance permeates. . . .

70. Ed. Margulies, p. 767, and see S. Lieberman, *Yevanit ve-Yavnut be-Ereẓ-Yisrael* (Jerusalem, 1962), p. 39.

71. R. Ḥiyya had a shop in Tiberias: see Y. Shabbat 6.2 and cf. Y. Taanit 1.2 ad inf. See also Safrai, "Fairs," p. 146, n. 51.

72. Carcopino, *Daily Life*, p. 274. He also refers us to *Digesta* 23.2.43.1.

73. On gambling in Rabbinic sources, my friend Joshua Schwartz is now preparing an extensive study.

74. See Tert. De fuga 13, Paul, Sent. 2.26.11, Cod. Just. 4.56.3 (225 C.E.), 9.9.28 (326 C.E.), 5.27.1 (336 C.E.); R. MacMullen, *Enemies of the Roman Order* (Cambridge and London, 1967), p. 338, referring to additional material;

idem, *Roman Social Relations 50 B.C. to A.D. 284* (New Haven and London, 1974), pp. 86–87, 182; Hermansen, *Ostia*, pp. 197–98, citing additional sources; J. P. V. D. Balsdon, *Life and Leisure in Ancient Rome* (New York, 1969), pp. 152–54; and the remark of J. G. Gager in his recent *Curse Tablets and Binding Spells from the Ancient Worlds* (Oxford, 1992), p. 153.

75. *CIL* 9.2689. See Stambaugh, *Ancient Roman City*, p. 182.

76. See Targum to Joshua 2.1, Ezekiel 3.44, I Kings 3.16 (in plural) and so too in Targum. Pseudo Jonathan to Genesis 42.6, telling that Joseph sent to search out his brethren in the market places (סרטיא פלטייא) and the brothels (בתי פונדקתא?). See Krauss, *Kadmoniyyot ha-Talmud*, vol. 1, part 1, p. 135, and Safrai, "Fairs," p. 146.

77. On this subject see my *Roman Palestine 200–400: The Land*, p. 167.

78. On the marketing and distribution of some perishable goods, such as pottery vessels, see D. Adan-Bayewitz and I. Perlman's joint article, "The Local Trade of Sepphoris in the Roman Period," *IEJ* 40 (1990): 154–72.

79. See Y. Maasrot 2.2.

80. For a different kind of market competition, see Lamentations Rabba 1.1, ed. Buber p. 44.

81. For a list of kinds of swindlers, see Eccles. Zuta 6.1, ed. Buber pp. 130–31.

82. See the passage in Y. Baba Meẓia 3.7, and cf. *Digesta* 1.15.3.1–2 on burglars, thieves, and robbers (Paulus, fl. ca. 200 C.E.). Taverns were famous for their swindlers. See Genesis Rabba 44.6, ed. Theodor-Albeck p. 1144–45.

83. CIL 4.64.

84. Cited in Shelton, p. 71.

85. See my *Dictionary of Greek and Latin Legal Terms in Rabbinic Literature* (Jerusalem, 1984), pp. 79–82 s.v. דיאטגמא.

86. See S. Lieberman, *JQR* 35 (1944) 6–10. On the publication, or promulgation of edicts, see ibid., p. 7, n. 40, and Jones, *Greek City*, p. 238.

87. Often the bathhouse was situated close to the marketplace, such as in Tiberias and Beit Shean, where the bathhouse is close to a broad street flanked by stones.

88. Cited in Shelton, pp. 217–18.

2

Administration and Organization of the Market

Permission to Open a Market

To operate a market, or fair, individuals and communities needed the sanction of the Roman senate or the emperor. We are told that the Emperor Claudius held markets on his estates.[1] Pliny mentions in one of his Letters[2] that "Sollers, a man of praetorian rank, petitioned the Senate to be allowed to establish a market on his estate. His petition was opposed by envoys from Vicetia—no doubt because there was a market in that town which stood to lose from Sollers' competition."[3]

An inscription from 138 C.E.[4] describes how a new market was established at Casae in the Roman province of Africa Proconsularis. The founding of this market required a specific vote of the Senate at Rome and granted Lucilius Africanus, a senator, permission to hold a market twice a month on a regular basis. The official decision of the Senate was formulated as follows:[5]

> Concerning this matter the senate decreed as follows: that Lucilius Africanus, *vir clarissimus*, be permitted to establish and maintain a market at Casae in the province of Africa, Beguensian district, territory of the Musulamians, on November 2 and 20 and every month there in the fourth day before the Nones and the twelfth day before the Kalends, and that people from the neighbourhood be permitted to gather and assemble there for the convenience of *attending market only*, without harm or inconvenience to anyone. . . .[6]

But what was the real effect of the decision of the Roman Senate? John E. Stanbaugh gives us a hint in his book *The Ancient Roman City*: "Lurking clearly between the lines of the inscription are the prospect of big profits for Lucilius and the desire of the authorities that the market not become the focus of any political activity."[7]

Normally, after receiving permission to establish a market, it became subject to the authority of the city prefect. Cicero writes that "there will be *aediles* who will oversee the city's markets, merchandise, and food supplies. . . .",[8] while from the *Digesta* we learn that "It is his job to see that meat is offered for sale at a fair price, and for this reason the swine market is . . . under his supervision. Similarly other livestock which are used to provide meat are within his jurisdiction."[9] We saw at the end of the preceding chapter that all foodstuffs (and indeed all products) were subject to the prefects' supervision; quality control, price control, and market availability, were not. The official responsible for these duties is a familiar figure in Rabbinic literature and goes primarily under his Greek title, *agoranomos*. He had to be sharp, quick witted, and decisive, dealing as he did with a variety of different types of scams and swindles, such as admixture in wines and condiments, false weights, and manipulated scales.[10]

Market Days

There were primarily three types of markets: daily, weekly, and biweekly, with occasional fairs sometimes continuing for a few consecutive days.[11] Thus, in M. Baba Meẓia in a disucssion on the question of what length of time after having received a defective coin can one return it, the Mishna says:

> In the cities, until one can get to a money-changer (*shulḥani*, τραπεζίτης, banker, who will check it); and in the villages, until the following Friday.

The Tosefta (M. Baba Meẓia 3.20, ed. Zuckermandel pp. 377–78; ed. Lieberman p. 78) adds as an explanatory note, "for village markets function from Friday to Friday," meaning that the village markets functioned mainly on Fridays to allow the local farmers to buy provisions for the Sabbath.[12] Apparently, the towns had regular market days, and the villages had only a weekly market (either in the village or in the town? See note 12). The villagers themselves came to market their produce in the town on Mondays or Thursdays, days when communal activities took place, such as the reading of the Torah in the synagogue in the mornings and the court sittings during the day.[13]

Relationships between Jews and Pagans on Market Days

Occasionally these market days fell on a Roman (pagan) festival, such as the *Saturnalia* or the *Kalendae*,[14] and under such circumstances Jews could do only business with those who did not observe or participate in the idolatrous ceremonies. Hence, Rabbi Abbahu, living in Caesarea in the late third and early fourth century C.E., ruled that Jews could be allowed to transact business with the heathen members of the *officium* of the *dux*—proconsul—on the *Saturnalia* and the *Kalendae* because, apparently, they did not worship idols. However, they could not engage in transactions with the Samaritan members of the officium, who because they were afraid of losing their position, would not disregard the required ceremonies and did not fail to worship the idols on these days.[15]

There were also occasional market days, or fair days, officially dedicated to a specific god. On such days Jews did not participate at all in market activities, since the income from business transactions accruing to the city (either through rental of space or taxes and percentages of transactions) was dependent on idolatry. However, outside the city when presumably no taxes or rental rates were claimed, Jews were permitted to engage in buying and selling.[16] Thus, we find Resh Lakish (Tiberias ca. 260–75) explaining that what goes on in the fairs within the city is subject to *meches*, tax, and what goes on outside the city is not.[17] Jews had, then, carefully to examine several aspects of such market days: whether taxes assessed for placing the stalls in the city forum went to the funding of idolatrous pagan activity, whether or not the merchandise had been brought into the city before the fair (in which case they might be permitted to buy it),[18] and whether or not the merchants themselves practiced idolatry.[19] Food products, on the other hand (called דבר שהוא חיי נפש), something that life depended upon, could be bought without hesitation according to Rabbi Yoḥanan (Tiberias, died 279 C.E.).[20] The most famous fairs mentioned were those of Gaza, Akko, and Butna.[21]

Here I might also add that the public areas of the cities were often decorated with idolatrous statuary. The rabbis discussed the question of whether or not they were allowed to walk past the statues, usually ruling that they could do so with closed or turned aside eyes (see Y. Avoda Zara 3.11). This was the ruling of Rabbi Yoḥanan on passing the statue in the building of the municipal council (*boule*) and of his contemporary, Rabbi Gamliel Zuga; however Rabbi Joshua ben Levi of the same generation was of a stricter view and would not pass near idolatrous statuary.

City Taxes and Free Markets

The city's income, whether it went to individual entrepreneurs who set up their own seasonal fairs or to the city authorities for regular market activities, was derived from taxes and rental of space for shops and stalls (see chap. 1). On occasions, however, there were special free markets, that is, tax-free markets. These are called in the Rabbinic literature אטלים, אטלס, or אטליז, which are different forms of the Greek ἀτελής, that is, πανήγυρις ἀτελής, a tax-free fair or market day. The overhead for such an event was usually donated by an individual or by the local authorities, either to celebrate a religious festival or to honor an important individual such as the emperor. Jewish merchants had to ascertain the exact nature of the tax exemption. If it were in honor of a local deity, they would benefit (by not paying the tax) from idolatry and hence would be forbidden to participate in such a fair. On the other hand, if the fair were dedicated to an important individual or to the emperor, there would be no reason why they should not take full advantage of such a tax-free opportunity. This apparently was the case with the fair at Tyre, dedicated by Diocletian to his brother Heraclius Maximus and mentioned in the Yerushalmi.[22]

Having seen something of the organization and administration of the market, its rights to function, and its audit sources of revenue, I will now return to question of market control. For clearly so complex an institution required constant supervision and control, and this was carried out by the *agoronomos*, a position to be discussed in the next chapter.

Notes

1. Suetonius, *Life of Claudius* 12.1.

2. Book 5, no. 4.1.

3. N. Lewis and M. Reinhold, *Roman Civilization, Sourcebook II: The Empire* (New York, 1955), p. 337.

4. *CIL* 8.23246.

5. Ibid.

6. Lewis and Reinhold, *Roman Civilization*, p. 337.

7. J. E. Stanbaugh, *The Ancient Roman City* (Baltimore and London, 1988), p. 250. Cf. ibid., p. 371, n. 13, referring to B. D. Shaw, "Rural Markets in North Africa and the Political Economy of the Roman Empire," *Antiquités Africaines* 17 (1981): 37–83.

8. Ulpian, *Digesta* 1.12.11.

9. De Legibus 3.3.7.

10. See Eccles. Zuta 6.1, ed. Buber pp. 30–131, for a description of different kinds of market cheating, including moving the scale along its pivot to falsify measurement: קנה מאזנים ארוך מצד זה וקצר מצד זה, the arm of the scale long on this side and short on the other. On the steelyard see B. Kisch, *Scales and Weights—A Historical Outline*[2], Yale Studies in the History of Science and Medicine, vol. 1 (New Haven and London, 1965), p. 56 et seq..

11. Z. Safrai wrote a fine study entitled, "Fairs in the Land of Israel in the Mishna and Talmud Period," which appeared in *Zion* 49, no 2 (1984): 139–58. It is certainly the most comprehensive examination of the subject to date.

11. Also in Torat Kohanim, be-Har, 3.8, 107d.

12. However, some commentators explain that the villagers came to town to buy provisions once a week, on Fridays for the Sabbath, and since there were no money exchangers in the villages, they had to delay the examination of the coin until their next visit, a week later. See Rabbi David Pardo, *Ḥasdei David* ad loc., 26c, who further explains that "Friday" does not mean Friday, but whichever day the villagers will go into town. The towns, on the other hand, had regular daily markets, and on those days when the money changer was available, any town dweller could check his coins for weight and fineness. This explanation is based on B. Baba Meẓia 52b, with a formulation as follows: In the villages, where there is no money-changer until the [following] Friday—when they go to market. The latter words, "when they go to market," are a Baylonian addition, in Aramaic, while the rest of the passage is in Hebrew.

13. See M. Megila 1.1. Safrai, "Fairs," 154–55, suggests that the Monday and Thursday, *Yemei Kenissah,* was an early Hellenistic institution that was subsequently replaced in Roman times by other types of markets. See I. Schepansky, *The Takkanot of Israel*, vol. 1 (Jerusalem and New York, 1991) [in Hebrew], p. 187 et seq. on the Ordinances of Ezra, brought in B. Baba Kama 82a. See Safrai, "Fairs," 144–45, on traveling merchants that moved about between the various fairs and commercial cities, at times with special and expensive merchandise. See T. Avoda Zara 1.9.

14. On pagan festivals in Rabbinic literature, see M. Hadas-Lebel, "Le paganisme à travers les sources rabbiniques de IIe et IIIe siècles. Contribution à l'étude du syncretism dans l'empire romain," in *Aufstieg und Niedergang der römischen Welt*, ed. M. Temporini and W. Haase, vol. 19, part 2 (Berlin and New York, 1979), p. 426 et seq. This subject needs further examination.

15. Y. Avoda Zara 1.2,39c. See S. Lieberman's brilliant analysis in his article "The Martyrs of Caesarea," in *Annuaire de l'Institut de Philologie et d'Histoire Orientale et Slave* (1933–34): 405–407.

16. See M. Avoda Zara 1.3–4. In Tanḥuma Numbers 9, ed. princeps, we read: ומה עיבורה? סטיות וסנדקאיות שהן חוץ למדינה על הדרך. The Mantua edition has פנדקאיות, and Yalkut Shimoni Numbers 683: ופונדקיות, ed. Buber ופונדקיות, Aruch ופונדקין (Lieberman, *Tosefta Ki-fshuṭah*, vol. 3 (New York 1962), p. 354, n. 55). This would suggest that there were such inns or eating places outside the city. However, Lieberman proposes an emendation to סנדמאיות, instead of סנדקאיות, suggesting that this is from the Greek σανιδώματα, with an Aramaic plural termination, meaning a kind of covered shelter (see *A Greek-English Lexicon*, compiled by H. G. Liddell, R. Scott, and H. S. Jones, 9th ed. [Oxford, 1940] (abbr. LSJ^9), p. 1583a, s.v. σανίδωμα, planking, framework) offering protection to travelers from sun and rain. He sees this as equivalent of פיגמין (see chapter 8, section on projections from the walls). However clever this suggestion may be, I find it somehow unconvincing. As to סטיות, variant חטיות in the same Tanḥuma text, which Lieberman (n. 54) corrects to סטיות, plural of סטיו, that is, stoa, covered walks outside the city (see chapter 4, note 15). The Buber edition has חנויות, which Lieberman sees as a mistake. However, this reading goes well with פונדקאיות and should perhaps be reconsidered. See chapter 4.

17. Y. Avoda Zara 1.2,39c. See Safrai, "Fairs," pp. 141–44, 146–97.

18. Y. Avoda Zara 1.2,39c, Safrai, "Fairs," 147–50.

19. See S. Lieberman, *Studies in Palestinian Talmudic Literature* (Jerusalem, 1991) [in Hebrew], p. 445 et seq. According to B. Avoda Zara 13a, in the name of Rabbi Nathan (fl. 134–80 C.E.), on the day special tax allowances for the benefit of idolatrous practices announcements advised persons wishing to participate in this quasi-religious activity to wear a wreath on their heads and to place one on the head of their mules. In M. Avoda Zara 1.4 we read of shops that were decorated and of those that were were not. "And such was the case with Beit Shean, and the rabbis ruled: 'The decorated ones are forbidden, those not decorated are permitted.'" Thus, there were externally recognizable signs indicating the degree of a trader's involvement in these (forbidden) idolatrous practices. See Safrai, "Fairs," pp. 144, 147.

20. Y. Avoda Zara 1.2,39c. However, maybe this reflects the period of privation and famine in the sixties of the third century; see my *Roman Palestine 200–400: The Land* (Ramat-Gan, 1978), pp. 70–99.

21. Y. Avoda Zara 1.4,39d. For a discussion on each of these fairs and others, see Safrai, "Fairs," pp. 152–53. Butna has been identified with Beit Ilonim, close to Hebron. See S. Klein, *Sefer Ha-Yishuv*, vol. 1 (Jerusalem, 1949), p. 158; two miles north of Hebron, also called אילת = Τερέβινθος. According to Sozomenus (fifth century C.E.), Hist. Eccl. 2.4., this market was not a place of licensiousness, unlike the many other fairs where prostitution was rampant. See Safrai, "Fairs," pp. 145–56, referring, inter alia, to Genesis Rabba 37, p. 348. However, despite this the rabbis forbade Jews to participate in this fair because

of its pagan character. Nonetheless, in effect, Jews did go there. See Safrai, "Fairs," 149–51.

22. Y. Avoda Zara 1.4,39d. This issue was discussed in detail by Lieberman in *Studies*, pp. 442–48 (first published in *Eshkolot* 3 (1959): 75–81), with full references and bibliography. Here I shall not repeat the sources or his scintillating argumentation. See also Safrai, "Fairs," pp. 139, 154–55, who has a slightly different interpretation of the chronological development.

3

Market Control

The Agoranomos

He is indeed a familiar personality in classical literature and frequently appears in literary epigraphic and papyrological sources. His duties are fairly well defined and have been competently described on a number of occasions.[1] Likewise, we know him from Rabbinic sources, in which he appears[2] under the guise of different spellings and even different names.[3] Here I shall try to sum up Rabbinic evidence on the subject and thus define the office and duties of the *agoranomos* in Roman Palestine.

Control of Weights and Measures

The notion of authoritative supervision of the weights and measures in use in a market is ancient and is found in Biblical law. Deuteronomy 25:14–15 prescribes that "Thou shalt not have in thine house diverse measures, a great and a small. But thou shalt have a perfect and a just weight, a perfect and just measure shalt thou have. . . ." Although this is formulated as a direct injunction upon the individual, clearly the practical implementation of such a commandment posits some kind of controlling authoritative framework.[4]

Tannaitic law (i.e., up to ca. 220 C.E.) exegetically expounds this latter verse as follows (Sifrei Deuteronomy, sec. 294):[5] "[But] thou shalt have [a perfect and just weight]. . . ."—appoint an *agoranomos*[6] for this (or according to some readings: for measures).[7] Although this ruling is based upon the Biblical verse, the actual institution of the *agoranomos* is clearly Hellenistic in origin; the use of a Greek loanword, as apposed to some local (Hebrew or Aramaic) term, is ample testimony. From the Sifrei we learn of the *agoranomos'* duty to control the standards of weights and measures in the market. Indeed, T. H. Dyer reminds us in his Pompeii[3] (London, 1871) that in Pompeii "in a recess at the north-east end of the temple under the colonnade of the Forum stood the public measures for wine, oil, and grain. These consisted of nine cylindrical holes cut in an oblong block of tufa: There are five large holes for grain and four smaller ones for wine. The former had a sliding bottom that the grain when measured might easily be removed. The latter are provided with tubes to draw off the liquid. These measures were placed near the *horrea* or public granaries" (p. 131).

Thus far we may deduce no more than that Tannaitic law ruled against there being such an official. This, however, is not proof that there were such officials actually operating in the markets of Roman Palestine. The actual day-to-day implementation of this ruling (or perhaps an identical practice independent of this ruling) may be deduced from a number of Rabbinic texts. For example, in Yalkut Shimoni Numbers (Ḥukkat) section 763[8] we read:

> [It is like] unto an *agardemis* (= *agoranomos*) who went out to inspect the measures, and found the shopkeepers locking up [their shops] (in order to avoid his inspection). He seized the first one and beat him,[9] and the others, on hearing this, opened [their shops] of their own accord.

This lively little text informs us not only that there existed market controllers in Rabbinic Palestine but also that they wielded a goodly measure of authority.

Furthermore, in Pesikta de-Rav Kahana, Aser Te'aser 2,[10] we read of the following episode:

> R. Ḥaggai in the name of R. Isaac (fl. later third century C.E.): . . . [It is like] unto an *hagronimos* who went out to inspect the measures and one [shopkeeper] saw him and started to hide from him. Why are you hiding from me? Let your measures be inspected and do not fear. . . .

Our shopkeeper's fear may be explained in the light of the preceding text, in which we saw that the *agoranomos* had the authority to punish offenders and the like and on occasion did so with some brutality. However, a further cause of his fear no doubt lay in the well-known fact that not all the functionaries who held this office were the epitome of ethical rectitude. Quite the contrary: A position of this nature, with the power and authority it carried, naturally tended toward corruption. The *agoranomos* would most likely demand his measure of "graft" in return for which the shopkeeper's license would be ratified. Lack of "cooperation" no doubt meant a suspension of the license (or perhaps prison?)[11] and even grievous bodily harm. Hence, the shopkeeper's fears, even if he felt his measures were fair and honest and in agreement with the standard kept in the office of the *agoranomos*, may have been justified.[12] In this case, the *agoranomos*, understanding the poor shopkeeper's fears, allays them by assuring him that he wishes nothing more than to inspect his measures. If they are found to be sound, all will be well with him.

The above interpretation, which may at first sight appear to be highly speculative, becomes preeminently obvious from the following texts. Although they do not use the term *agoranomos*, it is apparent that they are speaking of the same functionary. In Tanḥuma Leviticus, Ẓav ad init. we read:[13]

> [He was like] unto a butcher who was selling in the marketplace, and his shop was full of meat. The *logistes*[14] went past, and stared at the meat. The butcher saw him staring at the meat and said to him:

> Master, I have already sent a present[15] to your home in the hands of the servant.

The *logistes* is without doubt identical to the market controller. Thus the scholion to Aristophanes reads: ἀγορανόμους οὕς νῦν λογιστὰς καλούμεν.[16] (We shall return to this point again below.) Here we see that he takes his measure of "graft" or "squeeze." The butcher, who sees him gazing avidly at his well-stocked store, hastens, with mocking respect, to assure him that he had already sent him his "percentage." Small wonder that even innocent shopkeepers would dread the market controller's visits and on seeing him approach would close up shop and hide.

The corruption of these market controllers becomes even more evident from yet another text that is similar in style but contains a different term to describe our functionary. Numbers Rabba 20.18:

> It is like unto a banker who was cheating with his measures. The *ba'al ha-shuk*[17] (= market manager) came and became aware of the fact. He said to him: You are cheating with your measures.[18] He replied to him: I have already sent a present[19] to your house.[20]

Apparently, it was common practice among Palestinian *agoranomoi* to augment their regular salary with such income.

Control of Prices

Thus far we have seen the *agoranomos* (*logistes* or *ba'al ha-shuk*) in his function as inspector and controller of weights and measures but have not mentioned his role in controlling prices. Indeed, in the early Rabbinic period prior to the destruction of the Second Temple (in the year 70 C.E.) this office specifically excluded control over prices. In the Tosefta, Baba Meẓia 6.14 we read:[21]

> There were *igranamin* in Jerusalem, and they were not appointed [to control] prices, but only measures.[22]

This is, in fact, quite understandable in a system that encouraged free trade in the fullest sense of the word.[23] With the economic anarchy of the mid-third century C.E.,[24] however, certain changes came about in the Roman economic system,[25] including a variety of attempts to bring down prices. The most famous of these were expressed in Emperor Diocletian's famous Edict of Maximum Prices of the year 301 C.E.[26] It is fully understandable that any responsibility for such price control would pass to the jurisdiction of the market master.

With this background in mind we may perhaps more fully understand the following text from the later third century C.E. B. Baba Batra 89a:

> Thou shalt not have in thine house diverse measures, a great and a small. . . . (Deuteronomy ibid.)—This teaches us that one appoints an *agardemin* (= *agoronamos*) for measures, but one does not appoint an *agardemin* for prices. The house of the Nasi[27] appointed[28] *agardemin*

> both for measures and for prices. . . . Said Rami b. Ḥama, R. Isaac (or according to some readings: R. Yoḥanan)[29] said (both later third century C.E.): One appoints an *agardemin* both for measures and for prices because of swindlers.

It is clear that the earlier ruling, which we have already seen in the Sifrei (and its parallels), ruled with regard only to measures, while sometime during the third century C.E.[30] Rabbinic opinion (Rabbi Isaac or Rabbi Yoḥanan), reflecting or directing current practice,[31] broadened the sphere of the market manager's activities to cover also prices.

In times of difficulty and want the market master had to make sure that adequate supplies of basic provisions reached the market.[32] In order to do so he would at times force merchants whom he knew to have large stocks hoarded away to sell at a reduced rate.[33] We find a reference to this practice in Y. Demai 2.1:

> R. Samuel b. Isaac (fl. ca. 290–20 C.E.): . . . . You may explain it (referring to the discussion preceding in the context) as a case when a great (i.e., powerful) *agronimos* forces him to sell it cheaply. . . .

This entailed pressuring wealthy, powerful, and often ruthless landlords who held such stocks for speculative purposes in lean times. It is certain that they would not easily sell their stocks at a cheap rate.[34] It doubtlessly took a powerful *agoranomos* to carry out such a measure effectively.

Inspection of the Quality of Market Goods

Earlier on we saw that the market master also controlled the *quality* of goods sold in the marketplace, a function directly related to price control. This duty is also reflected in Rabbinic sources. We find evidence of such inspection already in the mid-second century C.E. Thus, in Tosefta Kelim Baba Kama 6.19:[35]

> R. Meir (fl. ca. 130–160 C.E.) declares [wine] ritually impure when there is a reed rope (*gemi*) [in it] because the *igranamin* inspects the wine.

This is not the place to give a detailed explanation of the complex halachic background to this text. It is sufficient to note that the *agoranomos* would go about tasting wine in order to inspect its quality. Here we are speaking of a non-Jewish *agoranomos* and, in the course of his doing so, he might cause it to become ritually impure.[36]

In yet another text we find a similar ruling that teaches us much the same thing. Tosefta Avoda Zara 7.5 declares that:[37]

> An *agronimon* who tasted [wine] from a cup and put [the cup] back into the barrel—presumably the cup was suspended from the barrel on a string, *gemi*, as above—it (i.e., all the wine in the barrel) is forbidden, because one drop of *yayin nesech* (literally libated wine, in this case meaning: wine drunk, touched, or held by a non-Jew) is forbidden and causes [the wine with which it comes into direct contact] to be forbidden, even [though it be] a minute amount.

Here too we are talking about a non-Jewish inspector. The ruling as such could equally apply to any non-Jew coming into contact with kosher wine. Normally, however, wine merchants were very careful not to let their wines (intended for Jewish customers) come into any kind of contact with non-Jews. In the case of a market official they could hardly withhold their wines from his inspection, however. (We have already seen what was liable to happen to those who attempted to avoid or to evade the *agoranomos'* attention!) Probably for this reason the *agoranomos* was singled out for special mention in both these texts. The picture that emerges is one of an official going from shop to shop inspecting the wines, in this case testing the wines for admixture from tasting cups that dangled from the barrels.

Not only wine but also bread was subject to inspection. It is for this reason that low-grade bread (called *kibar* bread)[38] was not sold in the shops on the marketplace but only in those back streets which were largely out of the market master's control. We can therefore understand the text in Canticles Rabba 1.6.4, on the verse in Jeremiah 37:21: ". . . and that they should give him daily a piece of bread out of the bakers' street" (*mi-ḥuẓ ha-ofim*, literally: outside the bakers [street]):

> Said R. Isaac: This *kibar* [= subquality] bread which is sold outside the *plateia* (i.e., market),[39] or (according to other readings),[40] *palter* (meaning either: πωλητήριον or πρατήριον),[41] which is black and made out of barley bran.

For our purposes the correct reading (*plateia* or *palter*) and the right etymology make little difference since all these places were subject to official inspection, so that low-grade breads were not sold.[42]

Assurance of Adequate Supplies

Among the duties of the market master was the assurance of regular and adequate supplies of basic food products, such as wheat and bread. This was normally done through the agency of *sitonae*, corn buyers, who were appointed to purchase cheap stocks of corn from diverse areas and to ensure sufficient reserves in the cities' granaries.[43]

Not only did the granaries have to be well stocked, but also the bread had to be baked regularly, usually through the night, so that there would be an uninterrupted supply of loaves in the market every morning. The supervision of this, too, lay within the duties of the *agoranomos*. We read in a text found in the Yalkut Shimoni, Deuteronomy sec. 808:[44]

> It is like unto a city that was in need of bread. The people cried out to the *ḥashban* (literally: calculator, a loan translation from the Greek *logistes*).[45] Two bakers came foreward and ground [flour] all through the night. [Then] they wished to make the dough, but their candle went out, and they could not see. What did they do? They kneaded the

> dough and baked it [without properly seeing what they were doing. Next morning] they brought it out, and filled the market [with bread]. The *ḥashban* came and saw that the bread was mixed with *kibar* (= stuff of inferior quality),[46] [and] said to them: Really you deserve to have the axe put across your necks and you should be paraded round the whole city.[47] But what can I do to you since you have filled the city [with food] in the hour of need.[48]

From the above we may learn (a) that it devolved upon the *ḥashban-logistes* to see that the market was supplied with adequate amounts of bread, (b) that the *ḥashban* normally inspected and controlled the quality of this bread, and (c) that he had the authority to punish and even execute (!) any baker who produced a substandard product. The control of the quality of goods was part of the duties of the *agoranomos* (*logistes*), as we have already seen. *Ḥashban*, as previously indicated, is a literal loan translation of the Greek λογιστής. Clearly, then, *ḥashban*, *logistes*, and *agoranomos* are all one and the same position, and all correspond to the *ba'al ha-shuk* (= market master). At different times and in different sources this same official is given different titles.[49]

I again remind the reader of the earlier text in which a great and powerful *agronimos* forces a merchant to sell his grain supply cheaply. This, too, was no doubt to ensure a steady supply of basic provisions during times of famine. It was probably this aspect of the *agoranomos*' activities that caused his office to be regarded as of the highest importance. In Leviticus Rabba 1.8[50] we read:

> It is like unto a king who entered into a city. With whom does he speak first? Is it not with the city-*agronomon*?[51] Why? Because he is engaged with the provisioning (literally: life) of the city.

Import Control

During times of severe famine when it was no longer possible to find grain locally and after the city stocks had been exhausted and the granaries emptied, wheat had to be imported from neighboring countries. This task was apparently within the jurisdiction of the *agoranomos*. One of the most natural candidates for supplying famine-ridden Palestine with grain was, of course, Egypt, which was rich, fertile, and close at hand. However, from the post-Augustan period onward Egypt had to satisfy Rome's enormous wheat demand; after meeting this demand, little surplus was left for others.[52] For this reason, any import from Egypt was subject to special imperial license. And having supplied the corn, the cities naturally maintained very strict price control over it. It could not be sold to middlemen, who were likely to turn this cheap supply to their own profit, but had to be sold directly by the importers to the local dealers. No further resale was permitted. Additionally, the millers and bakers were controlled to make sure they did not misuse this cheap grain.

In the light of this information, based on A. H. M. Jones's description,[53] we may now understand a difficult and hitherto insufficiently appreciated text. In Genesis Rabba 76.11[54] we read:

> "[We came to thy brother Esau], and also he cometh to meet thee, and four hundred men with him," (Genesis 32:7). R. Levi (fl. ca., 290–320 C.E.) said: He went and received an *agrami* (?) from Egypt. He said: If I can overcome him [by force], it is well. And if not, I will say to him, "Give me *meches* (= import dues)," and in this way I will kill him.

The word *agrami* has long been something of a puzzle. Some variant readings listed in Theodor-Albeck's apparatus[55] have *agrominim* (obviously *agronimin*) or *agronimon*.[56] Others offer a medley of readings all close to *agrami*, such as *agromi*, *agrami*, *igramo*, *igrami*, and *ogdami* (= *ogrami*, since in Hebrew manuscripts, D(ד) and R(ר) are virtually indistinguishable).

From the context it is clear that Esau received from Egypt some kind of control over imports, one which gave him the right to exact custom dues (*meches*) on imported goods. In the event that Esau was unable to overcome Jacob by force, he planned to extort such enormous import duties that it would be impossible for Jacob to bring grain from Egypt. Famine was a common enough occurrence in Palestine and especially during the lifetime of our homilist.[57] Esau could readily rely upon the fact that there would be famine within a reasonable period of time, and armed with this weapon, he would be able to kill off Jacob by "squeezing" him into starvation. In the light of this passage, the suggestion offered by scholars that we read *agoranomia* as meaning the right to control the import license from Egypt becomes very acceptable,[58] especially since we have seen that this control fell within the right of the *agoranomos*. Accordingly, we can state that the license to import foodstocks from abroad and the controlled marketing of these stocks lay under the direct supervision of the office of the *agoranomos*.

Agoranomi and Astynomi

I have already related a number of occasions in which the *agoranomos* wielded a considerable amount of power. He flogs "dissidents" and threatens careless and unhygienic bakers with the most serious punishments. Even the innocent live in dire fear of him. In all likelihood he did not do all these things by himself but through the agency of the local police.[59] In a larger city, where there were many markets,[60] an entire office employing a number of officials probably carried out all the duties of market control. In smaller cities, on the other hand, the special board that controlled the town and its civic services (for example, drainage system, water supply, [and] street lighting)[61] probably also supervised the market's activities. Hence, it is likely that at times the ἀστυνόμοι(controllers of the town) also served in the function of ἀγορανόμοι.[62]

An indication of this arrangement may be found in a text in Y. Ma'aser Sheni 5.2: There we find Rabbi Hoshaya (I? fl. first half of third century C.E.) using three *istononsin* for redeeming the fruit of "Fourth Year planting." According to the Mishna (Ma'aser Sheni 5.4) the rule is that the owner lays a basket before three people who know the price of fruit and asks them certain questions concerning the value of the fruit. Clearly, the *istononsin* whom Rabbi Hoshaya (in Tiberias, where he lived much of his life) approached were in some way connected with the market in that they were fully cognizant of market prices.

What were these *istononsin*? It has been suggested[63] that we correct the text to read *sitonesin*[64] (plural of σιτώνης). However, the correct identification is undoubtedly with *astynomi*.[65] The *astynomi* which Rabbi Hoshaya used for his redemption procedure were fully acquainted with market prices. It is therefore reasonable to assume that among their many other duties they served as *agoranomoi*,[66] who, as we have already seen, supervised prices in the marketplace.

Conclusion

In this chapter the *agoranomos*, or market master, has appeared in a number of different terminological guises, *agronomin* (in all its different spellings, *logistes*, *ḥashban*, *istononsin*, and *ba'al ha-shuk*). We have seen that at different times his office controlled weights, measures, and prices; inspected the quality of goods; ensured a steady supply of basic food products to the market, at times even forcing merchants to sell below the normal price; and controlled the license to import from Egypt (or other neighboring countries). We find him vested with the authority to punish and even to inflict capital punishment. We catch him in his moments of corruption, gloating over prospective graft or inspiring terror in timid innocents. We have noted the respectful but mocking irony in those who forcedly "cooperated" in augmenting his basic income. We have seen him utilizing his control over import licenses to further his own personal ends and to help him cast down his enemy. But we have also seen him in moments of honor and rectitude, supporting the community in times of need, exercising his authority to bring down prices, and using all his powers to slash at profiteers and speculative hoarders.

We know of additional functions of the market master from non-Rabbinic sources, such as keeping the fabric of the market in good repair, collecting rents from shops and stalls in the marketplace,[67] and fixing the hours of the market.[68] However, these functions do not seem to appear in Rabbinic literature. What survives in Rabbinic literature, a body of material with a very peculiar nature and character, is, after all, largely a matter of chance.[69] Hence, little can be deduced from the silence of the sources,[70] but much may be learned from their vivid, eloquent, and, at times, almost intimate passages.

Notes

1. See for example A. H. M. Jones, *The Greek City from Alexander to Justinian* (Oxford, 1967), pp. 215–17. Josephus, *Wars* 18.6.2.149, mentions this position as being held by Herod in Tiberias for a short while. His precise duties there are left undefined. Further material on the *agoranomos* may be found in Pauly-Wissowa, *Real-Encyclopaedie des klassischen Altertums* [:PW *RE*], vol. 1 (Stuttgart, 1894), pp 883–85 with bibliography; R. Haderli, *Die Hellenischen Astynomen und Agronomen, Jahrbuch für classische Philologie,* Suppl. 15, (Vienna, 1886); W. Liebernam, *Städtsverwaltung im römischen Kaiserreiche* (Leipzig, 1900), pp. 363–68, 339–42; and most recently the excellent article by B. R. Foster, "*Agoranomos* and *Muḥtasib*," *JESHO* 13 (1970): 128–44, especially p. 131, where the duties are summed up.

2. A list of references to the relevant sources may be found in S. Krauss, *Griechische und Lateinische Lehnwörter im Talmud, Midrasch, und Targum,* vol. 2 [*LW*[2]] (Berlin, 1899; reprint, Hildesheim, 1964), pp. 11ab–12a, s.v. אגרדמוס and אגרנימוס. A casual perusal of this list will readily reveal the considerable variety of spellings and readings of this term in Rabbinic literature. See further idem, *Talmudische Archäologie*[2], 3 vols. (Leipzig, 1910–12), pp. 374, 698, n. 418–22. (These two invaluable works have been strangely neglected by classicists.) A discussion of this office in Babylonia may be found in M. Beer, *The Babylonian Exilarchate in the Arsacid and Sassanian Periods* (Tel-Aviv, 1970) [in Hebrew], pp. 123–28; a good deal of Palestinian material is also referred to and discussed in these pages. See also J. Neusner, *A History of the Jews in Babylonia,*[2] *The Early Sasanian Period,* (Leiden, 1966), pp. 111–15, with bibliography, and more recently, A. Ben-David, *Talmudische Ökonomie, Die Wirtschaft des jüdischen Palästina zur Zeit der Mischna und des Talmud,* vol. 1 (Hildesheim and New York, 1974), pp. 214–18, 409–10 (who shows a lack of acquaintance with the relevant literature).

3. See below.

4. On the control of markets in ancient Mesopotamia, see A. Oppenheimer in *JESHO* 10 (1967): 5–6 (referred to by Foster, "*Agoranomos* and *Muḥtasib*," 136, n. 1). B. Kisch, in his *Scales and Weights—A Historical Outline*[2], Yale Studies in the History of Science and Medicine, vol. 1 (New Haven and London, 1965), p. 4, writes: "Two problems were of constant concern to governments: to safeguard the proper manufacture and use of weights and measures, and to urge uniformity of standards, at least within their individual realms. They not only kept a watchful eye on the accuracy of weights and scales but they appointed experts as officers entrusted with the duty of checking their instruments. Among the oldest laws against the fraudulent use of weights and scales are the different Biblical commandments (Lev. 19:35 ff.; Deut. 25 ff.). . . ." It should be noted that "standards" for weights and measures could be little more than of a local nature. The notion of exact measures was alien to people of that time, and mostly measures were of a rule-of-thumb nature (see my remarks in my article "Weights and Measures," in *Encyclopaedia Judaica* (Jerusalem, 1971), vol. 16, column 389), hence the diversity of standards. See also B. Eruvin 83a, and my discussion in "Costs of Living in Roman Palestine I," *JESHO* 8 (1965): 266–71. I hope to discuss this very important issue in detail elsewhere.

5. Ed. Finkelstein (Berlin, 1939; reprint, New York, 1969), p. 313. Paral-

lels are to be found in Sifra Kodashim 8.8, ed. Weiss (Vienna, 1862; reprint, New York, 1946), and 91b; Y. Baba Batra 5.8; B. Baba Batra 88a.

6. For many variant readings see Finkelstein's apparatus ad loc.

7. This latter reading is partly borne out by the continuation of the text: On the basis of this they said: The *siton* cleans his measures once every thirty days, and the [private] householder once a year (Sifra Kodashim 8.8; M. Baba Batra 5.10). On the *siton* see below.

8. Yalkut Shimoni, standard ed. (Berlin, 1926); ed. princeps. Saloniki 1521, Psalms sec. 819. This is a late compilation of Midrashic sources containing both early and late material. This particular text, though not closely datable, probably comes from the Amoraic period (third and fourth century C.E. in Palestine). (On the Yalkut Shimoni in general see Jacob Elbaum's article in *Encyclopaedia Judaica*, vol. 16, columns 707–9, with bibliography.) On the form *agardemos*, see Krauss, *LW*[1], p. 102, sec. 173. See also Schorr, *He-Ḥaluẓ* 13 (1899): 112, suggesting that this form is based on **agoradomus* (?).

9. On the connection between the office of the *agoranomos* and the police, see below. On the roughness of Palestinian police during the Amoraic period, see chapter 4. On flight out of fear for the brutality of the market controllers and also flogging of bakers see A. H. M. Jones, *The Later Roman Empire*, vol. 2 (Oxford, 1964), p. 735; Foster, "*Agoranomos*," p. 131; and Libanius Or. 1, 206–8. (= *Libanius' Autobiography* [Oration 1], ed., introd., trans., and nn., A. F. Norman (Oxford, 1965), pp. 111–13, and cf. *Autobiography* p. 208).

10. Ed. Mandelbaum (New York, 1962), pp. 162–63.

11. See chapter 6.

12. See Foster, "*Agoranomos*," referring to V. Bernardi, "Tegée et la Tagéatide," *Bulletin de Correspondance Hellenique* 17 (1873): 4–6; Haderli, *Die Hellenischen*, p. 76; and Jones, *Greek City*, p. 216. Note, for example, the "*Kesita*" (= *xestes*) of Sepphoris mentioned in B. Pesaḥim 109a, (discussed in my "Costs of Living in Roman Palestine I," in p. 267). This subject requires further examination. In the meantime see the material cited by Ben-David, *Talmudische Ökonomie*, pp. 215–18, 410, and the reference in Foster, "*Agoranomos*," p. 136. Attention has been called to the term *resh korei*, found in B. Kiddushin 76b and stated there to be a Palestinian institution. Rashi, ad loc., explains that this means a person in charge of measures—the *kor* is a measure of capacity—and so does a marginal gloss (presumably following Rashi) found in Ms. Vat. Ebr. 111, fol. 175d top ("Makor" facsimile *The Vatican Collection of Talmudic Manuscripts*, vol. 6 [Jerusalem, 1973], p. 268). See also Beer, *Babylonian Exilarchate*, p. 125, n. 28. However, an examination of the reading of this term in Ms. Munich ad loc. reveals that one should read כוורי (with two vavs) rather than כורי (with one vav). This suggests quite a different meaning, since כוורא is a fish (see M. Jastrow, in his *A Dictionary of the Targumim, the Talmud Babli and Yerushalmi, and the Midrashic Literature* (New York, 1903), p. 617b s.v. and M. Sokoloff's review of S. A. Kaufman's *The Akkadian Influences on Aramaic* (Chicago, 1974) in *Kiryat Sefer* 51 (1974): 469. I would suggest that *resh kavrei* is the head of the guild of fishermen. We know of such guilds in Talmudic Palestine (see my remarks in my article, "Some Observations on Fish and Fisheries in Roman Palestine," *ZDMG* 118 (1968); 267–68). The term is probably a Babylonian adaptation of an original Palestinian notion, which was perhaps expressed quite differently. Possibly there were in Babylonia similar such guilds

headed by a person called a *resh kavrei*, and the same term was applied to the Palestinian countepart. On fisheries in Talmudic Babylonia see more recently M. Beer, *The Babylonian Amoraim: Aspects of Economic Life* (Ramat-Gan, 1974) [in Hebrew], pp. 150–55.

13. Parallels in Yalkut Shimoni, Proverbs sec. 555; Midrash Tanḥuma, ed. S. Buber, Wilna, Lev. Zav 1, p. 12.

14. See Tanḥuma, ed. Buber, Lev. p. 12, n. 8.

15. *Ofsonin* = ὀψώνιον, so one should read. Cf. Tanḥuma, ed. Buber, Lev. p. 12, n. 9, whose interpretation is clearly incorrect. The word generally means an allowance but here bears the meaning (or implication) of a bribe. See my remarks in "*Calculo-Logistes-Ḥashban*," *Classical Quarterly* 19 (1969): 377, n. 9, and also "*Le-gilgulo shel Ḥeshbon*," in *Tarbiẓ* 39 (1969): 97, n. 10.

16. Acharn. 720, cited by S. Lieberman in "Roman Legal Institutions in Early Rabbinics and the Acta Martyrum," *JQR* 35 (1944): 37, n. 241 (who refers one to W. Liebernam in *Philologus* 56 (1897): 317, n. 115; M. Gelzer in Arch. Pap. 5 (1906): 358). This text is also quoted by the editors of *Hesychius* 62, n. 14. See my article "*Calculo-Logistes-Ḥashban*," where I discussed this term in detail. Haderli, *Die Hellenischen*, p. 69, writes that in Egypt *logistes* became another term for *agoranomos*; see also Foster, "*Agoranomos* and *Muḥtasib*," 135, 137 (P. Antin. 38, P.O. 83). From this Egyptian term in this meaning may derive the later Islamic term *muḥtasib*. (See H. Z. Dimitrovsky in "Hearot le-gigulo shel Ḥeshbon," *Tarbiẓ* 39 (1970) 317 and note 45 below.) On the *logistes* see PW *RE*, vol. 25, part 1, pp. 1926, 1020–21. See also W. Smith, W. Wayte, and G. E. Marindin, *A Dictionary of Greek and Roman Antiquities*[3], vol. 1 (London, 1890), p. 49 s.v. *agoranomi* (citing inter alia the gloss referred to above and giving the reference as Acharn. 688).

17. This term corresponds to the Islamic *sahib al-suq* found in a Geniza fragment (TS10J) and cited in S. D. Goitein's monumental *A Mediterranean Society*, vol. 1 (Berkeley and Los Angeles, 1967), p. 483, n. 64. See also Foster, "*Agoranomos* and *Muḥtasib*," p. 139, and C. Cahen and M. Talbi in *EI*[2] 3 (1971), 487a. Note also that in a Palmyrene bilingual inscription (G. A. Cooke, *A Textbook of North-Semitic Inscriptions* [Oxford, 1903], p. 180, n. 121 = Vog. 15) dated 242–43 C.E., we come across רב שוק equaling ἀγορανομήσαντα (noted by S. Lieberman in "Roman Legal Institutions," p. 37, n 241). These terms are loan translations from the Greek *agoranomos*. However, they may be no more than terminologically derivated from the Greek term, although doubt has been cast on this, too. See Foster, "*Agoranomos* and *Muḥtasib*," p. 139.

18. Bankers (money exchangers) checked coins and weighed them, dealt in bullion, and bought up gold, hence their use of weights (see my article "Money Changers" in *Encylopaedia Judaica*, vol. 12, columns 243–44). See my remarks in *Roman Palestine 200–400: Money and Prices* (Ramat-Gan, 1974), p. 240, n. 51, p. 311 note to p. 140.

19. Doron—δῶρον = present, here paralleling ὀψώνιον of the previous text (see note 15 above).

20. Undated text, probably of the later fourth century C.E. (cf. "*Calculo-Logistes-Ḥashban*," p. 377, n. 9). Almost all the texts we have cited thus far have been in the form of parables. These parables reflect the daily life of those times in a most remarkable fashion. For an examination of one class of these parables, see I. Ziegler, *Die Königsgleichnisse des Midrasch beleuchtet durch die römische Kaiserzeit* (Breslau, 1903) and most recently the fine work of D. Stern,

Parables in the Midrash; Narrative and Exegesis in Rabbinic Literature (Cambridge and London, 1991).

21. Ed. Zuckermandel, p. 384.

22. See Beer, *Babylonian Exilarchate*, p. 124, and especially note 22, where he examines the issue in some detail, demonstrating that in Babylonia price control was part and parcel of this office. (Correct his comment in note 22 on the word "*ofsonin*" in the light of note 15 above.) This Tosefta text, although formulated in the period after the destruction of the Temple, describes (in all probability accurately) a situation occurring prior to the destruction. The degree of emphasis placed on the fact that there was no price control but only control of weights and measures suggests that this text was formulated during a time when price control was the prerogative of this office, and our editor compares the earlier situation with the current one.

23. See my comments in "Laesio Enormis and the Talmudic Law of Ona'ah," *Israel Law Review* 8 (1973): 270, n. 31, citing *Digesta* 19.2.22.3; 4.4.16.4. Further indication of the lack of organized price control during this early period may be found in a Mishna in Keritot 1.7: Once in Jerusalem a pair of doves (for sacrifical purposes) cost a gold dinar. Rabbi Simeon b. Gamliel said: By this Temple! I will not suffer this night to pass before they cost but a [silver] dinar, (twenty-five times less!). He went into the Beit-Din (law court) and taught: If a woman suffered five miscarriages that were not in doubt or five issues that were not in doubt, she need bring one offering, and may then eat of the animal offerings; and she is not bound to offer the other offerings. And the same day the doves stood at a quarter (= half a denarius each). Thus, Rabbi Gamliel had no other way to reduce the price but through the medium of his legal exegesis, which had the immediate effect of radically cutting down the demand for this commodity.

24. I have discussed this matter in a number of articles and most fully in my book *Roman Palestine 200–400: Money and Prices*², Ramat-Gan, 1991.

25. See, for example, my article "Laesio Enormis," pp. 254–74 and again my *Roman Palestine 200–400: The Land*, p. 136 et seq. I have not discussed here techniques of price control or the process of price fixing (artificial or natural). This I hope to deal with elsewhere.

26. This has more recently been reedited by S. Lauffer in his *Diokletians Preisedikt* (Berlin, 1971), with a full bibliography. In *Roman Palestine 200–400: Money and Prices*, p. 37, I suggested that this edict was known in Palestine.

27. Beer, *Babylonian Exilarchate*, p. 123 note and p. 125, argues that this term refers to the Babylonian exilarch and may be referring to Rav's appointment to this position (in the second quarter of the third century C.E.) mentioned in Y. Baba Batra 5 ad fin. (bibliography ibid.). See also J. Neusner, *History of the Jews*², p. 112, n. 2, referring to S. Liebermann, *Hayerushalmi Kiphshuto* (Jerusalem, 1934), pp. 175–76. This view is based upon the context we find this event debated and discussed by Babylonian authorities.

28. According to certain manuscript readings: used to appoint, that is, a regular procedure, rather than a one-time event. See R. Rabbinovicz, *Variae Lectiones in Mischnam et in Talmud Babylonicum* [*VL*] (Munich and Mainz, 1868–86), to Baba Batra (Munich, 1881), p. 275, n. 6.

29. The readings at this point are both complex and confused. See Rabbinovicz, *VL*, p. 276, n. 8: Rami b. Aba said R. Yoḥanan . . . , R. Aba b. Avin said R. Yoḥanan. Chronologically, there is little difference between these readings,

since Rabbi Yoḥanan and Rabbi Isaac were contemporaries, Rabbi Yoḥanan's dying in the year 279 C.E., and Rabbi Isaac's living on some time after Rabbi Yoḥanan's death. All these readings show that we are talking of Palestinian personalities.

30. See note 22 above. It is not clear when the text in Tosefta Baba Meẓia 6.14 was formulated, although it appears to reflect a current practice of the *agoranomos*' controlling prices. Perhaps it is a late Tosefta of the early third century C.E., or perhaps it is earlier, in which case the practice in Palestine may have begun (regionally?) prior to the third century. Or does this text perhaps reflect a knowledge of Babylonian practice in this sphere, in which case it can cast no light on the date of the advent of this procedure in Palestine (see Beer, *Babylonian Exilarchate*, p. 123 et seq.).

31. As in Babylonia. See note 27 above on the reactions of Babylonian scholars to the House of the Nasi's (= Exilarch's) appointment of Rav to this office. Rabbi Yoḥanan was very active in the field of socioeconomic legislation. Apparently, his power and authority in the civil domain was (indirectly?) very great. See my articles "Laesio Enormis," pp. 254–74, and "Flight and the Talmudic Law of Usucaption: A Study in the Social History of Third Century Palestine," *Revue internationale des droits d'antiquité* 3, no. 19 (1972): 29–42 (= *Bar-Ilan* 9 [1972]: 290–96, in Hebrew).

32. This was very common during the third and earlier fourth centuries C.E., with their almost continuous runs of drought, famine, and plague. I have described the situation in detail in my article "Drought, Famine, and Pestilence in Amoraic Palestine," *JESHO* 17 (1974): 272–98, and again in my *Roman Palestine 200–400: The Land*, p. 70 et seq.

33. For parallels in classical sources see Jones, *Greek City*, pp. 216–18, 350, n. 11, 12, 16; Jones, *Later Roman Empire*, vol. 2, p. 844, vol. 3, p. 283, n. 48; and M. Rostovtzeff, *Social and Economic History of the Roman Empire* [*SEHRE*²] (Oxford, 1956), p. 599, n. 9. For a parallel in Babylonia, see B. Baba Batra 90b (cited by Neusner in *History of the Jews*², p. 113 and see also p. 114, n. 1 for further bibliography). On hoarders in third century Palestine, see my remarks in *Roman Palestine 200–400: The Land*, pp. 88, 90, 128, and Rostovtzeff, *SEHRE*², pp. 700–701, n. 21.

34. See my discussion in "Patronage in Amoraic Palestine (ca. 220–400): Causes and Effect," *JESHO* 14 (1971): 233–37, and again in *Roman Palestine 200–400: The Land*, p. 119 et seq. It is interesting to note that there are a number of references in Rabbinic literature to speculators who attempt to manipulate prices through their control over large reserves of basic commodities. Thus, for example, in B. Megilla 17b we read: Why did they [who compiled the *Amida* (= eighteen benedictions)] see fit to fix the "benediction of the years" as the ninth one? Said R. Alexandri (flr. mid-third century C.E.): Against those who manipulate the prices, as is written, "Break Thou the arm (*zero'a*) of the evil men. . . ." (Psalm 10:15). (Note the association with *ba'alei zero'a*, the strong ruthless patrons discussed in my *Roman Palestine 200–400: The Land*, pp. 89, 121–25, 132–35, 186–87.) Further references in Genesis Rabba 13.12, p. 121, and parallels: Midrash Ḥaserot vi-Yeterot, in S. A. Wertheimer, *Batei Midrashot*, vol. 2 (Jerusalem, 1956), p. 237, sec. 12, and Jones, *Later Roman Empire*, vol. 2, p. 735, vol. 3, p. 234, n. 53, referring one to Greg. Naz., Or. 43, according to which Basil influenced the landowners "to disgorge."

35. Ed. Zuckermandel, p. 576.

36. Probably there were no significant differences between the authority of a Jewish and a non-Jewish *agoranomos*, as has already rightly been pointed out by Beer in *Babylonian Exilarchate*, p. 125, n. 24.

37. Ed. Zuckermandel, p. 471.

38. See my discussion in my article, "Pat Kebar," *Tarbiz* 33 (1967): 199–201 (which requires some further modification).

39. See chapter 2.

40. In Yalkut Shimoni to Cant. sec. 982.

41. Krauss, *LW*², p. 458ab, s.v., and I. Löw's remarks ad loc.

42. It should be noted that in all probability most food products were subject to such inspection and control, but no clear evidence of this survives in the Rabbinic sources. Indeed, wine gained mention only because of its very specific legal status and, as it were, ritual vulnerability, while mention of bread survived in a chance homily by singular good fortune. On control over bakers, see Libanius Or. 4.35; 27.27; 54,42.

43. See Jones, *Greek City*, pp. 217, 350, n. 15. For references to Rabbinic sources mentioning *sitonae*, see Krauss, *LW*², pp. 381b–82a s.v. *sitonae*, and Schürer, *A History of the Jewish People in the Time of Jesus Christ*, Division 2, vol. 1 (Edinburgh, 1893), p. 38, n. 158. I hope to discuss this issue in detail elsewhere. In the meantime see Krauss, *LW*², p. 102b s.v. אפותיקי; my remarks in my article "Ḥikrei Millim ve-girsaot," *Erchei* 2 (1974): 110–11; Krauss, *Talmudische Archäologie*², pp. 194–95, 579–80, n. 312; and Jones, *Later Roman Empire*, vol. 2, p. 735.

44. This text derives from the Byzantine (?) Midrash Deuteronomy Zuta. See my comments on this in "*Calculo-Logistes-Ḥashban*," p. 377, n. 10 (I have discussed the whole text on pp. 377–78) and in "le-gilgulo shel Ḥeshbon *Tarbiz* 39 (1969): 96–97. See also S. Lieberman's discussion in "Roman Legal Institutions," pp. 37–38, 57.

45. Lieberman, "Roman Legal Institutions," p. 37, n. 241; H. Z. Dimitrovsky, "Hearot le-gilgulo shel Ḥeshbon," p. 317 (citing an oral communication from Lieberman); and again my own remarks in "*Calculo-Logistes-Ḥashban*" and "*Le-gilgulo shel Ḥeshbon*" (see also note 16 above). In my "Le-gilgulo shel Ḥeshbon," p. 97, I called attention to the parallelism with the Islamic term *muḥtasib*, also a "calculator, and in charge of the market." And indeed, so did Lieberman in "Roman Legal Institutions," p. 52; see also Dimitrovsky, "Hearot le-gigulo shel Ḥeshbon," p. 317. Despite the clear terminological relationship, the connection between the *muḥtasib* and the *agoranomos*, the dependence of the former upon the latter has been called into doubt. See Foster, "*Agoranomos* and *Muḥtasib*," p. 139, referring to Cahen and Talbi in *EI*², 3 (1970): 487a, and E. Tynan, "Histoire de l'Organisation judiciaire en pays d'Islam," *Annales de l'Université de Lyons*, 3 ser. (1943): 449. However, I am not completely convinced by the argumentation, which is partly *ex silentio*. See my remarks below in note 70.

46. See note 38 above.

47. See Lieberman in "Roman Legal Institutions," pp. 37–38 on this procedure. On the flogging of bakers, see Jones, *Later Roman Empire*, vol. 2, p. 735.

48. *Be-sh'at ha-zifzuf*. See Lieberman's comment in "Roman Legal Institutions," p. 38, n. 245. See also H. Yalon, *Studies in the Hebrew Language* (Jerusalem, 1971) [in Hebrew], p. 139.

49. *Agoranomos* (in its various spellings) is the earliest and most original

of these terms. *Ba'al ha-shuk* is derivative and its appearance thus seems relatively late, even though it is paralleled by the Palmyrene third century C.E. *Rav Shuk* (see note 17 above). Usage of *logistes* in this meaning may have appeared as early as the fourth century in Palestine (see my remarks in "Le-gilgulo shel Ḥeshbon," 1969, p. 97, and cf. material cited in note 16 above). *Ḥashban* is of course later, being a loan translation from *logistes* (see also note 45 above).

50. Ed. Margulies p. 22.

51. Ben-David, *Talmudische Ökonomie*, p. 216, seems not fully to have understood the phrase *agronimon shel medina*. It means no more than the city's *agoranomos*. This is the only meaning one can attach to the word *medina* in this context. So it is used the first time in this text: . . . a king who entered into the *medina*. It would be rash and unsound to reach any conclusions on the basis of this text about the nature of the *agoranomos*' appointment.

52. For a discussion of this point see my article on trade between Palestine and Egypt in Roman times "Objects of Trade between Palestine and Egypt in Roman Palestine," *JESHO* 19 (1976): 113–17.

53. Jones, *Greek City*, pp. 216, 218, 350; idem, *Later Roman Empire*, vol. 2, p. 844; and Rostovtzeff, *SEHRE*[2], p. 700, n. 21; and PW *RE* vol. 7, p. 186, s.v. frumentum.

54. Ed. Theodor-Albeck, p. 894.

55. Ibid., to line 2.

56. But these, of course, may be emendations to a more familiar word (or form). According to the principle "praestat lectio difficilior," we should prefer the group of readings (below) close to *agrami*.

57. See note 32 above.

58. See Theodor-Albeck's discussion in the notes on p. 894, with bibliography; Krauss, *LW*[2], p. 11b s.v. אגרומי and Löw's notes ad loc. (ἀγρονομία = *aedilitas*); S. Krauss, ed., *Additamenta ad Librum Aruch Completum Alexandri Kohut* (Vienna, 1927), p. 9a s.v. *agrami* (contra Kohut in Aruch Completum, 1, p. 29a s.v.); and likewise L. Ginzberg, *Additamenta*, p. 419b, s.v. It may well be that *agrami*, rather than being a corruption of *agronomi* (or some similar form), is a dialectical inflection of *agronomi*, just as we find the form ἄγρινοι in Hesychius (67, *LSJ*[9], p. 15, s.v.) equaling ἀγορανόμοι. See note 56 above.

59. See note 9 above. See also Jones, *Later Roman Empire*, vol. 2, p. 734; vol. 3, p. 234, n. 52.

60. For example, Tiberias; see S. Klein, *Galilee* (Jerusalem, 1967) [in Hebrew], pp. 97–98, who lists five *shuks*—markets, or streets with shops (see chapter 2).

61. See Jones, *Greek City*, pp. 213–14; Foster, "*Agoranomos* and *Muḥtasib*," p. 130. There is much work to be done in all these avenues of research. Meanwhile, the pioneer studies of Krauss remain the best general guides to these subjects: his articles "Mayyim li-shtot," *Ha-Shiloaḥ* 20 (1909), 17–26, 115–22 (on water) and "Ha-Kerach, ha-Ir ve-ha-Kfar ba-Talmud," *He-Atid* 1 (1900–1), 1–50 (on cities); *Talmudische Archäologie* throughout, especially vol. 1; and *Kadmoniyyot ha-Talmud* (a revised translation into Hebrew of part of *Talmudische Archäologie*, vol. 1 (Berlin and Vienna, no date but ca. 1924). See my *Material Culture in Ereẓ-Yisrael during Its Talmudic Period* (Jerusalem, 1993) [in Hebrew], pp. 29–45.

62. Jones, *Greek City*, p. 215; Foster, "*Agoranomos* and *Muḥtasib*," p. 133, n. 1, referring to Strabo 15.707–08, and also p. 137.

63. Jastrow, *Dictionary*, p. 57b, s.v. איסרטה.

64. In Y. Ma'aser Sheni 4.1 we read of Rabbi Yannai (fl. early third century C.E.) redeeming through the agency of *ḥatonaya* (so in the printed editions, including the ed. princeps). Some commentators (Pnei Moshe ad loc.) suggest reading *teḥunaya*, millers (see also Ratner, *Ahavat Ẓiyyon ve-Yerushalayim*, ad loc. (Wilna, 1917), p. 185). However, the correct reading is surely *sitonaya*, as in Ms. Vat. 133 (cited by Ratner). Note that in the Leiden Ms. (Cod. Scal. 3, p. 256) this passage is missing and was added in the margin by a glossator who was also among the editors of the ed. princeps. This gloss appears to read *ḥitonaya*. On the glossator and editor, see S. Lieberman, *Hayerushalmi Kiphshuto*, p. 15 et seq.

65. See J. Levy, *Neuhebräisches und Chaldäisches Wörterbuch über die Talmudim und Midraschim*, vol. 1 (Leipzig, 1876), p. 135a s.v. אסתוניא; A. Kohut, *Aruch ha-Shalem*, vol. 1 (Vienna and New York, 1878–92), p. 207a s.v. איסתוננסין; Krauss, *LW*², p. 38b s.v. איסתוננסין; p. 98a s.v.; and reject H. Guggenheimer, "La-Milon ha-Talmudi," *Leshonenu* 39 (1975): 61–62.

66. See Levy, *Neuhebräisches*, p. 135a.

67. Perhaps it was for this reason that the *agoranomos* came to be called a *logistes*, since he became ever more involved in the business of accounting. See also G. McLean Harper, *Village Administration in Syria*, Yale Classical Studies, vol. 1 (New Haven and London, 1928), p. 155 (referring to IGRR, iii, 1020), and cf. p. 150 on the lack of evidence that villages in Syria may have derived a small irregular income from renting their public buildings.

68. Jones, *Greek City*, pp. 215–16.

69. See note 42 above.

70. See McLean Harper, *Village*, p. 147: "The *logistes* is an official who does not appear in the villages of Syria." But more significant is the fact that the *agoranomos* hardly appears in inscriptions from (Syria and) Palestine. If we were to depend for our material solely on epigraphic sources, we would have to rely on very meagre evidence (Wadd. 2330 = CIG 4612 referred to by Foster, "*Agoranomos* and *Muḥtasib*," p. 136, n. 4) and might reach very different conclusions.

4

Pubs, Drunkards, and Licensing Laws

We now move on from the marketplace to the pubs and drinking houses, which as we have already seen, were to be found in the periphery of the market area. Here again we shall see that at times a brief homily in a Midrash can give us a glimpse into social situations in Roman Palestine; when coupled with classical sources, these homilies can help create a picture of how society functioned in that period. I will begin with a passage from Leviticus Rabba, which although it has the hallmarks of a sermon and therefore may not be strictly accurate historically, nonetheless captures the feeling of the times and is thus most instructive to the historian. In order fully to understand this text, we must first preface our discussion with some introductory remarks.

Sumptuary Laws

The problem of Roman sumptuary laws has been discussed by a number of scholars.[1] Ramsay MacMullen in his *Enemies of the Roman Order* has written as follows:

> From the 70's A.D., the governing classes, heavy eaters themselves and sometimes, like Nero, addicts of dives and bars, tried to improve the character of the lower classes by intermittent legislation to shut up taverns and to prohibit the sale of cooked meats and pastries. That left vegetables, their definition at one time being narrowed to peas and beans. After Vespasian, public morals were given up as a bad job for three centuries. In the 370's, when prefects renewed the war, they limited wine shops in what they could sell and in the hours they could stay open. . . .[2]

Of particular importance in this connection is the statement of Ammianus Marcellinus[3] that Ampelius, governor of Rome (371–72 C.E.), gave orders that no wine shop should be opened before the fourth hour (about nine o'clock in the morning), in other words, that wine shops should be shut up at night.

It is clear from these examples that an examination of pubs and licensing hours can offer valuable insights into social conditions of the time. Since there is relatively little primary material in the classical sources on this subject, I will bring to bear some contemporary Rabbinic findings, which may further expand the evidence on this issue.

Pubs

In Leviticus Rabba[4] we read the following tale:

> It happened once that a certain man, who used regularly to drink twelve xestes of wine a day, one day drank [only] eleven. He tried to go to sleep, but sleep would not come to him. [So] he got up in the dark (= night) and went to the wine-shop,[5] and said to [the wine seller]: "Sell me one xestes of wine." [The latter] replied to him: "I cannot, for it is dark." He said to him: "If you do not give [it] me, sleep will not come to me." [To which the wine seller] replied: "Just now the watchmen have passed from (= by) here, and I am afraid[6] of the watchmen and can [therefore] not give [it] you." [The man] raised his eyes and saw a hole in the door. [So] he said to him: "Hold the bottle[7] up to this hole; you pour from the inside and I shall drink from the outside." He was insistent. What did he (the wine seller) do? He put the spout[8] [of the bottle] through the crack[9] in the door and poured from the inside while the other drank from the outside. As soon as he finished [drinking], he fell asleep in a corner in front of the door. The watchmen passed by him before the door, and thinking him a thief, beat him. [But] he did not feel [it]. They wounded him, and he did not notice [it]. They reddened[10] his eyes, and he saw nothing. [People][11] applied to him the verse:[12] *Who hath wounds without cause*? meaning: Who has undeserved wounds? *Who hath redness of eyes*? Who has swollen eyes? Who has all these?—*They that tarry long at the wine*. Those who are first to enter the shop[13] and last to leave. Those who make searches after the wine, and learn where there is a good brand[14] and chase after it, saying: "The wine of so and so is good. The wine of so and so is red. Give us and we shall drink of it. The wine of so and so is hot (or bubbling).[15] Give us and we shall drink of it."

Licensing Laws

This passage belongs to the genre of moralistic homilies that were preached in the synagogues on the Sabbath before a mixed crowd. It belongs to a group of antidrinking sermons,[16] and although it may be tendentious in style and character, the reliability of the information it contains on conditions in Palestine during the Roman period can hardly be doubted. Unfortunately, the text cannot be closely dated, and the geographic location of the event described cannot be fixed with any certainty. All one can state is that it is from between ca. 270 and 380 C.E. and that it probably comes from one of the larger Palestinian towns, such as Tiberias or Caesarea.[17] In other words, it is not clear from where in Palestine it comes or whether or not it antedates the *leges sumptuariae* of Rome of the 370s. It certainly, however, refers to some kind of licensing-hour regulations and indicates that such regulations were enforced by the local police.

Night Police

The exact status of these night watchmen police is not clearly defined in the text. It is known that in Palestine there were private *saltuarii* (= *saltarii*—σαλτυάριοι),[18] who were payed and supported by the owners of (or renters in) villages and townships.[19] There was also a class of night watchmen called *nuktostrategoi*;[20] however, these were primarily used for controlling thieves and brigands[21] rather than for enforcing local (sumptuary) regulations. It seems more likely that night watchmen were official policemen, with the job of enforcing all rules and regulations. The fact that their behavior was somewhat rough and that rather than take the would-be suspect into custody they beat him up[22] should not suggest they had no authority to imprison[23] suspects and hence were not official policemen. We have clear evidence that this kind of behavior was quite the rule among the official police, too. In an undated text (cf. between ca. 270 and 350 C.E.) we read:[24]

> It once happened in Caesarea that there was a great man who had a reputation in the city. One night, the city guards, while patrolling, found a certain stranger[25] and seized him. He said to them: "Do not hit me. I am a member of the household of so and so" (i.e., the great man). When they heard this, they left him alone [merely] taking him into custody for the night. In the morning, they brought him to that man, and said to him: "We found this member of your household last night." He said to him: "My son, do you know me?" "No," he replied. "In that case how are you a member of my household?" "I put my trust in you. For were I not to have said that I was a member of your household, they would have beaten me up." He said: "Since he put his trust in me, leave him alone."

Police Brutality

Thus we see that when the Caesarean police found someone at night whom they considered suspicious, they beat him up, probably suspecting burglary. We have evidence that in Caesarea the authorities were especially strict with these types of criminal offenders. In Leviticus Rabba 6.2, ed. Margulies pp. 128–29, we read of a certain authority (*shilton*) in Caesarea who flogged (*malkeh*) thieves and executed "fences" (recipients of stolen property—*kablanim*). It would thus appear that local police were acting in accordance with official policy when they beat up a vagrant they found wandering about the city at night. It was only through ready wit and the invocation of a powerful name that our stranger saved himself from this treatment.

Palestinian cities were, in fact, patrolled by both day and night watches usually in different shifts.[26] These watchmen give the impression of having been very efficient and systematic. As one text states:[27] ". . . Just as the guards of the city do, passing during the night before every single door." Small wonder then that the wine seller feared these watchmen; he claims that "they have *just* passed by here" but is nonetheless afraid. He seems to have known that they would be returning shortly. This suggests that their "beat" was relatively short—shorter than a "long drink"—and constant. The picture that emerges from our analysis of this text is one of a well-manned,[28] vigilant police force that is somewhat rough—the same portrait that emerged from the Caesarean text.

It would be expected that the area around the wine shops would be well patrolled, since as MacMullen puts it: "Taverns and cookshops . . . lay under a more enduring suspicion as dens of criminals and prostitutes, centres of extravagance and loose living."[29] The police, aware of the nature of the place, had it under observation and, upon finding a suspicious-looking character lying at the door of the wine shop, assumed him to be a thief. Perhaps they thought he was feigning drunkenness to escape their attention. Without further ado, they set about beating him. Only when they saw that he was insensible to their treatment did they realize that he was truly drunk in a heavy alcoholic stupor and left him alone, bruised and cut up with blackened eyes.

Drunkenness

It would appear that it was no crime to be drunk, and vagrancy per se was not a criminal offense. Moreover, vagrancy was apparently unusual—the stranger in Caesarea was immediately suspect—and streets were quiet and empty at night. This, as we have already seen, was precisely the point of sumptuary laws: to prevent an outbreak of drunken violence, to preserve calm and peace, and to enforce law and order in a restless and disorderly period. A drunken brawl could easily assume more serious dimensions, even trigger a riot. We read in yet another undated text[30] (cf. between ca. 270 and 370 C.E.):

> It happened once that a band of "no-goods"[31] were sitting around drinking wine half-way through the night. But they did not get [properly] drunk. Wine was brought to them, and they said to the wine-server (= waiter) "We want wine mixed with wine."
>
> They continued to do (= drink) so until they were really saturated. Then they got up and started beating one another up in their drunkenness. There was an outcry[32] in the city. The loper[33] came, took them in and handed them over to the imperial authorites,[34] and they were all lost (= executed).

It seems clear that this "gang" was drinking in a tavern rather than in a private house, where they were served by a waiter with a choice of wines. Yet they were able to drink through the night. Evidently, no licensing laws existed at this time and place. Sumptuary laws were introduced as measures to prevent just such episodes, and since "troubles begin when people congregate, especially drunken men,"[35] the law closed potential trouble spots for the night. The police were zealous in their enforcement of these laws, and the penalties were no doubt severe.[36] We can now appreciate the wine seller's well-justified fears.

Wine Shops

What exactly were these regulations that the police so vigilantly enforced? In order to answer this question accurately, we must first determine the kind of place referred to in our text. The term *beit kapilia* is used, literally: the house of a wine seller or, in other words, a wine shop. Indeed, in the exegetical part of the homily the term *ḥanut*—shop—is used. However, the terms καπηλεῖον and *ḥanut* are also used for eating places,[37] and a *ḥenvani* (from *ḥanut*), literally: a shopkeeper, is also a restaurateur;[38] people used to eat in "meat shops." So also the καπηλεῖον, although strictly speaking a wine shop,[39] is a place where people sit around and drink—a pub.[40] In our case, too, a pub is referred to, since the homilist says of our drunk that he is one of "those who are first to enter the *shop* and last to leave." Clearly, such people spent their whole day on the premises, drinking themselves into a total stupor. The licensing rules probably forbade the publican to keep his "shop" open after dark and, consequently, to sell liquor after hours. Our publican could, however, not withstand the insistent requests of a regular (?) customer and, much against his better judgment, plied him his drink through the crack in the door.

The Amusing Tale of a Dipsomaniac

One can readily imagine the piteous entreaties of a person wholly addicted to his liquor. Indeed, an amusing tale is related of just such a dipsomaniac in Leviticus Rabba 12.1, ed. Margulies pp. 245–47, which I shall cite in full:

> R. Aḥa (Palestinian Amora of Lydda, fl. ca. 320–50 C.E.) said: Once there was a man who was wont to sell all his household belongings in order to [buy] drink with the proceeds, even unto the roof-beams of his house (i.e., even his own house). His children were forever complaining, "This old man will surely leave the world, leaving [us] nothing after his death. What shall we do with him? Come, let us ply him with wine until he is totally inebriated, then carry him off and take him out [of the city], lay him in a grave and claim that he died." They did so, took him, got him drunk, removed him and placed him in a cemetary [outside town].[41] A small group of wine-merchants (*ḥamarin*)[42] were passing by on their way to town when they heard there was an angareia (ἀγγαρεία, cumpulsory conscription, corvée labor)[43] in the city. (Fearing that they would be conscripted and their merchandise confiscated) they said, "Let us unload our wine-skins[44] and hide them

> in this grave and be off." And indeed that is what they did; they unloaded their merchandise, placed it in the graveyard, and went off to see what were the latest rumors in the city. That [old] man was [lying] there, and they saw him and thought he was dead. When he woke up from his [drunken] stupor, he saw the wine-skins placed above his head. He untied [the stoppers] and drew [the nozzle] to his mouth, and began to drink deeply. When he was sated he began to sing. Three days later (meaning: some time later) (apparently suffering from pangs of conscience) his children said, "Should we not go and see what our [old] father is doing, [and find out] whether he is alive or dead?" They came and found him sitting there with a wine-skin in his mouth, drinking [away]. They said to him, "[We see that] even here among the dead your Creator has not forsaken you. Surely among the living he will not forsake you! Since from heaven you were given [wine to drink], we know not what to do with you. Come let us take him back home, and arrange for him to have a regular daily ration (*katastasis*) [of wine]." They arranged that each day one of them would provide him with his drink.

Clearly, for one such as this no sumptuary laws could be effective!

The evidence I have presented is partial, fragmentary, and of uncertain date. However, when assembled, it suggests a mood of tension and urban unrest—a conclusion fully borne out by a wealth of independent classical and Rabbinic evidence[45]—which came as a natural consequence of the growing economic and social deterioration of the third and fourth century.[46]

Notes

1. See T. Kleberg, *Hotels et Cabarets dans l'Antiquité Romaine* (= Bibliotheca Ekmaniana 61) (Uppsala, 1957), pp. 101–103, 121–22, and G. Hermansen, *Ostia: Aspects of Roman City Life* (Edmonton, 1982), pp. 185–203.

2. R. MacMullen, *Enemies of the Roman Order* (Cambridge and London, 1967). More recently, Hermansen, *Ostia*, pp. 201–202, refers to Dio 60.17.8 (Claudius), Suetonius, Tiberias 39.1, Nero 16, Dio 62.14.2; Dio 65.10.3, Vespasian, Dio 60.6.6–7, Claudius.

3. 28.4.4.

4. 12.1, ed. Margulies pp. 250–52 and parallels (Esther Rabba 5.1). Cf. Tanḥuma Shemini 5. J. Israelstam's translation (Midrash Rabbah, Leviticus, 1939, p. 154) is too free to be of use to us.

5. See below for a discussion of the term.

6. וצאדי לי. Cf. Y. Berachot 1.1, 2a: דצדי לון. See M. Sokoloff, *A Dictionary of Jewish Palestinian Aramaic of the Byzantine Period* (Ramat-Gan, 1990), p. 458 s.v. 2 צדי, and D. Sperber, *Roman Palestine 200–400: The Land* (Ramat-Gan, 1978), p. 53, n. 20.

7. There are a number of variant readings here (see Margulies' apparatus); I find this the most satisfactory one.

8. The text reads *suntema*, which has been emended and interpreted in a number of different ways. The most convincing suggestion thus far is that of Y. Brand, in his *Klei Haḥeres Besifrut Hatalmud* (Jerusalem, 1953), p. 143, who

suggests that the word *suntema* equals the Greek *συστομα, meaning a narrow-spouted vessel. Elsewhere in a detailed discussion of the problem in my article, "Ḥikrei Millim ve-Girsaot," I have suggested *συστομα—the narrow spout (of the vessel). See *Leshonenu* 36 (1972): 259–61 (and again in my *Essays on Greek and Latin in the Mishna, Talmud and Midrashic Literature* [Jerusalem, 1982] [in Hebrew], pp. 47–49).

9. Correct from *ẓira* (= hinge) to *ẓaria* (= crack) as suggested by I. Löw, in S. Krauss, *Griechische und Lateinische Lehnwörter im Talmud, Midrasch und Targum*, vol. 2 [*LW*^{2}] (Berlin, 1889; reprint, Hildesheim, 1964), p. 377a, s.v. סונטמא and since borne out by manuscript readings (see Margulies' apparatus).

10. We would say: blackened.

11. See Margulies' apparatus.

12. Prov. 23:29.

13. See below in note 37 for a discussion of this term.

14. Literally: a good wine.

15. A reference to *calida*? See Kleberg, *Hotels*, p. 104.

16. This kind of antidrinking homily occurs from the mid-third century through the first half of the fourth century C.E. See Leviticus Rabba 12. 1, ed. Margulies pp. 243–56; Tanḥuma Shemini, passim; Numbers Rabba 10. 8. Nights of drunken orgiastic revelry are alluded to by the early fourth century Rabbi Yehuda b. Simon in Leviticus Rabba 33.6, ed. Margulies p. 767, as interpreted by S. Lieberman, in his *Yevanit ve-Yavnut be-Ereẓ-Yisrael* (Jerusalem, 1962), pp. 36–39.

17. Leviticus Rabba was compiled and edited in the Galilee and Tiberias; most of the material it contains is Galilean. See Margulies' introduction (Jerusalem, 1960), XXVII–XXXI. However, it also contains non-Galilean material, and there is evidence which points to Caesarea as being the location of our story.

18. See M. Baba Batra 4.7: If a man sold a town, he also sold the *santer* (an early second century text). *Santer* = *saltuarius* (contra Talmudic lexica); see S. Krauss, *Talmudische Archäologie*, vol. 2 (Leipzig, 1911), pp. 106, 501, n. 734, pp. 185, 570, n. 235; idem, *Additamenta ad Aruch Completum*, p. 298 s.v. סנטר. For sources, see idem, *LW*^{2} p. 403a, s.v. סנטיר. The other meaning of *saltuarius*, a bailiff (e.g., *Digesta* 32.1.58, 7.8.16, 33.7.15), is found to be used by Resh Lakish (Palestinian scholar, fl. ca. 250–76 C.E.) in B. Sanhedrin 98b. The *santer* is not identical to the "city watchman"; see Y. Baba Meẓia 9.1,12a32 and Y. Ḥagiga 1.7,76c34.

19. M. Baba Meẓia 9.1 (but cf. T. Baba Meẓia 9.11, where the watchmen are not listed). See MacMullen, *Enemies*, pp. 257–59. On privately owned villages, see previous note. On the payment of the watchmen by house renters, see A. Gulak, *Le-Ḥeker Toldot ha-Mishpat ha-Ivri bi-Tekufat ha-Talmud*, vol. 1 (Jerusalem, 1929), p. 28, and G. McLean Harper, *Village Administration in Syria*, Yale Classical Studies, vol. 1 (New Haven and London, 1928), pp. 160–62. On private nightguards, see J. Chrysostom *Ad Stagirium* 6 = PG 47, 458 (380 C.E.) (cited by MacMullen, *Enemies*, pp. 201–202).

20. Elsewhere (in *Leshonenu* 53 (1989): 60–61) I have suggested that נעשה טרטגוס in Midrash ha-Gaddol to Genesis 29.1, ed. Margulies p. 493, should be corrected to read נקטסטרטגוס: νυκτοστράτηγος. In accordance with this correction the text would read as follows: ". . . He that keepeth thee will not slumber. Behold, He that keepeth Israel shall neither slumber nor sleep"

(Psalm 121:3–4). . . . Furthermore, a *nuktostrategos*—night watchman—sleeps by day and guards by night. . . . See note 28 below.

21. They tended to be rough; see Y. Sheviit 4.2, 35b 18.

22. Cf. Numbers Rabba 10.8, cited below (see section on drunkenness) in extenso. See also Libanius, Epist. 532 to Firminus (ed. Foerster X, 501, 11. 1), where the chief of police of the Negev town Elusa, called Baithos, is mentioned (356 C.E.). See M. Schwabe's discussion of that text in *Bulletin of the Israel Exploration Society, Reader*, part 2 (1965): 153–64 [in Hebrew].

23. People were imprisoned pending their trial. Rabbinic literature has numerous references to the "*pilki*" (= φυλακή). See Krauss, *LW*², pp. 448–49, and also chapter 6.

24. Midrash Psalms 4.20, ed. Buber p. 211. The correct reading, however, is to be found in J. Mann's article "Some Midrashic Genizah Fragments," *HUCA* 14 (1939). 316.

25. *achsanai* = ξένος. (Mann, "Some Midrashic," p. 316.) This is the preferred reading as opposed to the variant מגייד, crucify. See editor's note ad loc.

26. On night patrols and patrol shifts, see T. Sukka 2.3 = B. Sukka 26a = Y. Sukka 2.5. Cf. Lamentations Rabba 2.

27. Midrash Psalms 48.2, ed. Buber p. 275.

28. But cf. MacMullen, *Enemies*, p. 337, n. 4. On νυκτοστράτηγοι, see F. Oertel, *Die Liturgie* (Leipzig, 1917), pp. 281–83 and note 20 above; Vigiles, MacMullen, *Enemies*, pp. 103–107, 257–60, 336–37; A. H. M. Jones, *The Later Roman Empire*, vol. 3 (Oxford, 1964), p. 228, n. 29; idem, *The Greek City* (Oxford, 1940), pp. 252, 360, n. 80. On εἰρηνάρχης see D. Magie, *Roman Rule in Asia Minor* (1950), p. 514, n. 46. On παραφύλακες and ὀραφύλακες, ibid., pp. 647–48, 1515–16, n. 47. See also *Chronique D'Egypte* 88 (1968): 347–52.

29. MacMullen, *Enemies*, p. 167. On taverns (*kapelia*) where one could eat and drink, see Midrash Samuel 7.3, p. 66, and Genesis Rabba 3.1, ed. Theodor-Albeck p. 170; Midrash Psalms 4.13, p. 48, B. Ḥulin 6a, where we find rich menus, including different kinds of bread, good wine, oil, eggs, chicken, meat, legumes, and other vegetables. Clearly, sumptuary laws prohibiting the sale of meat, for example (alluded to in Hermansen, *Ostia*, pp. 201–202—see note 2), did not apply in third- and fourth-century Palestine, from which period these texts come. Incidentally, the ברכות הרבה של דגים וכל דבר, which the visitors in Midrash Psalms 4.13 see in the *pundak*—πανδοχεῖον, are not pools of fish, which makes little sense in a hotel. Instead, I believe we should read: כריכות (like מחרוזות של דגים in T. Baba Meẓia 2.3–4, et al.), meaning strings of fish (hanging from hooks on the wall) and other foods. Indeed a well-known picture from Pompeii shows a group of travelers sitting round a table eating and drinking while behind them, suspended from a tack, are cheeses, sausages, and other unidentifiable edibles. See H. Tanzer, *The Common People of Pompeii: A Study of the Graffiti* (Baltimore, 1939), pp. 47–48 and fig. 25. On the *pundak*, see S. Krauss, *Kadmoniyyot ha-Talmud,* vol. 1, part 1 (Berlin and Vienna, 1924), pp. 136–38. Sometimes these taverns were dangerous places, where clients were robbed or even killed. See Krauss, *Kadmoniyyot ha-Talmud* vol. 1, part 1, p. 133 (on the basis of Targum Yerushalmi to I Chronicles 1:20). Cf. L. Friedlander, *Roman Life and Manners under the Early Empire* (London, 1907), p. 293. Often the travelers brought their own food to the "hotels" (perhaps for fear of their health); see *Kadmoniyyot ha-Talmud*, vol., part 1, pp. 138–39, and *Roman*

Life, p. 293. Friedlander, On the dangers of leaving a tavern to travel at night, see Genesis Rabba 92.3, ed. Theodor-Albeck pp. 1144–45.

30. Numbers Rabba 10.8.

31. *Zalim.*

32. Ẓevaḥ ed. Urbach, *Kobeẓ Al Yad* VI (XVI) 1, 1966, p. 53, line 55.

33. = rufilus, according to Krauss, *LW*², pp. 311–12; idem, *Monatsschrift für Geschichte und Wissenschaft des Judenthums* (Breslau, 1894), p. 151f. and idem, *Paras ve-Romi ba-Talmud u-ba-Midrashim* (Jerusalem, 1948), p. 103. However, this identification is not altogether certain. See J. Guttmann, "Rabbi Elazar b. Rabbi Shimon in the Service of the Roman Government in Palestine" [in Hebrew], *Zion* 18 (1953): 3–4.

34. *Malchut.*

35. MacMullen, *Enemies*, pp. 167–68, and Hermansen, *Ostia*, pp. 198–200, who writes; "drink made the guild brothers bold, irresponsible, and conspiracy prone, which led to public unrest. . . . So the closing of the guilds as well as of taverns was nothing but a political move, and all the provisions to curb the activities of the taverns and inns and limit the services that the taverns were allowed to offer were introduced for the sole purpose of making them less attractive to the public."

36. See Kleberg, *Hotels*, p. 122 (citing Dio Cassius 59.11.6).

37. Genesis Rabba 19.1 (170), *kapilo* = Midrash Proverbs 7, 3 (60), *ḥanut*. See also Ecclesiastes Rabba 1.18.

38. Tanḥuma, ed. Buber, Balak 24, 145

39. Pesikta de-Rav Kahana, ed. Buber p. 122b, where swindlers who water down their wine before selling it are described. See also Lamentations Rabba 1.4 (to I.1); Y. Shevuot 7.5, 38a13; Y. Baba Meẓia 5.8 (10c 53).

40. See M. Rostovtzeff, *Social and Economic History of the Hellenistic World*² [*SEHHW*²], p. 1628, n. 196. It should be noted that a *kapila* was not an inn, that is, a place where one spent the night. Such were called *pundak(in)* = πανδοχεἰον; see Krauss, *LW*², p. 428. In such places animals were stabled (T. Avoda Zara 3.2. = M. Avoda Zara 2.1), and people spent the night (T. Yevamot 1.10). Such places, often just outside the town on the main road (Y. Demai 22c87, Tanḥuma Numbers 9; ibid. Naso 15; Numbers Rabba 2.12), also served, of course, food and drink (Genesis Rabba 21.33, ed. Theodor-Albeck p. 583, Targum [= Aramaic translation] to (IChron. 1:20). See Krauss, *Kadmoniyyot ha-Talmud*, vol. 1, part 1, pp. 55, 131–43.

41. On cemeteries outside town, see B. Taanit 16a; M. Baba Batra 2.1; and cf. Semahot 14.10. This was often true of Greek and Roman towns, too. See E. J. Owens, *The City in the Greek and Roman World*² (London, 1992), pp. 153, 184, n. 23. On cemeteries in Roman Galilee, see Zeev Weiss, "Beit ha-Kevarot ha-Yehudi ba-Galil bi-Tekufat ha-Mishnah ve-ha-Talmud: Nituaḥ Architektoni be-Siyua MeKorot Talmudiim" (master's thesis, Hebrew University, 1989) and his recent article, "The Location of Jewish Cemeteries in the Galilee in the Mishnaic and Talmudic Periods," in *Graves and Burial Practices in Israel in the Ancient Period*, ed. I. Singer (Jerusalem, 1994) [in Hebrew], pp. 230–40.

42. חמרין, which is literally muleteers, but also perhaps an (unconscious) wordplay on חמר, wine; hence, muleteers transporting wine. The wine was transported in skins of different sizes (see Lamentations Rabba 50.2, נזקין בחמר. See H. Tanzer, *The Common People of Pompeii* (Baltimore, 1939), p. 39, fig. 2;

M. Rostovtzeff, *SEHHW*[2], plate XXVII (p. 163), plate XXXIV (p. 199), and plate XLVIII (p. 265).

43. See my article on this term in *Ant. Class.* 5, no. 38 (1969): 164–68.

44. See note 42 above.

45. See MacMullen, *Enemies*, "Urban Unrest," chap. 5, and my article "On Social and Economic Conditions in Third Century Palestine," *Archiv Orientalnì*: 38 (1970): 1–25.

46. See my studies in social and economic conditions in the third and fourth centuries in *Roman Palestine 200–400: Money and Prices* (Ramat-Gan, 1974), p. 1991, and in *Roman Palestine 200–400: The Land.*

5

On the Bathhouse

We will now move away from the market and forum area to that other central institution of the Roman city, the bathhouse. We have already mentioned in passing (see chapter 1) that the bathhouse was usually near the market, as indicated in the passage from Apuleius, and as is evident from numerous excavations, including those of Tiberias and Beit Shean.[1]

This may further be seen in a passage in Exodus Rabba 15.22:[2]

> . . . Like unto a servant whose master said to him, "Wait for me in the marketplace." But he did not tell him where [exactly] he should wait . . ., near the basilica or near the bathhouse . . . or near the theatre. . . . [His master] said to him: I sent you [to wait for me] near the entrance to the palace of the *eparchos*.

There is a wealth of archeological evidence from the Roman world in general and from Roman Palestine in particular on almost all aspects of the bathhouse and its activities. Nonetheless, a number of issues remain unclear, and Rabbinic sources can further clarify to them. Likewise, points of halachic obscurity may be solved by reference to contemporary literary sources and archeological findings. Apparently, the bathhouse was one of the landmarks in the market area, and the larger the city, the more bathhouses there were.

Annointing and Bathing

We shall now take as our point of departure a brief passage in B. Shabbat 41a (= B. Baba Batra 53b), which reads as follows:

> If he bathed and did not annoint [himself] this is like water in a barrel (and not in it, i.e., the water is wasted and so too the bathing is purposeless).

A plain reading of this aphorism would seem to indicate that the process of annointing comes *after* bathing, and indeed the Tosafists (ad loc.) remark that "throughout the Talmud bathing precedes annointing." So likewise in M. Sanhedrin 7.6 (in a description of idolatrous practices) we find the order: "bathes, annoints, clothes, and puts on his shoes." However, many early authorities attest to a different reading in our text,[3] namely: If he bathed and *had not* [*already*] annointed himself *earlier* (ולא סך תחלה—literally, in the beginning), indicating that one annoints oneself *first and then washes*. And if one does not annoint (that is, soap) oneself first, there is little point to the washing. Indeed, this was the reading that Rashi knew (M. Sanhedrin 40b): And I wished to annoint myself from it *before bathing*. The same passage in the Tosafot that we mentioned earlier indicates that the Tosafists also knew of a similar reading but rejected it. Thus, they write ". . . and we do not read מעיקרא, at the start,[4] for in the whole Talmud bathing precedes annointing . . . ." Let us see whether there is any way in which we can determine which is the more correct reading.

A text in Derech Ereẓ Zuta 7.2, which discusses the way in which a scholar should comport himself, states that he "should be modest in eating, and in drinking and in bathing and in annointing . . . ."[5] This would appear to bear out the reading that suggests the natural order is bathing and then annointing. In Biblical texts this seems to be the case. In Ruth 3:3 we read: "Wash thyself therefore, and annoint thee. . . ."; similarly in Ezekiel 16:9–10, "Then I washed thee with water . . . and I annointed thee with oil, I clothed thee also with broidered work. . . ."; and in Judith 10:3, ". . . and [she] washed her body all over with water and annointed herself with ointment. . . ."

This same order is also found in Rabbinic literature. So we read in Avot de-Rabbi Nathan I, chap. 41, p. 133: "Wash her and annoint her, and dance before her until she reaches her husband's house" and earlier in chapter 16, p. 63 ". . . and he sent him two beautiful women; he washed them and annointed them and bejewelled them like brides. . . ."

Although these sources describe feminine activities, the same seems to be true for men. In B. Berachot 32b Rabbi Yoḥanan tells (in a homily) of a man who had a son whom he washed and annointed and to whom he gave food and drink. And so also in B. Kiddushin 22b (= B. Baba Batra 53b) we read in a baraita. ". . . and he untied his shoe. . . , undressed him, bathed him, annointed him, rubbed him down (*gerado*), dressed him, put his shoes back on. . . ."

Procedure in the Bathhouse

A detailed description of the order of events in the bathhouse is to be found in Derech Ereẓ Rabba 10.1:

> And before entering [the bathhouse], what should he do? He [first] removes his shoes,[6] and then his cap, and then his cloak (*tallit*), his girdle, his shirt, and his underwear (*epikarsion*). When he has bathed and they bring him a towel, he [first] rubs (*mekaneaḥ*) his head, and then other parts of his body. [Then] they bring him the oil, [and] he annoints [first] his head, and then the other parts of his body. After that he puts on his underwear, his shirt, his girdle, and his cloak, and his cap and his shoes. . . .[7]

This seems to have been the standard procedure in Roman baths. First one undressed in the *apodyterium*, the undressing room. Judging from the *apodyterium* in the baths at Pompeii, there were seats for dressing and undressing along the sides of the walls, in which wooden pegs were fixed for hanging up clothes. (The holes for these pegs may still be seen in Pompeii.)[8] One entered into the *apodyterium* from a corridor leading to a door to the street. In the corridor a small niche may be seen, which presumably served as the station of the *balneator*, who collected the money from those entering.[9] Such an attendant is mentioned in Y. Berachot 2.1,4c; he was called יעקב תרמוסרה: Jacob the θερμοσάριος, the bath attendant.[10] The attendant collected the money, a small sum, and exchanged it for a token (*tessara*), which was then handed to the *olearius*.[11] Next one went through a series of warm, hot, and cold baths (*tepidarium*, *caldarium*, *frigidarium*), though not necessarily in that order.[12] The sweat was scraped off with a *strigil*[13] (a metal hooklike scraping instrument), and one was rubbed down with towels (*lintea*). Finally came the annointing with oil,[14] the latter in a special "oiling room" (called the *unctorium*) by oilers or masseurs (*unctores*).[15] Again this description suggests that the "oiling" comes at the end of the bathing process and not before it; this appears to be borne out by classical sources, too. In Celsus, *De Medicina* 1.3.4 (ed. Loeb 1, p. 53), we read: "When there is a bath, he should first sit in it in the warm room, then after resting there a while, go down into the tubs; next after being annointed freely with oil, and gently rubbed down, again descend into the tub; finally he should foment the face, first with warm, then with cold water."[16]

When Does One Annoint Oneself with Oil?

The matter of the bathing process is a little more complex than the preceding description would suggest, however. The Mishna in Shabbat (1.2) teaches us that one may not indulge in certain kinds of activity close to the advent of the Sabbath; however, if one has started, one does not have to stop. On this the Yerushalmi (Y. Shabbat 3a; = Y. Kiddushin 1.7,61a) comments as follows:

> What is [called] the beginning of the bathhouse [activity]? R. Zerikan in the name of R. Ḥanina said: From the moment he loosens his girdle. Rav said: From when he takes off his shoe.[17] This is like R. Joshua b. Levi who was used to listening to a chapter [of the Bible] (read to him) by his grandson every week before Shabbat. On one occasion he forgot [to do this], and went to bathe in the bathhouse of Sepphoris [shortly before Shabbat]. He was supporting himself on the shoulder of R. Ḥiyya b. [A]bba, when he remembered that he had not [yet] heard the chapter from his grandson, and he turned and left [the bathhouse].[18] What was this (i.e., according to which opinion did he act)? R. Darosi said: He was annointing himself (סך הוה).[19] R. [E]leazar b. R. Yossi said: He was removing his clothes. R. Ḥiyya b. Abba said to them: If they began they do not stop (or interrupt).

We see then that Rabbi Darosi and Rabbi Eleazar bar Rabbi Yossi were of differing opinions as to what constitutes the beginning of the bathing process; the one says: annointing, the other says: even earlier on when one removes one's clothing. Now clearly annointing cannot come after bathing[20] but must come before bathing and hence constitutes, according to one opinion, the *beginning* of the bathing process.

Indeed, we can demonstrate that people used to annoint themselves with oil *before* entering the baths. In Tosefta Shabbat 16 (17).16, ed. Lieberman pp. 78–79, we read:

> A person should not annoint his hair with oil and then go to the bathhouse, but rather he should annoint all his body, limb by limb.[21]

So too in Y. Sheviit 8.2, 38a:

> One does not annoint oneself with oil of the Sabbatical year in the bathhouse, but one may annoint oneself [with it] outside and then enter.

Two Kinds of Annointing

Lieberman shows that it was the accepted practice to annoint oneself with oil, enter the bath for a real wash, scrape oneself with the strigil, exercise a little, and then again annoint oneself (probably with aromatic unguents)[22] (fig. 5.1). The first annointing was with an agent that served

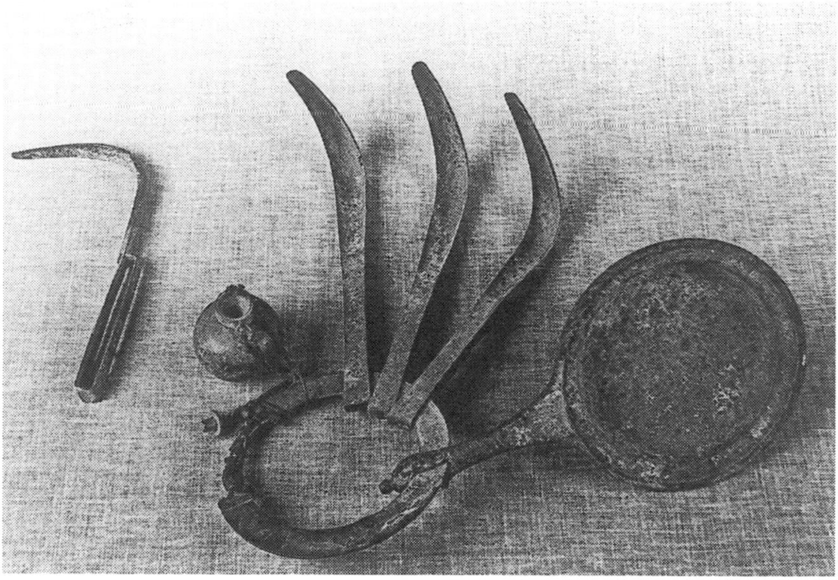

Figure 5.1 Four strigils and ungientarium (ampulla olearia) and patera on rings. Basic bathing apparatus. Pompeii. Taken from *Gallus on the Roman Scenes of the Time of Augustus*, by W. A. Becker. Translated by F. Metscalfe. (Longman, 1907), p. 394.

as soap; the second annointing gave off a pleasant fragrance. The first soaping-oiling is mentioned in classical sources, as we have previously seen. And in a recently published text, *From Ausonius' Schooldays*,[23] the order is as follows: oiling, sweat bath, hot bath, cold swim (sauna!), strigil, drying, dressing, and good wishes. It was then two different kinds of oiling, argues Lieberman, that led to the confusion in Rabbinic sources, causing the Tosafists to reject the reading suggesting a prebath oiling and accepting only a postbath oiling. Indeed, in the fragment of an Uncannonical Gospel we read: μυρί[ζ]ου[σιν κ]αὶ λούσουσιν και σμήχουσι,[24] meaning they annoint themselves, wash themselves, and soap themselves.[25] But, perhaps here σμήχουσι means: wipe off (by help of soap or unguent) or wipe clean.[26]

However, the truth may be summed up in the words of Becker. "The annointing with oil took place both before and after the bath, and even have after they had already stepped into the bath they sometimes left it again, to be annointed a second time, after which they again betook themselves to the bath (Celsus 1.3)."[27] Lieberman further suggests that these two different oilings led to confusion (or interchange) in Rabbinic sources between two different rooms, the oiling room (usually the *tepidarium*) and the sweating room (*sudatorium*), where the bathers were then scraped with a strigil and reoiled. In Y. Kilaim 9.4,32b (= Y. Ketubot 12.3, 35a) we read that a certain absent-minded scholar was given two students to look after him when he entered the סכותא, the annointing room,[28] while in the parallel in Genesis Rabba 33.3, ed. Theodor p. 307, we are told that they would accompany him to the אשונא, sweatroom, *sudatio*.[29] In this latter room the oil was also warmed up for the annointing, as indicated in Y. Sheviit 8.2,38c, where we are told that Rabbi Ḥezkiah went to bathe and gave the jar [of oil] to Zosimi (the *olearius* (אוריירא)—oiling man) and said to him: bring it to me to the אשונא, the sweatroom.

In many cases the bather also exercised with weights and performed gymnastics[30] to induce extreme perspiration. This would seem to emerge from the caution in Derech Ereẓ Rabba 10.2, (ed. Higger p. 300):

> He who enters the bathhouse should not exercise (= gymnastics) nor should he scrape himself, nor should he massage himself[31] on the marble. And it once happened that Rabban Gamliel felt weak, and they offered him (or spread for him—חלפו לו) oil on the marble, but he refused it.

The scraping would seem to remove the first soaping-oiling and the sweat of exercising, after which came a massage (by the *unctor*) on an oiled marble slab and probably the annointing with fragrant unguents.[32]

Sale of Aromatic Unguents

These aromatic oils were apparently sold to the client in the bathhouse. So we learn from T. Kelim B.M. 10.4, p. 588, which speaks of "the box [*tevah*] on which they sell oil in the bathhouse." This may be identical to the box of the bath attendants [בלרין], mentioned in T. Kelim B.M. 10.32,[33] upon which they laid out the bottles of oil, selling them to the bathers for their (final?) annointing.

The Typical Visit to the Bathhouse

Putting together all the snippets of information we have managed to extract from the various sources, we can reconstruct a fairly complete picture of a typical visit to the bathhouse by the "average Palestinian Talmudic citizen." He first enters from the street into a corridor where he is met by a doorkeeper who admits him upon receiving a minimal payment and gives him a token (tessara). He then enters an undressing room where he sits down on a bench next to the wall, removes all his clothes, hangs (some of) them on a peg above the bench (or places them in a niche in the wall, as in some Roman baths), and then is oiled-soaped, probably by an attendant. Presumably at this point he gives the tessara to the attendant, but this matter is not altogether clear. He then moves on through a series of tepid, hot, and cold (?) baths (perhaps not in this order) and on occasion exercises vigorously to build up even greater perspiration. He is subsequently dried with towels and "scraped" down with a strigil by a special attendant, who drops some oil on the edge of the strigil so as not to cut his client. After this he (enters the cold bath? and then) lies down on an oiled marble slab and is massaged and rubbed with fragrant ointments. He subsequently returns to the undressing room to retrieve his clothing and dresses, leaving the bathhouse clean, refreshed, and fragrant to go about his business.

Beggars at Main Entrance

Having reached this point we can now add details from a variety of sources that will help flesh out the extent of activities that took place in the bathhouse in Roman Palestine.

People coming into the bathhouse off the street would probably be met by a crowd of beggars at the main gate.[24] Evidence of this emerges from a story told in Y. Pea 8.5,21b, which relates how Rabbi Yoḥanan (died ca. 279 C.E.) and Rabbi Simeon ben Lakish (died ca. 275 C.E.) were accosted upon entering the bathhouse at Tiberias by a beggar who turned out to be a "phoney." When the beggar died, they found he had a purse full of gold coins strung round his neck.[35]

Time of Bathing

Bathers probably entered the bathhouse sometime during the latter part of the afternoon, which seems to have been the preferred time for bathing, as indicated in sources cited above that describe rabbis visiting the bathhouse close to the onset of the Sabbath and in a variety of Roman sources (such as Vitruvius 5.1, Loeb ed. 1, p. 303).[36]

Order of Rooms in the Bathhouse

From the entry gate bathers went into a vestibule where they were greeted by the doorkeeper, who collected their entrance fee. At this stage, of course, the bathers were still dressed. They then moved on to the changing room, where they sat on a (marble) bench[37] and disrobed, hanging their clothes on a hook placed above the bench or storing them in a special niche built for this purpose (as in Pompeii).[38] After bathing in the various baths, tepid, hot, and cold, they returned to this same changing room to retrieve[39] their garments and to dress (fig. 5.2). Hence, in this room[40] one finds both people dressed and undressed.[41] Bathers next went into the bathing and sweating chambers, where they

Figure 5.2 Excavated foundations of the Roman thermae at Heerlen (= Coriovallum). Key: 1. Entrance; 2. Massage rooms; 3. Dressing room; 4. Cold bath; 5. Sudatory; 6. Tepid bath; 7. Hot bath; 8. Firing room; 9. Open air swimming pool; 10. Drain; 11. Gymnasium; 12. Colonnaded arcades. (From J. J. M. Timmers, *Mirrors of Roman Cultures* [Heerlen, 1966], p. 14. Used with permission.)

washed, sweated, and were scrubbed and annointed. Here, of course, everyone wandered about quite naked (except perhaps for a towel).[42] This nakedness may be deduced from a text in T. Berachot 2.20, p. 5 (ed. Lieberman p. 10), where we read as follows:

> He that enters the bathhouse, in that room (literally: place) where people stand dressed he may study Bible[43] and pray and, of course, greet people . . . ; in that room where people stand about both dressed and undressed one may greet but one may not study Bible or pray . . . ; in that room where people stand about naked one may not [even] greet. . . .[44]

Likewise, in Derech Ereẓ Rabba 10.5 (ibid. p. 305; van Loopik p. 144) we read:

> One does not discuss the Law in a room [in the bathhouse] where most of the people are undressed, nor in a room where most of the people are dressed. . . .

Indeed, it was even considered bad form to sit in the sweatroom in one's cloak (Derech Ereẓ Rabba, ibid. 8, p. 305), perhaps because the warm clothing absorbed the humidity.[45]

Dangers of Bathing in the Bathhouse

There was thought to be a certain element of danger involved in entering a bathhouse. The newly constructed ones were as yet untested, and the floor, which rested on small pillars and under which the fire was stoked to heat the hot room (*caldarium*), could easily collapse and cause the bathers to be badly burned. In B. Pesaḥim 112b Rabbi Yose b. Rabbi Judah warns Rabbi Judah [ha-Nasi] (probably at the end of second century C.E.) against entering a new bathhouse because of the danger of the floor's collapsing.[46] Old bathhouses, if they were in a state of disrepair, presumably were dangerous for this same reason (fig. 5.3). Indeed, in B. Ketubot 62a (et alia) we read of Rabbi Abbahu's (Caesarea, died 309 C.E.) going one day into the bathhouse supported by two servants.[47] The floor collapsed under him. He was saved by one of the supporting pillars, which miraculously raised itself to prevent him from falling into the fire.[48] In the light of this incident we may understand why Rabbi Mana is said to have made a will on entering a heated bathhouse.[49] Likewise, we may better understand the prayers made on entering and exiting the bathhouse, as recorded in Y. Berachot 9.6, 14b:

> On entering one says: May it be Thy will . . . that you rescue me from being burned upon the fire and from the harm brought on by the heat (היזק החמים),[50] as from a collapse (המפולת) . . . and when one goes out one says: I thank Thee . . . for saving me from the fire.[51]

Rabbi Abbahu, who suffered that unfortunate incident mentioned earlier, remarks on the dangers as follows: This [i.e., the recitation of these prayers] refers to a heated (vapour?)[52] bathhouse. We even have a his-

Figure 5.3 Large bathhouse at Masadah. View of the *caladarium* at the end of the excavation. In the center are the remains of the small columns that supported the floor. On the left is the entrance to the *tepidarium*. (From M. Gichon, "Roman Bath-Houses in Eretz-Israel" [in Hebrew], *Qadmoniot* 6/2–3, no. 42–43 (1978): 41. Used with permission.)

torical record that the bathhouse of *Sachuta* (סכותא)[53] actually collapsed on Ḥol ha-Moed, and Rabbi Abbahu (!) ruled that the locals were permitted to repair it on Hol ha-Moed.[54]

Massages and Exercise

We have seen that bathers were oiled (soaped) before washing and again oiled (annointed) after washing. They were vigorously massaged or oiled on marble slabs or sometimes on a leather mat.[55] The marble or tiled floors at times must have been covered in oil and awash with water, making the danger of falling on the slippery hard surface surely great. A bath attendant was required to keep the place clean, as we learn from a parable in Genesis Rabba 63.8, p. 687 (in the name of Rabbi Abbahu?), which tells of a פירכיטא—παραχύτης,[56] a bath attendant, who has to wash down the bathhouse (שמשטף את המרחץ).[56] Nonetheless, the danger of slipping was real, and perhaps for this reason it was ruled (Derech Ereẓ Rabba ibid. 2, p. 302) that one should not bring oil in a glass flask into the bathhouse. If it fell, the splinters of glass could injure many people. Rather, one bought oil from a salesman on the spot (T. Kelim BK 10.4, p. 588, line 34), and professional attendants applied it.[57] There is, however, other evidence indicating that sometimes clients brought their own oil with them (T. Shabbat 16.17, p. 136, line 2). In all events, it is clear that a goodly amount of oil was used in the bathhouse and was supplied regularly (apparently in "Galilean jars").[58]

Decorations

Deiss, in his fascinating study of Herculaneum, writes as follows: "Every effort was made to decorate the baths as beautifully as possible. In the cities the baths had arcades or garden paths for strolling, fountains and music for soothing harassed nerves, statuary and paintings to please the eye."[59] In general this description seems to be true for Palestinian bathhouses of Roman times, according to our literary sources. There, too, one strolled down pleasant arcades or garden paths. Indeed, such walks were permitted on the Sabbath, too. T. Shabbat 3.8, p. 113, l. 25 (B. Shabbat 40a) describes city baths (אמבטאות corresponds to ἐμβάτη)[60] through which one may stroll on the Sabbath.[61]

And as to the lavish decorations, these frequently included a variety of ornamentations, busts, and statuary, which the Jews regarded as idolatrous. The bathhouse at Akko was famous for its statue of Aphrodite which stood at the mouth of a water basin, overshadowing the bathers.[62] In fact this statue has been identified with the Aphrodite figure appearing in mid-third century C.E. from Akko Ptolemais.[63] In the later third century Rabbi Yoḥanan orders Bar Darosa to break up all the statues placed in the bathhouse at Tiberias.[64] Such statues can be found in any major Roman bathhouse but were religiously unacceptable to Jews.

A Technical Point

A final point of halachic interest is to be found in T. Shabbat 3.3, p. 113:

> A bathhouse whose apertures (נקבים) were closed on the eve of the Sabbath, may be bathed in immediately after Sabbath (i.e., one does not have to wait after the Sabbath, that period of time that it would take to warm up the baths, and one is not considered as benefiting from [forbidden] work carried out on the Sabbath). And if they closed its aperture on the eve of a festival, one may enter the bathhouse on the festival [itself], sweat, go out and rinse oneself down with cold water . . . (for different rules apply to the festivals).

Lieberman explains that the apertures were closed so that the heat would not come into the bathhouse.[65] He further explains[66] that the Yerushalmi (T. Shabbat 3.3,6a) speaks of closing up the קמין (καμίνιον),[67] the furnace that supplies the heat.

It could well be that these sources are describing merely the closing off of the pipes which conveyed heat from the furnaces through the *hypocaustum* to the *caldarium*. However, there may be an additional element to be understood in this passage.

Roman sources tell us that at one end of the *caldarium* there was a chamber called the *laconicum* (Vitruvius 5.10–11). This *laconicum* is covered by a dome in the middle of which is an opening from which a "bronze tray (*clipeus*) is hung with chains, and by raising and lowering the tray from the opening, the sweating is adjusted" (Vitruvius 5.10.5). Becker argues convincingly that the *laconicum* was a "cupola-like" (*hemisphaerium*) *hypocaustum*, which rose in an alcove above the floor, and that it was closed by the *clipeus*. When that was drawn up by the chains, or let down within, the heat and the flame itself streamed out more vehemently, and heightened the temperature of the alcove." Thus when lowered, the *clipeus*, "served to let the heat confined in the *laconicum* stream out, and increase the temperature of the *sudatio*."[68] Perhaps, then, our texts are speaking of a similar kind of device with apertures that were opened and closed to modify the temperature of the baths.

We have by no means exhausted the testimony in Rabbinic sources on the bathhouse and its structure and activities.[69] We have only occasionally compared the evidence with contemporary Roman sources and only briefly made reference to the relevant archeological evidence. Nonetheless, I hope I have demonstrated that by piecing together the fragments of information from different kinds of sources it is possible to reconstruct a fairly coherent mosaic of "bath life" in Talmudic Palestine.

In conclusion we may state that a fuller understanding of the practices and order of events in the Roman-Palestinian bathhouse not only enables us to reconstruct a fairly coherent picture of a visit to the bathhouse in Talmudic Palestine but also to clear up a number of points of confusion in Rabbinic sources, as well as to clarify the Tosafists' dispute over the correct reading in a Talmudic passage.

Notes

1. So too the Forum Baths at Pompeii, just next to the Forum. On Roman baths in general there is a very considerable literature. For a typological survey, see W. L. MacDonald, *The Architecture of the Roman Empire*, vol. 2, *An Urban Appraisal* (New Haven and London, 1986), pp. 115–16, 210–19.

2. Parallel in Tanḥuma Genesis, Ḥayye Sarah 3 (where the reading is תאטרון as opposed to פיטרון in Exodus Rabba; see S. Krauss, *Griechische und Lateinische Lenhwörter im Talmud, Midrasch, und Targum*, vol. 2 [*LW2*, (Berlin, 1899; reprint, Hildesheim, 1964), p. 4426 s.v. פיטרון), idem *Kadmoniyyot ha-Talmud*, vol. 1, part 2 (Berlin and Vienna, 1924), p. 428. See chapter 6, note 29 for a further discussion of this term.

3. See R. Rabbinovicz, *Variae Lectiones* and Mischnam et in Talmud Babylonicum, to Shabbat p. 12 note 100, referring to Rabbi Isaac Alfasi's commentary and also to those of Rabbi Manaḥem Meiri and Rabbi Asher, major medieval Talmudic commentators. In Ms. Munich the word מעיקרא has been added in the margin.

4. As in Ms. Munich. See preceding note.

5. Ed. Higger, p. 122, ed. Sperber p. 149, in my English edition pp. 94–100, 118–20, and in ed. van Loopik pp. 281–82.

6. See Y. H. Sofer, *Zechut Yiẓḥak* (Jerusalem, 1992), pp. 61–62, in which he points out that in B. Shabbat 96 the beginning of the bathing process is the removal of the headgear and not the shoes. (But see B. Kiddushin 22b.) He explains that the removal of shoes would not necessarily indicate that a person

has come to bathe, since the removal of shoes was regularly practiced on coming indoors. We may add that an examination of the whole *sugya* will reveal why headgear is mentioned rather than shoes. See also ed. van Loopik p. 158. Elsewhere I have demonstrated that it was fairly common practice in Talmudic Palestine to walk about the house barefoot.

7. T. Derech Ereẓ 5.2, ed. Higger, pp. 296–99. See my English edition of Derech Ereẓ Zuta, p. 119, and ed. van Loopik, pp. 138–39.

8. See A. Rich *A Dictionary of Roman and Greek Antiquities*[4] (London, 1874), p. 44 s.v. apodyterium, and W. Smith, W. Wayte, and G. E. Marindin, p. 275. See also T. H. Dyer, *Pompeii*[3] (London, 1871), pp. 159, 183, 185. According to Cicero, pro Cael. 26.62, every person entering such a public establishment was compelled by law to strip himself before he passed into the interior rooms to check to robbery and to prevent concealment of stolen property.

9. See Smith, Wayte, and Marindin, *Dictionary*, p. 274.

10. See S. Lieberman's discussion in *Tosefta ki-fshuṭah* vol. 1 (New York, 1962), p. 26, in which he shows that the θερμοσάριος was farther from the bathing place (i.e., closer to the street) than the ὀλεάριος, whom he called the clothing attendant.

11. See in T. Maaser Sheni 1.4, and 4. ibid. 1.2,52d, B. Baba Meẓia 47b. See also Lieberman's brilliant explanation in *Tosefta*, vol. 2, p. 716. The box containing the entrance fees (*quadrantes*) was found in the baths at Pompeii; see Smith, Wayte, and Marindin, *Dictionary*, p. 274.

12. Smith, Wayte, and Marindin, *Dictionary*, p. 272, "It is difficult to ascertain the precise order in which the course was usually taken, if indeed there was any general practice beyond the whim of the individual."

13. This instrument was often hung up in the bathhouse on a string. See M. Kelim 12.6 (תלוי המגרדת) and more explicitly in T. Kelim BK 2.12, p. 580: תלוי מגרדת של אולירין, meaning the string on which the bath attendant's (oiler's) *strigil* was hung. Since the strigil was by no means a blunt instrument, its edge was softened by the application of oil, which was dropped into it from a small vessel called a *guttus*, which had a narrow neck, so as to discharge the oil drop by drop, hence its name (Smith, Wayte, and Marindin, *Dictionary* p. 279). Perhaps, the *olearius* was also the "scraper." In Pompeii they may have been hung on iron hooks on the wall; Dyer, *Pompeii*[3], p. 178.

14. An *unctor* appears in a graffito from Pompeii in *CIL* 4.6890. See H. Tanzer, *The Common People of Pompeii* (Baltimore, 1939), p. 55. The scraping room may also have been called the *destrictarium*, as found in a Pompeiian inscription. See Dyer, *Pompeii*[3], pp. 175–78.

15. See Pliny, Letters 2.17.11, ed. Loeb, vol. 1, pp. 136–37.

16. Of course, as a part of a medical treatment the succession of baths would be regulated by the nature of the disease, for which a cure was being sought. Cf. Celsus, Med. 1.4.2, ed. Loeb, vol. 1, pp. 68–69: deinde id aliquamdiu perfricare, novissime detergere et unguere, meaning that after the head had been rubbed for a while and wiped dry, it should be annointed. See J. Carcopino, *Daily Life in Ancient Rome* (London, 1964), chap. 9, sec. 2, pp. 284–85, and J. J. Deiss, *Herculaneum: A City Returns to the Sun* (London, 1968), p. 111.

17. Cf. with note 7 above for the parallel discussion in the Bavli.

18. This indeed is the meaning in some testimonies, and in the parallel in Y. Kiddushin: מן דימוסיא. See S. Liebermann, *Hayerushalmi Kiphshuto* (Jerusalem, 1931), p. 20.

19. Our printed editions have כך הוה, which makes little sense. But J. N.

Epstein, in his article "Mi-Dikdukei Yerushalmi" *Tarbiz* 6 no. 1 (1935): 48, states that one should read with Ms. Leiden: סך הוה. So, too, is the reading in a Genizah fragment, cited in L. Ginzberg, *Seridei ha-Yerushalmi* (New York, 1809), p. 315. See also Liebermann, *Hayerushalmi*, "Introduction," p. 10; "Commentary," p. 20.

20. Contr. Epstein, *Tarbiz*, p. 48.

21. See Lieberman, *Tosefta*, vol. 1, p. 472, and ibid., vol. 3, pp. 276–77.

22. See W. A. Becker, *Gallus*², trans. F. Metcalfe (London, 1907), pp. 378–79, 393. And cf. Lieberman, *Tosefta* vol. 1, p. 99 (to T. Berachot 5.32; Y. Berachot 6.6, 10d; B. Berachot 53a), that this was primarily to remove dirt and bad body odors.

23. A. C. Dionisotti, "Tom Ausonius' Schooldays," *JRS* 72 (1982): 116 ff.

24. Grenfell and Hunt, *Fragment of an Uncannonical Gospel from Oxyrhynchus*, (Oxford, 1908). See also citation in A. Büchler, *JQR O.S.* 20 (1908): 344.

25. See S. Lieberman, *Kiryat Sefer*, 13 (1936): 187.

26. *A Greek-English Lexicon*, compiled by H. G. Liddell, R. Scott, and H. S. Jones, 9th ed. [LSJ⁹] (Oxford, 1940), p. 1019b s.v. σμήχω II.

27. Becker, *Gallus*, p. 393.

28. Read thus, with Ms. Leiden in Y. Ketubot ibid., and not סכנתא danger, as in printed edition.

29. I am not totally convinced by Lieberman's argument on this point.

30. See M. Shabbat 22.6, but see Lieberman's *Tosefta* vol. 3, p. 277.

31. See M. Jastrow, *A Dictionary of the Targumim, the Talmud Babli and Yerushalmi, and the Midrashic Literature* (New York, 1903), p. 1517b s.v. שבר literally: have [his limbs] broken on the marble [slab].

32. On this whole issue of the order of events in the bathhouse, see A. Büchler's article *Sefer-ha-Yovel le-Professor Shmuel Krauss* (Jerusalem, 1936), pp. 38–45, which is rich in material and provocative in its ideas but not altogether convincing in all its conclusions.

33. See S. Liebermann, *Tosefeth Rishonim*, vol. 3 (Jerusalem, 1939), p. 66 to line 34.

34. See S. Krauss, *Talmudische Archäologie*, vol. 1 (Leipzig, 1910–12; reprint, Hildesheim, 1966), p. 675, n. 97: שערי מרחצאות, Sifrei Deut. 36, ed. Finkelstein, p. 67. תרעא in Y. Sanhedrin 7(14).9, 25b, on the other hand, he sees as an internal entrance.

35. See M. Hirshman's article "Stories from the Bathhouse of Tiberias," in *Tiveriah mi-Yisudah ad ha-Kibush ha-Muslemi*, ed. Y. Hirschfeld (Jerusalem, 1988) [in Hebrew], pp. 119–22.

36. See Becker, *Gallus*, pp. 396–97.

37. See M. Niddah 9.3; אצטבא של מרחץ

38. See M. Johnson, *Picture in Roman Life* (Chicago, 1957), p. 253 and p. 247 for the Stabian baths.

39. Their clothes were not taken away from them by attendants and placed in special baskets, as Krauss (*Talmudische*, vol. 1, pp. 223–24, 678, n. 801) thought. He based his analysis on T. Kelim BK 6.8, p. 585, line 15: סלין שבמרחץ, the baskets in the bathhouse. The correct reading should be במרחל, and the text is referring to baskets of figs. See Liebermann, *Tosefeth*, vol. 3, p. 53, and in his article "Pitron Millim ve-Inyanim," in *Seler ha-Yovel le-Profesor Shmuel Krauss* (Jerusalem, 1936), p. 304.

40. This room is not to be identified with the בית החיצון, the outer room in B. Shabbat 40a (cf. T. Baba Batra 3.3, p. 113), which is probably the *friqidarium*. See Krauss, *Talmudische*, vol. 1, pp. 218, 674–75, n. 95, p. 681, n. 168; ed. van Loopik p. 145 has a slightly different interpretation. The inner rooms were called בית פנימי. See sources referred to above.

41. There were several types of bathhouses in Talmudic Palestine. Some were arranged linearly, meaning that the way in was at one end of a series of chambers and the way out at the other end. Some were planned on a circular basis, meaning the exit and entrance were at the same point. See the detailed analysis of M. Gichon, based on the archeological evidence, in his article "Roman Bath-Houses in Eretz-Israel," *Qadmoniot* 11/1 no. 41, (1978): 37–53 [in Hebrew]. (Also cf. E. Netzer, *Qadmoniot* 8/2–3 no. 30–31, (1975): 56–60, on Cypros, Y. Tsafrir, *Ereẓ-Yisrael from the Destruction of the Second Temple to the Muslim Conquest*, vol. 2 (Jerusalem, 1984), pp. 106–14, and Schwartz, chapter 10.) This depended, among other things, on the topographical conditions. However, our sources indicate a type which is circular. In Derech Ereẓ Rabba 10.2 (ed. Higger p. 301) we read that in a bathhouse priority is given to him that enters over him that exits (i.e., he that enters has "the right of way"). Cf. Y. Baba Kama 3.5, 3d.

42. See Krauss *LW*[2], pp. 52–53 s.v. אלונטית—linteum.

43. We should bear in mind that most major public baths had libraries (Becker, *Gallus*, pp. 390–91), and literary discussions took place in them. See also Deiss, *Herculaneum*, p. 111.

44. The standard greeting included the word *shalom*, which was considered by the rabbis to be one of the epithets of God and thus should not be said in an unsuitable place.

45. So suggests ed. van Loopik, p. 150. However, I am not completely convinced that this is the correct explanation. There it is said that he who does so "is robbing the public" (גוזל את הרבים). Probably this means he is taking up someone's place in the sweat bath while he gets no benefit out of it, since he is robed. On the health aspects of sweating, see Avot de-Rabbi Natan 1, chap. 41, ed. Schechter 1.131: Three types of sweat are good for the body: the sweat of a feverish person, the sweat of the bathhouse, and the sweat of labor. The sweat of the feverish person is curative; the sweat of the bathhouse has no like.

46. The anonymous stratum in the Talmud there (*setama*), probably a Babylonian addition, defines "new" as within twelve months of opening. The passage in B. Avoda Zara 28b, which states that all bathhouses have an element of danger—כולהו בי בני סכנתא—refers to health matters, that is, the bath may be injurious to one's health. It is a Babylonian statement.

47. Goths, according to the partial parallel in Y. Moed Katan 1.2, 80b.

48. In the parallel in B. Berachot 60a we read that (miraculously) he saved one hundred and one people whom he supported on one arm. See Rashi's attempt to explain this statement rationally.

49. Y. Berachot 4.4,8b: מרחץ נסוקת.

50. Cf. above note 46 (?). Presumably, people with weak hearts could be adversely affected by the sweat bath.

51. A slightly different version is found in Derech Ereẓ Rabba 6.1, ed. Higger pp. 295–96, ed. van Loopik p. 137.

52. See Jastrow, *Dictionary*, p. 841a s.v. מרחץ.

53. This place סכותא appears in the Reḥov Inscription as having a northern

gateway [פילי] (line 7). See Y. Sussman, "Ketovet Hilchatit mi-Beit-Shean," *Tarbiz* 43 (1974): 115, n. 158, for a discussion of the identification of this place. It is not to be confused with the similar-sounding term above at note 28.

54. Despite the fact that normally there were severe restrictions on work on Ḥol ha-Moed. On the dangers of the bathhouse, see further Krauss, *Talmudische*, vol. 1, pp. 220, 676, n. 109; idem, "Le Traité Talmudique 'Derech Ereç'," *REJ* 36 (1898): 213.

55. See T. Terumot 10.10, p. 43, line 14, T. Sheviit 6.9, p. 69, line 9. See Krauss *Talmudische*, vol. 1, pp. 230, 684; idem, "Le Traité Talmudique 'Derech Ereç,'" 36 p. 212; and ed. van Loopik pp. 141–42. The leather mat was called a קיטבליא = καταβολή, and on it the massaged person would roll around (מתעגל) in order for the oil to get into all parts of his body. This process is also called משתבר, literally: letting one's [limbs] be broken; see Derech Ereẓ Rabba 10, 2, p. 300, ed. van Loopik p. 142.

56. Cf. περιχύτης λουτραὶ, P. Oxy 148 (sixth century C.E.)

57. See B. Shabbat 40b, which Rabbi Judah ha-Nasi says that he once entered the bathhouse and requested that they place a flask of oil in the bath for him (to warm up the oil). See Becker, *Gallus,* p. 393.

58. פכין גלילין, T. Kelim BK 2.9, p. 571. D. Adan-Bayewitz suggests that פכין גליליים mentioned in Mishna Kelim 2.2, T. Kelim Baba Kama 2.2, and Sifra Shemini 7.3 may perhaps be identified with a jug made at the Galilean settlement of Shikhin from the late first century B.C.E. through the mid-second century C.E. and possibly somewhat later. See D. Adan-Bayewitz and M. Wieder, "Ceramics from Roman Galilee: A Comparison of Several Techniques for Fabric Characterization," *Journal of Field Archaeology* 19 (1992): 189–205. On the date of the vessel, see D. Adan-Bayewitz, "The Pottery," in *The Excavations of an Ancient Boat in the Sea of Galilee (Lake Kinneret)*, ed. S. Wachsmann, *'Atiqot* 19 (1990), 89–96 and figure 11:11. The evidence for this identification—archeological, archaeometric, and literary—will be presented by Adan-Bayewitz in a forthcoming publication.

59. Deiss, *Herculaneum*, p. 111.

60. See Krauss, *Talmudische*, 1, p. 676, n. 112.

61. Cf. T. Shabbat 16.18, p. 136, line 3; טריקלין שהסיקה.

62. See M. Avodah Zara 3.4, B. ibid. 44b; and cf. M. ibid. 4.3.

63. See L. Kadman, *The Coins of Akko Ptolemais* (Jerusalem, 1961), pp. 71, types no. 204–205, 238, 253, 268 (in catalogue and plates).

64. Y. Avoda Zara 4.4,43d. See Lieberman's brilliant analysis of this passage in *JQR* 36 (1946): 366–70.

65. In his edition of the Tosefta, ad loc. pp. 11–12.

66. Lieberman, *Tosefta*, vol. 3, pp. 44–45.

67. See Krauss, *Talmudische*, vol. 1, p. 676, n. 105, 106.

68. Becker, *Gallus*, pp. 386–87.

69. We have not discussed the technical aspects of how the baths were constructed, the women's baths—the emperor Hadrian (117–38) forbade mixed bathing, but the Jews would in any case not have permitted it—or the three different typological layouts emerging from Palestinian archeological remains. In 1990 there appeared an excellent comprehensive work on this subject by Inge Nielsen, entitled *Thermae et Balnea: The Architecture and Cultural History of Roman Public Baths* (Aarhus, 1990), which contains much corroborative evidence. See especially vol. 1, pp. 125–47.

6

Public Buildings

Around the central market forum area, every Roman town with pride and pretensions to importance developed a number of public buildings that made up a standard set, the components of which we can glean not only from the remains themselves but also from Vitruvius' architectural treatise. In Book 5 he sets out "the arrangement of public places" (*publicorum locorum dispositiones*), listing almost exactly the buildings to be found in any Greek and Roman city: forum, basilica, treasury, prison and councilhouse, theater with adjoining porticoes, baths, palaestra, and harbor and shipyards.[1] We have already discussed the prominent nature of the bathhouse, the palaestra is specifically admitted by Vitruvius not to be a usual thing in Italy, and harbors and shipyards are obviously dependent on specific geographic location. Of the other buildings, the treasury and prison, although necessary, were probably of minor importance and therefore do not merit much attention in the sources, while the council- and senate-houses are expected features in a society in which a self-administering community was the standard form of political life. The one building that stands out as peculiarly Roman is the basilica, a large covered hall that performed the functions of the ubiquitous stoas of Hellenistic architecture, and is obviously loosely related to them, but had a form that appears to lack any clear parallel in the Greek world.[2]

We shall discuss and describe some of these focal points of the urban center, beginning with the most prominent, the basilica.[3]

Civic Services

The Basilica

The basilica is often identified with the courts of justice.[4] However, this identification is by no means clear. Indeed, it served either as a court of law and seat of the magistracy or as a place of meeting for merchants and men of business. These two uses were so mixed that it is not always easy to state which was the principal. The basilica at Fanum, of which Vitruvius was the architect (5.1.6–10), was entirely devoted to business, and the courts were held in a small building attached to it—the temple of Augustus.[5] In Pompeii the basilica was situated next to the public granaries (*horrea*),[6] indicating its commercial functions.

The basilica's architectural characteristics are very distinctive, and we have a number of Tannaitic texts from the mid-second century C.E. that although difficult and partially corrupt, can still give us a fair description of the basilica.

The Mishna in Tehorot 6.8 describes the basilica as follows:[7]

> A basilica is accounted private domain in what concerns [the laws of] the Sabbath,[8] and public domain in what concerns [the laws of] uncleanness.[9] R. Judah (flr. mid-second century C.E.) says: If a man stands at one entrance and can see persons entering and leaving at the other entrance, it is accounted private domain in what concerns both the [laws of the] Sabbath and the [laws of] uncleanness; otherwise, it is accounted private domain in what concerns the [laws of the] Sabbath and public domain in what concerns [the laws of] uncleanness.

And in Tosefta Tehorot 7.12–14, p. 668, the discussion is considerably amplified, containing additional elements:

> 12. Basilicas which are open by day and closed at night,[10] as long as they are open, they are [considered to be] public domain, [but when] closed [they are] private domain. Hence, you may say that by day they are clean and by night unclean. A basilica whose entrances face one another, and so also a stoa which is fenced (walled) on both sides and have space between the columns, R. Judah says: If a man stands on one side and sees persons entering and leaving on the other side,[11] it is accounted private domain in what concerns [the laws of] the Sabbath, and public domain in what concerns [the laws of] uncleanness. But if not, it is accounted private domain both concerning this and that (i.e., the laws of the Sabbath and uncleanness).
>
> 13. A basilica whose two entrances face one another, its central [area] is accounted private domain in what concerns [the laws of] the Sabbath, and public domain in what concerns [the laws of] uncleanness, and the side [areas] are accounted private domain to both this and that (Sabbath and uncleanness). Thus, according to R. Meir (mid-second century C.E.). And the Sages say: Both the central [area] and the side [areas] are accounted private domain both as concerns [the laws of] the Sabbath and [the laws of] uncleanness.[12]
>
> 14. And R. Meir would agree with the Sages in [the case of] a basilica whose two[13] entrances do not face one another (such as the court of beit *Gabi* and *Ḥamata*),[14] that both the central [area] and the side [areas] are accounted private domain concerning both the [laws of the] Sabbath and [the laws of] uncleanness. . . .[15]

These are very difficult texts, partially corrupt, with apparent contradictions between the Mishna and the Tosefta (see notes ad loc.). Without going into the detailed reasoning behind these rulings, which distinguish between the laws of the Sabbath and those of uncleanness with regard to the public and private domain, and without entering into the relationship between seeing across an area and its legal status in this regard,[16] we may nonetheless draw certain conclusions about the architectural characteristics of the basilicas referred to.[17]

We are dealing with a large area—it is not always easy to see from one side to the other—probably the whole of which was covered, that is, divided into three sections: the larger (and perhaps higher) central hall and two narrower (and perhaps lower) side halls (compared with stoas.) The whole structure is supported by columns, which also divide up the different areas. There are openings at the two ends of the central section, and a person standing at one end can see people entering and exiting at the other end. In some cases there are many openings in this building, not necessarily facing one another directly (see note 13), so that a person standing on one side of the basilica cannot necessarily see people on the other side.[18]

These findings correspond with what we know of Roman basilicas. They were stoa-like structures, and hence are often called στοὰ βασιλική or simply στοά, whose specific architectural characteristics were a rectangular space divided into a nave (*media porticus* = האמצעי, the middle of the Tosefta) and two side aisles (צדדים, sides of the Tosefta) each separated from the center by a single row of columns. The space between the columns is called in Greek μεσόστυλον, and in Y. Nedarim 4.3,37d (= Y. Shavuot 3.9,34d) we are told that Rabbi Judah [ber Simon] b. Pazi (fl. ca. 290–350 C.E.) claimed to have seen a snake skin that stretched over eight מסוסטולא (μεσόστυλα pl.) intercolumnations. Perhaps he was thinking in terms of the nave of a basilica.[19]

In some cases at the end of the central aisle was the tribunal of the judge (see below), either rectangular or circular[20] and sometimes cut off from the length of the grand nave (as in Pompeii). In such cases when one end of the basilica was closed, the entrances were on the "long" side. Indeed, there were two distinct types of basilicas: the "long" type (with the entrances on the short side) and the "broad" type (with the entrances on the long side).[21] In the long type there were usually only two entrances, whereas the broad type had many entrances along its length (see note 13).

Its lighting was provided by a clerestory supporting the roof of the nave, which was higher than the aisles. Such a mode of construction was particularly suited to buildings intended for the reception of a large concourse of people.

As to its functions, we have already noted that it served both as a court of justice and as a sort of chamber of commerce. Rabbi Yoḥanan (died Tiberias ca. 279 C.E.) informs us[22] that there are three types of basilicas: those of kings, of baths, and of storage chambers (אוצרות). The connection is further borne out by M. Avoda Zara 1.7, in which we read that one may not build with gentiles a basilica and a gradum—a court tribunal.[23] In addition, in T. Ahilot 18.18, p. 617 we are told that in Ashkelon they sold wheat in the basilicas.[24] In Esther Rabba 1.3 (20), on the other hand, Rabbi Samuel bar Naḥman (flr. Tiberias ca. 250–320 C.E.) says: It is like unto a great basilica full of people where the king sits holding court,[25] and all the populace prostrate themselves before him. This, presumably, was Rabbi Yoḥanan's "basilica of kings," the court of the local magistracy, whereas in Ashkelon the basilica was a granary exchange (perhaps among other things). And, indeed, in Pompeii, as already mentioned (see note 6), the basilica was situated next to the public granaries (*horrea*).

Over the course of time the term *basilica* was applied to other public walks of all sorts, such as those attached to temples, theaters, and baths.[26] This explains Rabbi Yoḥanan's use of the term in connection with the public baths מרחצאות.[27]

From Vitruvius (5.1.4) we learn that "the site of the basilicas ought to be fixed adjoining the fora in as warm a quarter as possible[28] so that in winter businessmen may meet there without being troubled by the weather." Here again we see the basilica in its central location, adjoining the forum and constituting a focal point in the city. We read in Exodus Rabba 15.22 (= Tanḥuma Genesis, Ḥayye Sarah 3):

> It is like unto a slave, whose master said to him: Wait for me in the marketplace (i.e., forum), but did not tell him where [in the marketplace] to wait . . . whether near the basilica or the bathhouse, or perhaps next to the theatre.[29]

Apparently, these were the key points in the city center, situated as they were around the market forum. Indeed, we have excellent archeological evidence for the proximity of the basilica to the forum, where the passageway linking these two places has been uncovered in Sebaste. Furthermore, at the eastern end of the basilica was a platform with a semicircular niche and four seats. Presumably, this was the seat of the court of justice. Similarly, in Ashkelon a small forum with a basilica has survived.[30] (See chapter 10, the City Center section, where additional archeological evidence is cited.)

Arche: Courthouse and Public Archives

The term *arche* in Rabbinic literature is used for two different institutions (as is basilica): law court and archive.[31] The courthouse, which was often located in the basilica or, as in the case of Pompeii, next to the basilica, was always close to the central forum area. Unfortunately, our sources offer little of substance about this institution, although a passage in Esther Rabba 1.3 (20) reads as follows:

> R. Eleazar (died Tiberias ca. 280 C.E.) and R. Samuel bar Naḥman: R. Eleazar said: It is like unto the *archion* of Geder,[32] where the king (מלך = magistrate?) sits up on high in judgment, and all the public sit before him on the ground. R. Samuel bar Naḥman says: It is like unto a great basilica full of people, where the king sits holding court,[33] and the populace prostrate themselves before him.

Clearly, *archion* here is a court of justice, and interestingly enough it parallels the court in the basilica.

As to the other meaning of *arche*, archive, Stuart S. Miller[34] has examined in detail "the old ארכי of Sepphoris." Apparently, the term refers to an ancient institution that existed before the destruction of the Second Temple (i.e., pre–70 C.E.). The adjective "old" (*yeshanah*) served to differentiate this particular archive from the latter more prevalent "archives of the gentiles" found in Rabbinic literature.[35] Here again we know little more than that such institutions existed,[36] but not what they looked like or where they were located. However, it is reasonable to assume that they would be found in the center of the city.

Prisons

In the beginning of this chapter I noted that Vitruvius listed prisons among the prominent public buildings found in every city. We know little of the physical characteristics of a Palestinian Roman jail other than that it was generally called a *pilke* (פילקי = φυλακή) and had a prison warden called a *pilkerin* (פילקרין = φυλακάρης)[37] or a *custodia* (קוסטדיא = κουστωδία).[38] Some of the cells were very dark,[39] and there were high-security cells for important (political) prisoners.[40] The cells were called קילין (*kilin* from *cella*, κέλλα), and sometimes the jailhouse is called a בית קילין, *beit kilin*, literally, house of cells,[41] suggesting a large prison with many "lock-ups." Second-century sources refer to a prison built with a vaulted chamber (כיפה, *kippah*, vault)[42] in which people were incarcerated for life as a sort of alternative death sentence. Perhaps these jails were attached to the police station, and possibly these were managed by the police force.[43]

In Pompeii the prison was situated at the northwestern corner of the forum; its exact spot was determined by the skeleton of two men left to perish in the general confusion. Their leg bones were found still within shackles.[44] Other dungeons of a more temporary nature were beneath the raised tribunal for the *praetor* or judge;[45] there were holes in the floor through which orders were transmitted to the person in charge of the prisoners.[46] Vitruvius (5.2.1) advises that "the treasury, *prison*, senatehouse are to adjoin the forum . . . ," again strengthening our assumption that the jailhouse was close to the marketplace.

We shall now turn our attention to buildings for entertainment. And for this I asked my good friend Dr. Zeev Weiss, who has specialized in the field, to contribute a section and he very kindly agreed. It is, in fact, part of a much broader treatment in which he is currently engaged. I have added some additional notes in square brackets initialed D. S.

Buildings for Entertainment

ZEEV WEISS

General

It is well known that games and spectacles held a prominent place in Roman life. This is evident not only from the ever-increasing number of festival days during the Roman period but also from the extensive construction of theaters, circuses, and amphitheaters (i.e., buildings for entertainment) throughout the empire during the first three centuries of the common era.[47]

Herod the Great was the first to introduce games and spectacles to the Roman East, dramatically changing the leisure habits of the population. Very few cities had theaters, hippodromes, or amphitheaters at the beginning of the Herodian period. However, from the end of the first century C.E. onward, and especially during the second and third centuries C.E., many buildings whose primary purpose was entertainment were erected in Roman Palestine.

Theaters have been revealed in twenty-three cities in this region. Every large city had at least one theater, and some, like Gadara, Gerasa (Jerash), and Philadelphia (Amman), had two or three. Occasionally, one of them was a smaller structure called an *odeon* (see discussion in Theater section later). Literary and other sources mention theaters in Jerusalem, Gaza, and Ashkelon, which have not yet been exposed.[48] In addition, Hellenized cities like Ptolemais (Acre), Eleutheropolis, and Jaffa must have contained at least one such building. This would bring us to a total of far more than thirty theaters in our region. It is noteworthy that a larger number of theaters have been uncovered in Transjordan and Hauran than in western Palestine. This does not necessarily mean that the cities in Transjordan were more oriented toward Hellenistic culture but rather that the generally good preservation of ruins there has resulted in more finds. All the available evidence suggests that the number of theaters in both these regions was probably similar.

Circuses, or hippodromes[49] as they were called in this part of the Roman world, have been found in seven cities to date, although literary sources indicate that such structures were also built in Jerusalem, Tarichaeae, Gaza, Ashkelon, and elsewhere.[50]

Amphitheaters, on the other hand, have been discovered in only five cities (or possibly six), and there is very little additional evidence of others, apart from Josephus' problematic reference to amphitheaters built by Herod the Great in Jerusalem, Caesarea, and Jericho.[51] The "amphitheater" in Caesarea is probably the Herodian hippodrome that is now being excavated. If this proves to be the case, we may conclude that those in Jerusalem and Jericho were in fact also hippodromes, which for various reasons he termed amphitheaters.

An analysis of these numbers, together with their distribution throughout the region, leads to the conclusion that in Roman Palestine theaters were more popular than the other types of entertainment structures. This disproportion does not seem to stem from an unfavorable attitude toward buildings such as the hippodrome, which was used for chariot racing and athletic contests, but from fiscal considerations. The outlay for their construction and maintenance, and for the support of their activities over a long period of time, in addition to the continuous upkeep of other public buildings, was apparently beyond the financial capability of most cities in Roman Palestine.

In most cases theaters were situated within the urban infrastructure, whereas hippodromes and amphitheaters were located on the outskirts, near the roads which led into the city. Thus, for example, the theaters in Scythopolis (Beit Shean), Neapolis (Sechem, Nablus), and Gerasa were incorporated within the urban infrastructure, while their hippodromes or amphitheaters were located outside the city (fig. 10.5, p. 160). On the other hand, all three types of entertainment structures in Caesarea and Bostra were erected outside the urban layout. The theater was a structure smaller than the hippodrome and amphitheater and did not require such a large public space within the city's center. Theaters were usually built when the city was founded and as public buildings were being constructed in its center. Hippodromes and amphitheaters were generally added later when the center was already crowded with public buildings and unable to accommodate another massive structure.[52] Moreover, hippodromes and amphitheaters could hold many more people than theaters could hold and might have been a potential site for the outbreak of riots. Therefore it was deemed preferable to locate them outside the city proper.

These buildings and the performances held in them were financed by the city using tax payments and revenues from municipal properties and the procurement of municipal offices.[53] Donations from magistrates, wealthy residents, and others, who sought to glorify their city in this way and win popularity among their fellow citizens, were the main source of income for public buildings, including those for entertainments.[54] In all likelihood, the cities of Palestine also relied on the the same means for financing the construction and regular operation of entertainment structures; private contributions in particular constituted the main source of income for this purpose. This is intimated in a few dedicatory inscriptions found in the southern theater of Gerasa and in the theater of Canatha (Qanawat).[55] To these can be added certain sources from the Talmudic literature, which also suggest that the Palestinian entertainment structures were erected with the aid of contributions from the cities' wealthy residents.[56] These Talmudic sources not only mention the actual payment for the construction of such structures but also attest to the financing of games, for example, in the case of gladiatorial and animal-baiting contests held in the amphitheaters.[57]

Theaters

The first theaters in Roman Palestine were built by Herod the Great in Jerusalem, Caesarea, and Jericho (fig. 6.1).[58] The earliest structures date from the end of the first century B.C.E., but the majority are from the second and third centuries C.E.

As noted, theaters were generally located in the city's center, near other public buildings. However, a detailed analysis brings to light various exceptions to this rule. A theater and an *odeon* were located near

Figure 6.1. Caesarea—general view of the theater. (Photo: Gabi Laron.)

one another, on either side of one of the main streets of Scythopolis.[59] At Philadelphia they were located on either side of the forum,[60] and two theaters flanked the acropolis at Gadara.[61] Theaters were also considered by the ancients to be part of the city center's landscape. In order to explain a verse in Psalms, one of the rabbis, making reference to the reality within the city, comments: "They were like a slave, to whom his master said: Wait for me in the marketplace (שוק), without specifying the spot. The slave then began to think: perhaps he wanted me to wait for him near the basilica, or near the bathhouse or near the theater. When he found him, his master slapped his face saying: I sent you to the entrance of the governor's palace (*Hipparchos*):"[62] From this we learn not only that the theaters were situated in the city's center but also that they served as a landmark, like any other public building.

The theater was not always aligned with the city's grid as in Scythopolis, Neapolis, and Gerasa, for example (fig. 10.5, p. 160).[63] Its positioning was determined by the specific mode of construction that characterized all theaters in our area, with the exception of those at Bostra and Philipopolis. It was based on the use of a natural slope, especially in the *ima cavea*. As a result, the structure often deviated slightly from the alignment of the city infrastructure.

Theaters in Roman Palestine fall into three groups. Huge structures with diameters of 90 to 100 meters and 6,000 to 8,000 seats were built in large cities like Bostra, Caesarea, and Scythopolis (fig. 6.1). Medium-sized theaters with diameters of 60 to 80 meters and 2,000 to 4,500 seats were found in a smaller cities which nevertheless played an important

Figure 6.2. General view of the Roman theater at Gerasa. (Photo: Gabi Laron.)

Figure 6.3. General view of the theater at Sepphoris. (Photo: Gabi Laron.)

role in their region, like Sepphoris, Sebaste-Samaria, and Gerasa (figs. 6.2 and 6.3). Small theaters with diameters of 30 to 50 meters and 1,000 to 1,500 seats were built in minor cities like Shuni and Hamat Gader, or as a second theater in large cities, as noted at Scythopolis and Philadelphia. In certain localities this type of building was possibly used as an *odeon*.[64]

From these data one grasps the direct relationship between the size of the theater and that of the city in which it was built. Large theaters were erected in the Palestinian metropolises with large populations. Such extensive construction was not characteristic of provincial centers, the seats of the imperial government, but it was linked with the size of the city, the number of its inhabitants, and its financial capability to meet their needs.[65] In other towns, which were of no lesser significance financially, culturally, and socially but had fewer inhabitants than the metropolises, only medium-sized theaters were built. The building of a small theater does not necessarily indicate a lesser inclination toward the theater and the performances presented in it but was rather connected with the city's needs and financial capability to undertake grand projects.

Theaters in Roman Palestine were built according to the Roman model known from other parts of the empire. This includes the use of vaults and arches to consolidate the upper parts of the *cavea*; the use of corridors (*vomitoria*) through which the audience passed to enter the theater; the division of the *cavea* into sections with aisles running lengthwise (*cunei*) and widthwise (*ima*, *media*, and *summa cavea*); the use of the stone-paved *orchestra* as a place for seating honored guests rather than for dances and performances, as in the Greek theater; the design of the stage building (*scaena*); and especially the use of architectural patterns decorating the rear of the *scaena frons* (fig. 6.4).[66]

By and large the theaters of Palestine fit into this general picture. Nevertheless, one can point to certain local features. The creation of a desirable incline for the *cavea* by utilizing a natural slope together with vaults is the most significant one. Every theater in this region shows a Roman influence and used Roman architecture as a model, but each has its own special characteristics. None of these buildings completely resembles another, even in a nearby city.

Certain similarities can be noted in the theaters of Transjordan that distinguish them from those in western Palestine, for example, the relationship between the *cavea* and the *orchestra* and the way the *cavea*, where the common people sat, was separated from the *orchestra*, which was reserved for the dignitaries (see below). Theaters in Transjordanian cities such as Gerasa, Bostra, and Philipopolis have common features which suggest that they were all influenced by the same architectural source. On the whole, however, one can say that the theaters of Roman Palestine were characterized more by architectural diversity than by similarity.

The seating arrangement in Roman theaters was based on rank.[67] Prominent people sat in the *orchestra*, and the others, according to their rank, in the *cavea*. As Paul Zanker states in his book *The Power of*

Figure 6.4. Scythopolis—northern view from the cavea toward the stage. (Photo: Gabi Laron, with courtesy of G. Mazor and R. Bar-Naton, IAA.)

Images in the Age of Augustus: "Even the architecture of the theater helped to include and make visible the principles of social stratification. The networks of arches, passageways, and staircases served not only to insure an easy flow of traffic in and out of the theater, but to separate the audience according to rank."[68] This also applied to the theaters of Roman Palestine. While the masses gained access to the *cavea* through the various *vomitoria*, the *parodoi*, on the side of the building, led distinguished guests directly to their seats in the *orchestra*. To maintain this division, a stone barrier was installed between the *orchestra* and the *cavea* in the theaters of western Palestine. The high *podium* at the bottom of the *cavea* served the same purpose in the theaters of Transjordan. This reality was probably noted by Resh Lakish, a third-century rabbi, who uses it to explain a verse in Ecclesiastes: "It may be like a king who entered a province accompanied by his *dux*, *hipparchos*, and *strategoi*. Although they all entered through the same gate of the *agon* [referring to the theater as a place of contest],[69] each went and sat in a row and place corresponding to his rank."[70]

Theater performances in the Roman world did not include classic comedy, tragedy, and satire. They were usually of a merrier and lighter bent, with an emphasis on mime, pantomime, and the Atellan farce, which provided amusement of the simplest kind.[71] There were also some agonistic performances, acrobats, jugglers, and clowns.[72]

The themes used for mime were taken from everyday life in the village or the town—romance, social satire, mythology, and religion. These shows combined movement, dance, mimicry, and clowning performed by an ensemble of actors. Rabbi Abbahu (died ca. 309 C.E.) makes reference to a short mime, originally consisting of a few acts, which was probably viewed by the inhabitants of Roman Caesarea, part of which runs as follows:

> . . . and they introduce the mime into their theater, with his head shaven. And they say one to the other: why is his head shaven? And they replies: These Jews observe the Shabbath. And all they toil for throughout the week they eat on the Sabbath. But they have no wood to cook on: so they break up their beds and cook on them. And they sleep on the ground rolling in the dust. And they anoint themselves in oil, and that is why oil is expensive. And apparently this is why he was shaven bald, because he could not afford to "soap" his hair in oil, so instead, for the sake of hygiene, he shaved all his hair. . . .[73]

The number of actors cited by Rabbi Abbahu, their role in the play, and the mention of animals brought up on the stage are in accord with known mime patterns and seem authentic. The hostility toward Jews as well as other minorities in the Roman world aroused by the mime finds expression in this passage.

Pantomime, on the other hand, was based on historical and mythological themes, and a single actor played all the roles.[74] These performances featured dance without words, accompanied by a chorus and music. One passage in the Palestinian Talmud refers to a leading pantomime artist who performed in the Caesarea theater.

> . . . This man commits five sins every day: he adorns the theater, engaged the hetaerae (i.e., musicians and dancers), brings their clothes to the bathhouse, claps hands and dance before them and clashes the cymbals up before them. [Rabbi Abbahu] said to him: what good did you perform? He replied (again referring to himself): This man once was adorning the theater (תייטרון) when a women came in and stood behind the columns [of the theater (referring presumably to the columns of *scaena frons*)] crying. I asked her: what is your business [here] (i.e., what do you want)? She said (about herself): They imprisoned the husband of this woman and she wants to see what she can do to release him (implying that she wants to be engaged to work in the theater). I sold my bed and curtain covering my bed and gave her the money I received for them, and told her: Here you have the money, release your husband and do not cry. . . .[75]

This man, whose real name is unknown to us, is termed *pantokakos* in the Talmud on account of his evil deeds. This *pantokakos* met Rabbi Abbahu in Caesarea and described to him his work in the theater. From his words we learn of the types of performances held in the theater. One of his jobs was to engage actors for the theater. The lady, who was lurking by the columns, was seeking work in the theater. She asked him to hire her in order to earn enough money to save her husband.

The Atellan farce presented short, amusing skits featuring fixed characters—clown, fool, glutton, old man, and idiot.[76] Evidence for such performances in Roman Palestine is scanty, but the Talmudic literature seems to indicate that they did take place in our region.[77]

Hippodromes/Stadia

Hellenistic-style chariot racing was one of the features of the athletic contests in Roman Palestine (see below). Chariot races as well as athletic contests were held in the hippodrome, in contrast to the practice in other parts of the Roman empire, where each of them was provided with its own structure.[78] The hippodrome, sometimes called a stadium in literary and other sources,[79] was adapted to meet these needs. Generally, the building was long enough for both contests, but it was necessary to widen it to make possible chariot racing.

The first hippodromes in Roman Palestine were built by Herod the Great in Jerusalem, Caesarea, and Jericho.[80] The stadium in Sebaste-Samaria was probably another of his projects.[81] The structures in Sebaste-Samaria and Jericho, despite their differences, have certain common features,[82] whereas the hippodrome in Caesarea is completely different.[83] It seems that during the Herodian period, there was no fixed plan for hippodromes. Some were designed according to the Roman pattern (see below); others combined diverse architectural elements in one structure, virtually creating a new plan. All of them, however, were intended to meet the needs of various games.

Most of the hippodromes built in our region date from the second and third centuries C.E. and can be classified in two groups. As in the case of the theaters, large hippodromes (approx. 120 × 450 m) were located in the biggest cities, whereas other cities had smaller ones (approx. 70 × 250 m). It is estimated that the large hippodromes could seat about 16,000 spectators and the small ones only about 10,000. From these data we learn of the direct relationship between the size of the hippodrome and that of the city in which it was built, as was the case with regard to theaters. In the metropolises of Caesarea and Bostra, which had large populations (approx. 70,000 inhabitants), large hippodromes were constructed. In other localities, such as Gerasa and Gadara, these structures were smaller, in conformity with the size of the of the city's population (approx. 30,000). This relationship in Roman Palestine between the size of the city and its hippodrome statistically matches that throughout the Roman empire.[84]

Most of the hippodromes in Palestine that have been excavated or surveyed were built beyond the city limits. The hippodrome was usually built adjacent to one of the main roads leading to the city. This made possible easy access when the inhabitants of the city and its surroundings came to watch the games and races. The hippodrome was sometimes built in a natural depression or next to a river channel, thus taking advantage of the natural slope for the construction of the *cavea*.[85] With

Figure 6.5. General view of the southern part of the hippodrome at Gerasa, looking toward the cavea and the carceres. (Photo: Gabi Laron.)

the aid of retaining walls and earth fill, a level area was created, a prerequisite for the holding of races in a hippodrome.

The Palestinian hippodromes constructed during this period had several common features.[86] The Circus Maximus in Rome, rebuilt by Trajan, inspired the erection of many structures of this type in the Roman empire, including those in our region. Several elements recur regularly in the plan of the hippodrome. It was a rectangular structure with one of its short sides ending in a semicircle and with the chariots' starting gates (*carceres*) located on the opposite side (fig. 6.5). A low barrier (*euripus*) decorated with basins (pools containing water), statues, columns, and obelisks separated the tracks, which the charioteers rounded several times. The tiered seating space (*cavea*) skirted the entire perimeter of the track except for the side on which the starting gates were located. Various entrances scattered along the structure (*vomitoria*) enabled the spectators to reach their seats in the *cavea*. This basic plan, with certain additional changes to meet the local needs, was characteristic of the Palestinian hippodromes built in the second and third centuries C.E. To the best of our knowledge, this building was used both for the chariot races and athletic contests held in various cities of Palestine.

Various games were held periodically in Roman Palestine.[87] In the second and third centuries C.E. cities organized these events in honor of the Caesars and local entities.[88] The cities provided the facilities and awarded prizes to the winners. Some of the athletes who participated in these contests even came from abroad. The number of games increased

Figure 6.6. Marble funerary relief from Caesarea depicting an athlete holding a victory palm and a prize vase. (Courtesy of the Caesarea Museum Kibbutz Sdot-Yam.)

dramatically toward the end of the second century and during the third century C.E. as new hippodromes were built.

The director of the games and the person actually responsible for their organization was the *agonothetes*.[89] It was his duty to invite to the games athletes and players from his own city and those who came from other localities, to see to all their needs, and in effect to supervise the program of games during the festival. The *agonothetes* had the honor of opening the games, and he awarded the prizes to the winners. The qualifications of the *agonothetes*, his personal involvement, and his attitude toward winners and losers alike were a prerequisite for the success of the games.[90]

The winner of an athletic contest[91] or chariot race was crowned with a palm branch as a sign of victory in addition to receiving a wreath or a cash prize (fig. 6.6). Rabbi Avin, a Palestinian Sage, compares the victory of a charioteer in the hippodrome and his coronation with a palm branch to the waving of the palm branch (*lulav*) on the Feast of Tabernacles (*Sukkot*) as an expression of victory in the judgment before God. And that what he says: "What kind of victory is meant in the phrase *in thy right hand there are pleasures of victory*? That kind in which the victor receives a wreath. For according to the custom of the world, when two charioteers (*heniochos*) race in the hippodrome, which of them receives the wreath? The victor . . . ."[92]

Among the games and contests known to have taken place in our region were the combatant sports—wrestling, boxing, and *pankration* (a combination of the two).[93] Wrestling was tame compared with boxing and *pankration*, where the fighters attached pieces of metal to their gloves. Nevertheless, these sports were no less brutal than the gladiatorial contests that the Romans enjoyed so greatly.

As is known, various types of combatant sports were held in many Palestinian cities throughout the Roman period.[94] Of all the athletic contests that took place in this country, combatant sport matches are given the widest mention in the Talmudic literature, but it is difficult to

Figure 6.7. General view of the amphitheater at Scythopolis. (Courtesy of G. Foerster and Y. Tsafrir. The Hebrew University, Jerusalem. Photo: Gabi Laron.)

determine from the descriptions at our disposal the exact nature of the contest to which reference is made: boxing, wrestling, or *pankration*. Moreover, some of these sources appear to describe situations taken from gladiatorial combats, spectacles no less cruel than the Roman combatant sports. The rules of combat in combatant sports were known to Rabbi Nehemia, who states: ". . . Who places himself in the arena (*le-zirah*) stands either to fail or win. . . ."[95] The winner was awarded a garland as a prize, as mentioned by Resh Lakish: "It can be compared to two prize fighters, one of whom was stronger than the other. The stronger prevailed over the weaker who placed a garland on his head. . . ."[96] In another passage the same Sage describes the emotions of the loser: ". . . Let's take as an example two athletes grappling with one another. One of them, sensing he was about to lose, said: 'Now he will beat me and I will be shamed in front of everybody'. What did he do? He kissed his rival's hand, thus gaining his pardon."[97]

Running various distances, mainly multiples of the *stadium* (approx. 192 m), was another type of contest.[98] Other competitions involved jumping, discus throwing, and javelin throwing. In the *pentathlon* athletes competed in a number of sports. Such contests were also held in Palestine, but we possess only scanty evidence of their existence.[99]

Chariot racing was another popular sport. Races were financed by private contributors and participation in them was not restricted to certain groups.[100] In the Hellenistic period the number of contestants in each race was variable, in contrast to the Roman tradition in which a fixed number of contestants were divided between four factions. Chariot races were first held in Palestine during the days of Herod.[101] The construction of hippodromes in certain cities here during the second half of the the second century and the beginning of the third century C.E. attests to the popularity of such races during this period. Chariot racing in Palestine during the first centuries of the common era followed the tradition prevalent in the Hellenistic period. Only later, during the fourth century, factions were introduced in Roman Palestine for various reasons. This greatly changed the character and organization of competitions in the region during the Byzantine period.

Athletic games and chariot races took place in the hippodromes, but it is possible that contests in the combatant sports were held in the theater, especially in those cities lacking a hippodrome. The athletes of Roman Palestine were probably organized in clubs,[102] and they practiced in a gymnasium or in open spaces in the city, such as the *palaestra* of the public bathhouse.[103]

Amphitheaters

Gladiatorial games and animal baiting, held in the amphitheater, were very popular throughout the Roman period.[104] According to Josephus, it was Herod the Great who built the first amphitheaters in our region.[105] An analysis of the historical and archeological data from the Herodian period leads to a different conclusion. The structures built by Herod were not Roman-style amphitheaters but rather hippodromes that Josephus confused with amphitheaters. The local population apparently objected to these kind of spectacles during the Herodian period, which explains why amphitheaters were not built until later.

Amphitheaters began to appear in Roman Palestine only during the second and third centuries.[106] They were initially built to satisfy the desire of the growing Roman population who had settled in the central administrative cities of Palestine at the end of the first century C.E. and especially during the centuries that followed.[107] It seems that once gladiatorial games and animal baiting were firmly established in the main cities, the local populace also began to enjoy these spectacles, despite their original disapproval.

The amphitheater, like the hippodrome, was built outside the city but adjacent to one of the roads leading to and from it. There was direct access to the building since it was surrounded by open space. Here the people assembled prior to entering the building before the games, and from here the crowds dispersed after exiting the amphitheater at the end of the contests.[108]

Very few amphitheaters have been discovered in our region, and even the known ones have not been adequately excavated or studied. Nevertheless, it is clear that amphitheaters in Roman Palestine generally followed the Roman style. They fall into two groups: those built as amphitheaters from the outset[109] and those which replaced older hippodromes.[110]

Both types have common features in keeping with the kind of performances held in them, although the shape of the *arena* and its measurements vary from building to building. Certain recurrent elements in several of these structures, such as the *podium* at the bottom of the *cavea*, the main entrances on the axis of the building, the animal cages scattered around the building, and the platform (*pulvinar*) with a shrine (*sacellum*) beneath it, allow us to conclude that they were the prevalent ones in the amphitheaters of Roman Palestine.

Gladiatorial games and wild animal baiting exhibited in the *arena* were the main spectacles viewed by the Romans in the amphitheater.[111] Slaves, prisoners of war, condemned criminals, and sometimes even hirelings participated in these contests.[112] The gladiatorial games (*munera gladiatorum*) involved two combatants. The *retiarius*, half-naked and armed with a net and a trident, fought against the *myrmillones*, who was armed with a shield and a sword and wore a helmet on his head. The battle continued until one of them was defeated or killed. Two kinds of animal baiting took place in the amphitheater aside from the simple exhibition of the animals. Wild animals were either baited and killed by men (*bestriarii*) or were preyed upon by other animals (*venatio*).

All these spectacles were known in Roman Palestine,[113] and are referred to in the Talmudic literature by their Greek names, *mono-*

machia, *kunegesia*, and *theriomachia*.[114] The types of contests, fighting techniques, and weapons used in the spectacles staged in the amphitheaters of our region were in accordance with the custom throughout the Roman world.[115] The list of animals participating in such games in Roman Palestine is long and includes bulls, lions, bears, and rams.[116]

The economic crisis that beset the Roman empire in the mid-third century C.E., leaving its mark also on Palestine, forced certain people to engage in gladiatorial combat, for which they received handsome payment.[117] The search for sources of livelihood during the crisis, together with the desire to gain glory that was not directly connected with the individual's legal or social status, led certain people, including Jews in Palestine, to take part in gladiatorial and animal-baiting contests during this period.[118]

The gladiators were trained in a special school headed by a *lanista*, who took charge of them and supplied combatants for the games.[119] On the night before the performance, the gladiators ate a special meal provided by the person who funded the games.[120] The next day, the events opened with a spectacular procession accompanied by music, during which the gladiators displayed their arms. Immediately thereafter, the animal-baiting contest began, followed by the gladiatorial games. The variety of the spectacles and their sequence were intended to hold the attention of the audience throughout the entire show.

Thus the character of games and spectacles in the Roman East of Herod's day was a revolutionary innovation. Not only were the monumental buildings new but so were the variety of games and spectacles. They caused a radical change in the leisure habits of the population in the Roman East. Thus, Herod's massive building projects left an imprint on the region for a very long time; his dream of integrating Palestine culturally with the rest of the Roman empire became reality far beyond his reign and the boundaries of his realm.

Notes

1. See J. Carter, "Civic and Other Buildings," chap. 2 in *Roman Public Buildings*, ed. I. M. Barton (Exeter, 1989), p. 32, and cf. J. Schwartz, chapter 10, section "City Center: Politics, Administration, and Economy."

2. Carter, *Roman*, p. 32.

3. We shall not discuss all the public buildings. For instance, the palace mentioned on numerous occasions in Rabbinic parallels is a subject that merits its own study. Most references to the palace in parables seem to be literary and probably do not reflect actual contemporary circumstances. See for example D. Stern, *Parables in Midrash: Narrative and Exegesis in Rabbinic Literature* (Cambridge, 1991), pp. 226–27, 231–32. The *bouleuterion* is infrequently mentioned in Rabbinic literature, although *boule- and bouleutes* occur often. See Schwartz's chapter 10 on this subject. As to the synagogue, there is a vast bibliography on this subject that need not be repeated. See for example M. J. S. Chiat, *Handbook of Synagogue Architecture* (Chico, 1982); *The Synagogue in*

Late Antiquity, ed. L. I. Levine (Philadelphia, 1987); *Beit ha-Knesset bi-Tekufat ha-Mishnah ve-ha-Talmud*, ed. Z. Safrai (Jerusalem, 1986); Z. Ilan, *Batei Knesset ba-Galil u-va-Golan* (Jerusalem, 1987).

4. See for example *Illustrated Dictionary of Historic Architecture*, ed. C. M. Harris (New York, 1977), p. 50 s.v. basilica, defining it as a Roman hall of justice. . . . See also S. Lieberman, "Roman Legal Institutions in Early Rabbinics and the Acta Martyrum," *JQR* 35 no. 1 (1944), 13: As the place of Roman trials the rabbis generally mention the basilica. . . . But trials of capital cases in the theater and circus are also mentioned. See Avot de Rabbi Nathan 21, ed. Schechter p. 74 (Lieberman *JQR* 35 no. 1 (1944), 13, n. 77).

5. See W. Smith, W. Wayte, and G. E. Marindin, *A Dictionary of Greek and Roman Antiquities*[3] (London, 1890), p. 287 s.v. basilica. See the introduction to my *Dictionary of Greek and Latin Legal Terms in Rabbinic Literature* (Jerusalem, 1984), p. 22.

6. T. K. Dyer, *Pompeii: Its History, Buildings, and Antiquities*[3] (London, 1871), pp. 124–31.

7. Mishna, Danby trans., p. 725.

8. Meaning: one can carry objects freely within this area; one cannot do so in an area designated as public domain.

9. Uncertain uncleanness in a public domain is ignored, that is, the person or object remain clean or pure; in a private domain they are considered unclean; see M. Tehorot 6.1. The definition of private and public domain differs between the laws of the Sabbath and those of uncleanness, as is evident from these texts.

10. Cf. Y. Eruvin 1.1,18d; S. Liebermann, *Hayerushalmi Kiphshuto* (Jerusalem, 1934), p. 226; idem, *Tosefeth Rishonim* vol. 4 (Jerusalem, 1939), p. 79, lines 11–12.

11. Cf. Tosefta Tehorot 7.8 ed. Zuckermandel p. 608: If there were two untended fields and a person standing at one end could see those entering and leaving at the other end, it is private domain for the Sabbath and public domain for uncleanness; and if not, it is private domain for both this and that. See Liebermann, *Tosefeth*, vol. 4, p. 78 to lines 2–3. This would seem to contradict Rabbi Judah's statement in the Mishna above. It is for this reason that the Gaon, Rabbi Eliyahu of Wilna, in Eliyahu Rabba, suggested emending our Tosefta text to read: If a man stands on one side and does *not* see. . . . However, see Liebermann's discussion in his *Tosefeth*, vol. 4, p. 79, lines 11–12 and pp. 79–80 to lines 12–15.

12. A similar difference of opinion between Rabbi Meir and the Sages may be found in M. Tehorot 6.9. The question is what is פרן in that Mishna. Most commentators and dictionaries understand it as φάρος (-ον), a lighthouse (see S. Krauss, *Griechische und Lateinische Lehnwörter im Talmud, Midrasch, und Targum*, vol. 2 [*LW*[2]] vol. 2 (Berlin, 1899; reprint, Hildesheim, 1964), p. 491 s.v. פרן II), but S. Liebermann in *Talmudah shel Kesarin* (Jerusalem, 1931), p. 13 (and again in his *Siphre Zutta* [New York, 1968], p. 132, 27) explains it as *forum*, which is much closer to the adjacent Mishna discussing the basilica and to the parallel Tosefta text. Indeed, on this basis Maimonides, in his Mishna commentary to Tehorot 6.9 concluded that the פרן is similar to the basilica. See Liebermann, *Tosefeth*, vol. 4, p. 80 to lines 15–18. Nonetheless, it is difficult to understand how a forum could be considered a private domain as regard the Sabbath. See chapter 1, note 3.

13. Tosefta 13 and 14 both mention a basilica with *two* entrances, whereas Tosefta 12 describes a basilica with *entrances*. Liebermann (*Tosefeth*, vol. 4, pp. 79–80 to lines 12–15) suggests that Tosefta 12 is describing a basilica that has *many* entrances facing one another, like the walled stoa with its columns. When the columns and entrances directly face one another, a person can see from one side to the other. But if the arrangement is staggered, for the most part he will not be able to see all the way through. For the legal implication of this, see the continuation of his discussion in *Tosefeth*.

14. Liebermann (*Tosefeth*, vol. 4, p. 80 to line 19) suggests that the correct reading is that of the medieval commentator Rabbi Simeon of Sens (the Rash), who omits these words, which have been mistakenly inserted from below line 21 (a passage we have not cited). On the identification of these sites, see S. Lieberman, *Tosefta ki-fshutah* vol. 3 (New York, 1962), pp. 384–85.

15. The continuation of this text, which is not required for our discussion, is extremely corrupt. See Liebermann, *Tosefeth*, vol. 4, p. 80 to lines 21–22.

16. See *Ḥasdei David* of Rabbi David Pardo, to T. Tehorot 7.12 (Jerusalem, 1977), p. 121 for a detailed halachic analysis of these texts.

17. I use the plural to distinguish between different types of basilica. See note 13 and below. See also S. Krauss, *Kadmoniyyot ha-Talmud*, vol. 1, part 2 (Berlin and Vienna, 1923), pp. 427–28.

18. Cf. T. Yoma 1.3., p. 180, Liebermann, *Tosefeth*, vol. 4, pp. 79–80, and *Ḥasdei David*, p. 121.

19. That is, looking along the nave, he thought in terms of the length of the space between eight opposite columns. Alternatively, he could be thinking in terms of a single row of columns, as in a stoa, and the length was the length between eight columns. See also Krauss, *Kadmoniyyot ha-Talmud*, vol. 1, part 2, p. 432.

20. This is the βῆμα, the prominent elevated platform, which served as the seat of the judge or judges. (See Tosefta Kelim Baba Meẓia 10.6, p. 589; Liebermann, *Tosefeth*, vol. 3, p. 66; and S. Lieberman, *JQR* 35 no. 1 (1944): 13.

21. See Carter, *Roman*, p. 43.

22. B. Avoda Zara, 16b.

23. See my *Dictionary*, pp. 76–78.

24. See Krauss, *Kadmoniyyot ha-Talmud*, vol. 1, part 1, p. 429, on the readings in the parallel texts. This reading seems to be the best.

25. במסיבו; cf. Canticles 1:12.

26. See Smith, Wayte, and Marindin, *Dictionary*, p. 287.

27. See Krauss, *Kadmoniyyot ha-Talmud*, vol. 1, part 1, p. 428.

28. As indeed was the case in Pompeii. See Dyer, *Pompeii*, p. 125.

29. Exodus Rabba has פיטרון, while Tanḥuma has תיאטרון. Krauss (*Kadmoniyyot ha-Talmud*, vol. 1, part 1, p. 428, n. 3) cites a variant (from *Ot Emet*, quoted by *Matnot Kehunah*): סטרין, which Krauss emends to סטדין = stadium. However, this is most unlikely since the stadium usually required a large area and was rarely in the center of the city, close to the forum. See Schwartz, chapter 10, section on Stadium (with reference to Tsafrir p. 121). See also Krauss, *LW*², pp. 442–43, where Löw prefers the reading תיטרון = theatre.

30. There are some additional Rabbinic sources thought to relate to the basilica. Krauss (*Kadmoniyyot ha-Talmud*, vol. 1, part 1, p. 427) cites from Sifrei Deut. 36, p. 67: שערי בסילקאות, which he understood as "entrances to basilicas." But Lieberman has cogently argued that this refers to water con-

duits—סילקאות. See chapter 9. Similarly, the text in Midrash Psalms 105.5, p. 451 and its emendations, remains problematic and as yet unsatisfactorily explained. See Krauss, *LW*², p. 3181b s.v. סידקי. This is also true of Midrash Psalms 22.3, p. 181; see Krauss, *Kadmoniyyot ha-Talmud*, vol. 1, part 1, p. 428.

31. ארכי or ערכי = ἀρχή; and ארכיון = ἀρχεῖον = archivum. I have collected all the relevant material relating to these terms in my *Dictionary*, pp. 62–65.

32. Gadera, east of Sea of Galilee, near Ḥamat Gader. Se S. Klein, *Sefer ha-Yishuv*, vol. 1 (Jerusalem, 1939), pp. 27–28.

33. See note 25 above.

34. S. S. Miller, "The 'Old' Archei," chap. 3 in *Studies in the History and Traditions of Sepphoris* (Leiden, 1984), pp. 46–55.

35. Miller, *Studies*, p. 51 and my *Dictionary*, p. 63. These would appear to be courts of law. The old archive of Sepphoris preserved records relating to personal status of individuals and therefore would probably have been attached to the court of law, which had to determine halachic questions of personal status.

36. S. Albeck's *Law Courts in Talmudic Times* (Jerusalem, 1980) [in Hebrew] does not deal with these aspects. The various studies on the history of the Sanhedrin are also not really relevant to this issue. See Y. Y. Greenwald, *Le-Toldot ha-Sanhedrin be-Yisrael* (New York, 1950); A. Büchler, *Ha-Sanhedrin* (Jerusalem, 1974) [Hebrew trans. of German *Das Synhedrion in Jerusalem* Vienna, 1902]; S. B. Hoenig, *Sanhedrin Gedolah*² (Jerusalem, 1975) [Hebrew trans. of his English *The Great Sanhedrin*, Philadelphia, 1953]; and H. D. Mantel, *Studies in the History of the Sanhedrin* (Cambridge, 1961), [Hebrew trans., *Meḥkarim be-Toldot ha-Sanhedrin*, Tel Aviv, 1969]. Much more relevant to our subject is Lieberman's brilliant study in "Roman Legal Institutions" (1944): pp. 1–57.

37. See my *Dictionary*, pp. 143–45.

38. See my *Dictionary,* p. 175.

39. Midrash ha-Gaddol to Genesis 27:1, ed. Margulies p. 463 and my *Dictionary*, p. 144: בפילקי חשיכה.

40. Lamentations Rabba 1.31, ed. Buber p. 67, and my *Dictionary*, p. 192.

41. Canticles Rabba to Cont. 8:13 and my *Dictionary*, p. 185. The more classical term, which also appears in Rabbinic literature, is בית האסורים, *beit ha-assurim*, literally: house of prisoners. The Latin terms *carcer* and *ergastulum* (= *carcer rusticus*) do not appear in Rabbinic literature.

42. M. Sanhedrin 9.3.

43. See chapter 4, on someone being locked up by the police for a night in Caesarea.

44. Dyer, *Pompeii*, pp. 100, 124. On chains and leg irons, see Krauss, *Talmudische Archäologie*, vol. 2, (Leipzig, 1911), pp. 96, 497; Pesikta Rabbati 29–30, 138a; and my *Dictionary,* pp. 102–3 s.v. כירו מניקייה.

45. See previous notes on basilica and arche.

46. Dyer, *Pompeii*, p. 126.

47. This chapter is based on my Ph.D. dissertation, "Games and Spectacles in Roman Palestine and Their Reflection in Talmudic Literature," written at the Hebrew University of Jerusalem in 1994, under the supervision of professors Gideon Foerster and Lee Israel Levine. Its a great pleasure to thank them both for their invaluable guidance and advice over the past years.

48. Jerusalem: *Ant.* XV, 268–73; *Chronicon Paschale*, ed. L. Dindorf, *CSHB*, vol. 14 (Bonn 1832), p. 474, lines 9–15. Gaza: Sozomenes, *Historia*

Ecclesiastica, 9.5. Ashkelon: *Catalogue of the Greek and Latin Papyri in the John Rylands Library, Manchester*, vol. 4, ed. C. H. Roberts and E. G. Turner (Manchester, 1952), no. 627, pp. 117–24, lines 212–22.

49. On the use of the hippodrome in our region as a stadium in which athletic contests were held, see the section on the hippodromes, below.

50. Jerusalem: *Ant.* XVII, 254–55; Tiberias: *War* II, 598–99; Gaza: Hieronymus, *Vita Hilarionis*, 16–20 (*PL* 23, 38); Ashkelon: *CIG* 4472. [Circuses together with theaters occur frequently in Rabbinic literature; see Krauss, *LW*², p. 571 s.v. קרקס II. D.S.]

51. See the section on the amphitheater below. [Interestingly enough, the term *amphitheater* does not appear to be found in Rabbinic literature. D.S.

52. J. C. Golvin, *L'amphithéâtre romain*, vol. 1 (Paris, 1988), pp. 408–12; E. J. Owens, *The City in the Greek and Roman World* (London, 1991), pp. 121–48, 155–56.

53. This is in contrast to the entertainment structures from the Herodian period, which were built by the king who also financed the games held in them; see *Ant.* XV, 268–74, 341. Agrippa financed the construction of the theater and amphitheater in Beirut, as well as the games that took place there; see *Ant.* XIX, 335–37.

54. According to Duncan-Jones, 58 percent of all the public buildings in the Roman cities of North Africa were erected with the aid of private capital; see R. P. Duncan-Jones, "Who Paid for Public Buildings in Roman Cities?" in *Roman Urban Topography in Britain and the Western Empire*, ed. F. Grew and B. Hobley (London, 1985), pp. 28–35. Bowman, in his discussion of public buildings in Egypt, reached a similar conclusion; see A. K. Bowman, "Public Buildings in Roman Egypt," in *JRA* 5 (1992): 495–503. See also A. H. M. Jones, *The Roman Economy* (Oxford, 1974), pp. 25–29; P. Garnsey and R. Saller, *The Roman Empire, Economy, Society, and Culture* (Berkeley, 1987), pp. 37–38; and J. Reynolds, "Cities," in *The Administration of the Roman Empire, 241 B.C.–A.D. 193*, ed. D. C. Braund (Exeter, 1988), pp. 34–38. On the other hand, Mitchell points to an imperial involvement in public construction in the east; see S. Mitchell, "Imperial Building in the Eastern Roman Provinces," in *Roman Architecture in the Greek World*, ed. S. Macready and F. H. Thompson (London, 1987), pp. 18–25. In his opinion, the emperor transferred funds directly for the erection of the structures, sometimes provided part of the building materials, and in other cases made available the taxes collected in the particular city for this purpose.

55. Flavius Dionysos contributed the sum of 3,000 drachmas for the construction of a bloc of seats in the southern theater of Gerasa. Another man in that city contributed money for the paving of the theater; see C. B. Welles, "The Inscriptions," in *Gerasa City of the Decapolis*, ed. C. H. Kraeling (New Haven, 1938), nos. 51–52. An inscription found in the theater of Canatha mentions that Marcus Ulpius Lysias, son of Icauros, head of the city council, of his own free contributed 10,000 dinars to his beloved birthplace for the construction of an *odeon* that resembled a theater; see W. H. Wadingtom, ed., *Inscriptions grecques et latines* (Paris, 1870), no. 2341. Polybius Quartinus, on the other hand, contributed a flight of stairs in the *odeon* of Canatha, as well as some other element whose name has not been preserved in the inscription there; see ibid., no. 2432. Not only parts of buildings but also statues were donated by individuals or specific groups; such statues were placed in the entertainment structures. This is

indicated by an inscription found in the southern theater of Gerasa, which relates that a group of local actors donated a statue in honor of Titus Flavius Gerrenus, the city's first *agonothetes*; see Welles, *Gerasa*, no. 192.

56. A Midrash offering an exposition of a verse in the book of Deuteronomy reads as follows: ". . . It can be compared to a young man who came to a city and found the people thereof collecting money for charity, and when they asked him also to subscribe, he went on giving until they had to tell him that he already gave enough. Further on his travels, he lighted on a place where they were collecting for a theater, and when asked to contribute toward it, he was also so generous that he had to be told, enough . . ." (Exodus Rabba 51.8). As mentioned, an individual's affluence was a significant factor in his election to municipal office, the assumption being that he would contribute funds from his private capital for the construction of public buildings or for the financing of their operation. Against this background, one can readily understand the rejoinder of Rabbi Yohanan, which characterizes the *modus operandi* of Rome: "*And, behold, in this horn were eyes like the eyes of a man*—this alludes to the wicked state, which casts an envious eye upon a man's wealth [saying]: So and so is wealthy, we will make him a city magistrate (*archon*); So and so is wealthy, let us make him a councillor (*bouleutes*) . . ." (Genesis Rabba 76. 7). On this phenomenon and other passages in Talmudic literature giving expression to this situation, see S. Lieberman, "Palestine in the Third and Fourth Century," *JQR* 36 (1946): 346–48.

57. "It is like a man who came to a city where he heard that a gladiatorial exhibition was about to be held. He asked the gladiator, when will the show take place? He replied: It is far off yet. Then he asked the one who was to give the show and he replied: Soon. He then said: Did I not ask the gladiator this, yet he said, It is far off? He replied: Is this your sense to ask the gladiator? Is he then anxious for me to stage the gladiatorial exhibition, knowing as he does that he may be slain when he descends into the arena . . . ?" (Exodus Rabba 30.24). The *philotimia* [see Krauss, *LW*[2], pp. 444–45. D.S.] mentioned by the Sage, a term also appearing on an inscription from Asia Minor, is a sum of money donated by one of the city's residents for the holding of games; see L. Robert, *Les gladiateurs dans l'orient Grec* (Paris, 1940), pp. 276–80. The *philotimia* generally relates to all contributions, but in the third century it was mainly connected with entertainment spectacles; see I. Lévy, "Notes d'historie et d'épigraphie," in *REJ* 41 (1900): 182–83. On the costs of gladiatorial and animal-baiting contests in the western parts of the empire, see R. Duncan-Jones, *The Economy of the Roman Empire* (Cambridge, 1982), pp. 245–46. *Leitourgia*, a public service or office imposed on wealthy or distinguished citizens, was another way of financing animal-baiting spectacles in the amphitheaters of our region, as follows from the words of the Sage who mentions how the nations of the world instructed Israel: ". . . Go out and get us wolves and lions and bring them into our arenas so that with these beasts we can stage contests (*kunegesion*) of the kind we enjoy. . . ." (Seder Eliyyahu Rabba 8).

58. Jerusalem: *Ant.* XV, 268–73. Caesarea: *Ant.* XV, 339–41; see also A. Frova, *Scavi di Caesarea Maritima* (Rome, 1961), esp. pp. 167–74. Jericho: *Ant.* XVII, 161–62; E. Netzer, "The Hippodrome That Herod Built at Jerusalem," *Qadmoniot* 51–52 (1980): 104–106 [in Hebrew].

59. G. Mazor, "City Center of Ancient Beth Shean—South," *Excavations and Surveys in Israel*, 6 (1987–88): 18–22; G. Foerster and Y. Tsafrir, "Nysa-

Scythopolis in the Roman Period: 'A Greek City of Coele Syria—Evidence from the excavations at Beth-Shean," *Aram* 4 (1992): 120–21.

60. H. C. Butler, *Ancient Architecture in Syria*, Devision IIa (Leyden, 1907), map no. 1.

61. T. Weber and R. G. Khouri, *Umm Qais, Gadara of the Decapolis* (Amman, 1989), pp. 17–18.

62. Exodus Rabba 15.22

63. For Scythopolis, see Mazor, "Beth-Shean," p. 11; Neapolis: Y. Magen, "The History and the Archaeology of Shechem (Neapolis) during the First to Fourth Centuries A.D," (Ph.D. diss., Jerusalem, 1989) [in Hebrew], pl. 34 Gerasa: C. H. Kraeling, ed., *Gerasa, City of the Decapolis*, vol 2 (New Haven, 1938), plan 1.

64. One of the confusing issues with regard to all theaters found in our region is the nomenclature to be used for these structures, especially the smallest ones, and their function. One should refer to the large ones as "theater," as we learn from several inscriptions; see: J. Pouilloux, "Deux inscriptions au théâtre sud de Gérasa," *LA*, 27 (1977): 246–54; Waddington, *Inscriptions*, no. 2136. The problem is how to name the smallest structures, which sometimes are identical to the large ones but on a smaller scale. Should they be termed a small theater or an *odeon*? Epigraphic and historical sources show that these terms were sometimes used interchangeably by the ancients. For example, an inscription engraved in the central part of the *podium* around the *orchestra* at Canatha refers to the building as an *odeon*; see Waddington, Inscriptions, no. 2341. On the other hand, an inscription from Haluẓa, in the Negev, refers to a building with the same dimensions as a theater and not an *odeon*; see A. Negev, *The Greek Inscriptions from the Negev* (Jerusalem, 1981), pp. 73–74. An examination of the evidence in our region has led to the conclusion that these buildings should be identified according to their function and not necessarily their size. The theater was the site of dramatic performances such as the mime and pantomime (see below), whereas the *odeon* was used for concerts, lectures, and other gatherings. Thus small buildings did not necessarily served as *odeons* unless there is clear evidence to that effect. Bowsher suggests that small theaters, or odeia as he calls them, served as *bouleteria*; see "Civic Organization Within the Decapolis," *Aram* 4 (1992): 265–81. [The term *theater* occurs frequently in Rabbinic literature (see Krauss, *LW*², pp. 260, 586), whereas the word *odeon* is never to be found, although the institution was known to the rabbis.]

65. Duncan-Jones, who attempts to estimate size of the population in the cities of North Africa, mentions that the size of the theater or amphitheater was determined by the city's financial capability and was not always proportional to the number of its inhabitants; see R. P. Duncan-Jones, "City Population in Roman Africa," *JRS* 53 (1963): 85.

66. For a general picture of Roman theaters, see M. Bieber, *The History of the Greek and Roman Theater* (Princeton, 1961), pp. 167–226; A. J. Brothers, "Buildings for Entertainment," in *Roman Public Buildings*, ed. J. M. Barton, (Exeter, 1989), pp. 97–112.

67. This is in contrast to the Greek theater in which the seats were apportioned according to the principle of the equality of all citizens; see L. Polacco, "Théâtres, société, organisation de l'état," in *Théâtre et spectacles dans l'antiquité*, ed. H. Zehnacker (Strassburg, 1982), pp. 5–15; O. A. W. Dilke, "The Greek Cavea," *ABSA* 43 (1948): 165–84. For the seating arrangements in the Roman

theater as an expression of social stratification, see J. Kolendo (Varsovie), "La repartition des places aux spectacles et la stratification sociale l'Empire Romain," *Ktema* 6 (1981): 301–15; D. B. Small, "Social Correlation to the Greek Cavea in the Roman Period," *Roman Architecture in the Greek World*, ed. S. Macready and F. H. Thompson (London, 1987), pp. 85–93. For comprehensive study of this aspect, especially with regard to entertainment structures in Rome, see E. Rawson, "Discrimina Ordinum: The Lex Julia Theatralis," *PBSR* 55 (1987): 83–114. On the social structure of Rome during the imperial period, see G. Alfoldy, *The Social History of Rome* (London, 1985), pp. 94–156.

68. P. Zanker, *The Power of Images in the Age of Augustus* (Ann Arbor, 1990), pp. 147–53, esp. p. 151.

69. Although the term *agon* is used by the Sages when referring to all contests and games, one can assume that Resh Lakish was referring mainly to the theater, which was the dominant institution in our region, in which the seats were apportioned, as we have noted, according to rank.

70. Ecclesiastes Rabba 12. 5.

71. Bieber, *Greek and Roman Theater*, p. 227; W. Bear, *The Roman Stage*[3] (London, 1968), p. 238. R. C. Beacham, *The Roman Theatre and Its Audience* (London, 1991), p. 150.

72. Bieber, *Greek and Roman Theater*, p. 238; E. J. Jory, "Continuity and Change in the Roman Theatre," in *Studies in Honour of T. B. L. Webster*, ed. J. H. Betts, J. T. Hooker, and J. R. Green (Bristol, 1986), pp. 145–46.

73. Lamentations Rabba, Proem 17 (ed. Buber p. 7b). [See M. D. Herr's analysis of the antisemitic elements in these scenes and their different literary structures in his article in *Benjamin de Vries* memorial volume, ed. E. Z. Melammed (Jerusalem, 1968) [in Hebrew] pp. 150–51. D.S.]

74. On the pantomime, see E. Wüst, "Pantomimus," *PW* 18.3 (1949): 834–70; Beacham, *The Roman Theatre*, pp. 140–153.

75. Y. Taanit, 1 4, 64b. Cf. Lieberman's comments on this story: S. Lieberman, *Greek and Hellenism in Jewish Palestine* (Jerusalem, 1984) [in Hebrew], pp. 24–25, and the notes there.

76. Bieber, *Greek and Roman Theater*, pp. 247–48; Bear, *Roman Stage*, pp. 137–48; A. Nicoll, *Masks, Mimes, and Miracles* (New York, 1963), pp. 65–74.

77. Several well-known characters from the Atellan farce appear in a list of players in the Tosefta and in some other parallel passages in the Talmudic literature. "He who goes to the stadium or to the camp to see the performances of sorcerers and enchanters or various kinds of clowns, *bucco, maccus mulio saeculares* and the like, this is a seat of the scoffers . . . ," T. Avoda Zara 2.6, ed. Zuckermandel, p. 462. Cf. Y. Avoda Zara 1.7, 40a; B. Avoda Zara 18b. The *bucco*, according to the Tosefta, played the role of the fool. The gluttonous *bucco* had a large mouth and swollen cheeks and spoke nonsense. The *maccus*, parallel to the *mukiyyon* (clown) in the Tosefta, was bald and also personified stupidity, even to a greater extent than the *bucco*. [This difficult text was discussed partly by S. Lieberman; see his studies in *Palestinian Talmudic Literature* (Jerusalem, 1991), pp. 378–80. D.S.]

78. J. H. Humphrey, *Roman Circuses—Arena for Chariot Racing* (London, 1986), pp. 535–39.

79. [The hippodrome is mentioned in a relatively late Byzantine Hebrew text; see Krauss, *LW*[2], p. 386, with bibliography and perhaps in Midrash Psalms; see below note 92. On the stadium in Rabbinic sources, see Krauss, *LW*[2], p. 1196. D.S.]

80. *Ant.* XV, 268; XVI, 137; XVII, 175–78. Although Josephus terms the structures amphitheaters, they should be regaded as hippodromes; see below, p. 12.

81. J. W. Crowfoot, K. M. Kenyon, and E. L. Sukenik, *The Buildings of Samaria* (London, 1942), pp. 41–49.

82. Netzer, "Hippodrome," p. 107.

83. Y. Porath, "Herod's 'Amphitheater' at Caesarea: A Multipurpose Entertainment Building," *The Roman and Byzantine Near East: Some Recent Archaeological Research* (ed. J. H. Humphrey), *Journal of Roman Archaeology* (Supplementary Series no. 14) (Ann Arbor, 1995, pp. 15–27).

84. See for example Humphrey's comment (*Roman Circuses*, pp. 334–35) about the North African circuses.

85. Humphrey, *Roman Circuses*, pp. 334.

86. Ibid., pp. 477–505, 528–39.

87. The first games were held by Herod in Jerusalem and Caesarea in honor of the emperor Augustus; see: *Ant.* XV, 267–71; XVI, 136–40. Caesarea is the only city where we find confirmation of their continuity in the time of Agrippa (*Ant.* XIX, 343), as well as from a dedicatory inscription of a Laodicean athlete who participated in the games of 221 C.E. held at Caesarea; see: *CIG* 4472. Cf. D. R. Schwartz, "'Caesarea' and Its 'Isactium': Epigraphy, Numismatic, and Herodian Chronology," *Studies in the Jewish Background of Christianity* (Tübingen, 1992), pp. 167–81. Games were held in other cities of Palestine throughout the second and third centuries C.E., for example, in Bostra or Gaza; see Wessely, *CPH*, 5.1, nos. 70, 74. For example, Aelius Aurelius Menander, an athlete from Aphrodisias, took part in the games held in Neapolis, Scythopolis, Caesarea, Gaza, and Philadelphia; see L. Moretti, *Inscrizioni Agonistiche Greche* (Rome, 1951), no. 72. At that time athletes from Alexandria participated in the games that took place in Gerasa; see Welles, *Gerasa*, nos. 193–94.

88. On the games in the Roman east, see: A. H. M., Jones, *The Greek City* (Oxford, 1940), pp. 227–35; H. W. Pleket, "Games, Prizes, Athletes and Ideology," *Arena* 1 (1975): 49–89; D. White, "Roman Athletics," *Expedition*, 27 no. 2 (1985): 30–40.

89. Jones, *Greek City*, p. 234; see also *PW* 1.1, Agonothetes, pp. 870–77. Herod contributed large sums for the maintenance of the games at Olympia and even served as an *agonothetes* in them; see *War* I, 426–28. According to Lämmer, Herod served only as honorary chairman, since the games in Olympia were directed by a council consisting of ten men chosen a long time before their opening; see M. Lämmer, "King Herod's Endowment to the Olympic Games," in *Proceedings of the Pre-Olympic Seminar on the History of Physical Education and Sport in Asia*, ed. U. Simri (Netanya, 1972), pp. 31–50.

90. We learn this from an inscription located in the southern theater of Gerasa, in honor of Titus Flavius Gerrenus, the city's first *agonothetes*; see Welles, *Gerasa*, no. 192.

91. [For the term *athlete* in Rabbinic literature; see Krauss, *LW*[2], p. 136. D.S.]

92. Midrash Psalms 17.5 (ed. Buber p. 64b); see also Buber's commentary there. [In the same text אפרכוס is probably corrupt for איפודרמוס, hippodrome. See Buber's note and Krauss, *LW*[2], p. 231 s.v. הנדיוסין. הפרכוס II. See also Genesis Rabba 10.4, ed. Theodor p. 78, for the charioteer. D.S.]

93. E. Gardiner, *Athletics of the Ancient World* (Oxford, 1930), pp. 181–221; H. A. Harris, *Sport in Greece and Rome* (Ithaca, 1972), pp. 22–27; M. Poliakoff, *Studies in the Terminology of the Greek Combat Sports* [Beiträge

zur klassischen philologie, Heft 146] (Königstein/Ts, 1982); idem, *Combat Sports in the Ancient World* (New Haven, 1987), pp. 23–87. [On training for wrestling see S. Lieberman, *Greek and Hellenism in Jewish Palestine* (Jerusalem, 1962), pp. 70–72. That the arena, κήρωμα, was sometimes of mud, πήλωμα, basing himself on M. Shabbat 22. 6. D.S.]

94. Wrestling matches were held in Gerasa at the beginning of the third century C.E.; see Welles, *Gerasa*, no. 194. Ashkelon was renowned for its good wrestlers; see *Expositio Totius Mundi et Gentium*, 32, ed. J. Rougé (Paris, 1966), p. 166. Aurelius Septimius Irenaeus, a boxer from the city of Laodicea, won several matches held at the beginning of the third century C.E. in Caesarea, Ashkelon, and Scythopolis; see *CIG* 4472. A third-century Palestinian wrestler named Aurelius Philadelphos took part in wrestling matches held in his city Panias and also elsewhere; see L. Robert, "Inscriptions de Didymes et de Milet," *Hellenica* 11–12 (1960): 440–43. Wrestling contests were held in Caesarea at the beginning of the fourth century C.E.; see Eusebius, *Martyrs of Palestine* [in Greek] 7, 4. Aelius Aurelius Menander from Aphrodisias was the victor in the *pankration* contests held in Damascus, Caesarea, Neapolis, Scythopolis, Gaza, Panias, and Philadelphia in the second century C.E.; see Moretti, no. 72. *Pankration* matches were held in Gerasa at the beginning of the third century C.E.; see: Welles, *Gerasa*, no. 193. In the fourth century Gaza gained renown for its excellent pankratists; see *Expositio*, 32.

95. Exodus Rabba 27.9.

96. Exodus Rabba 21. 11.

97. Tanḥuma Genesis, Vayigash 3. The victory inscription of Tiberius Claudius Marcianus, who won the wrestling contest at Antioch of Pisidia, reads: "When he undressed, his opponents begged to be dismissed from the contest"; see J. G. C. Anderson, "Festivals of mên Askaênos in the Roman Colonia at Antioch of Pisidia," *JRS* 3 (1913): 287, n. 12. For other examples of this phenomenon, see E. N. Gardiner, "Wrestling," *JHS* 25 (1925): 16–17.

98. Gardiner, *Athletics of the Ancient World*, pp. 128–43; H. A. Harris, *Greek Athletes and Athletics* (London, 1964), pp. 64–77; idem, *Sport in Greece and Rome*, pp. 27–33.

99. The third-century boxer Aurelius Septimius Irenaeus, mentioned above (note 94), also participated in and won three times the *dromos*, a race over a short distance of one *stadium*, in the games at Ashkelon and Scythopolis; see *CIG* 4472. An Alexandrian athlete won the *diaulos* and *hoplites* races held in Gerasa at the beginning of the third century C.E.; see Welles, *Gerasa*, no. 193. In the same period an athlete from Panias won the *dromos* and *hoplites* races at Rhodes, thus indicating that contests of this kind were perhaps also held in his city; see Robert, "Inscriptions de Didymes et de Milet," pp. 443–46. The sole evidence of the *pentathlon* has been preserved in an inscription from Gerasa; see Welles, *Gerasa*, no. 194.

100. A. Cameron, *Circus Factions* (Oxford, 1976), pp. 10, 202–19; Harris, *Sport in Greece and Rome*, pp. 173–212.

101. In Herod's time chariot races were held at Jerusalem (*Ant.* XV, 271) and Caesarea (*Ant.* XVI, 137).

102. On the organization of athletes in the Roman world, see Gardiner, *Athletics of the Ancient World*, pp. 107–10; C. A. Forbes, "Ancient Athletic Guilds," *CP*, 50 (1955): 238–52; H. W. Pleket, "Some Aspects of the History of the Athletic Guilds," *ZPE* 10 (1973): 197–227; M. B. Poliakoff, "Guilds of Per-

formers and Athletes: Bureaucracy, Reward, and Privileges," *JRA* 2 (1989): 295–98. Two inscriptions found at Gerasa confirm the presence of a gymnasium in the city; see Welles, *Gerasa*, nos. 3–4. The athletes joined a guild led by a *xysarch*; see Welles, *Gerasa*, no. 170. Even in the Roman period the gymnasium was headed by a *gymnasiarch* who was responsible for the training of the athletes. Such figures are known to us from Gerasa (ibid.) and Philadelphia; see P. L. Gatier, *Inscriptions de la Jordanie* (Paris, 1986), no. 29. To these should be added Seleucus (son) of Ariston, keeper of the ointments (*aleipths*), from Beth Shean, who was none other than a trainer of athletes in his city; see G. Foerster and Y. Tsafrir, "City Center (North)," *Excavations and Surveys in Israel*, 11 (1993): 8. *Aleipths* in the Roman period was the appellation of the athletes' trainer; see C. Foss, "Aleipterion," *Greek, Roman, and Byzantine Studies* 16 (1975): 217–26.

103. I. Nielsen, *Thermae et Balnea* (Aarhus, 1990), pp. 101–11, 149–52; P. Grimal, *Roman Cities*, trans. and ed. M. Woloch (Madison, 1983), pp. 68–72.

104. K. Hopkins, *Death and Renewal* (Cambridge, 1983), pp. 1–30; C. A. Barton, *The Sorrows of the Ancient Romans, The Gladiator and the Monster* (Princeton, 1993), pp. 11–81.

105. For Caesarea, see *Ant.* XV, 341; Jerusalem, *Ant.* XV, 268, 273–74; XVII, 194.

106. The amphitheater at Beit Guvrin, for example, was built during the second century C.E.; see A. Kloner and A. Hübsch, "The Roman Amphitheater of Bet Guvrin: A Preliminary Report of the 1992, 1993 and 1994 Seasons," *Atigot* 30 (1996): 85–106. The amphitheater at Neapolis, on the other hand, is dated to the third century C.E.; see I. Magen, *Neapolis* [in Hebrew], p. 184.

107. As a result of the reorganization of the province of Syria and the permanent settlement of many Roman soldiers there after the suppression of the Bar-Kochba revolt, the number of Roman soldiers residing in western Palestine was more than double that in the province of Arabia; see B. Isaac, *The Limits of the Empire* (Oxford, 1990), pp. 83–89, 99–100, 118. This demographic change accounts for the upsurge in the construction of amphitheaters in our region during the period under discussion. For the connection between the army and the erection of amphitheaters in the western parts of the empire, see P. Le Roux, "L'amphithéâtre et le soldat sous l'Empire romain," in *Gladiateures et amphithéâtres*, ed. C. Domergue, C. Landes, and J. M. Pailler (Actes du Colloque à Toulouse et à Lattes 26–29. Mai 1987, Lattes 1990), pp. 203–15. The building of amphitheaters in Roman Britain is also associated with an increased Roman presence there, especially the movements of the army; see G. Webster, *The Roman Imperial Army of the First and Second Centuries A.D.* (London, 1985), pp. 207–8; M. Fulford, *The Silcester Amphitheatre, Excavation of 1979–1985* (London, 1989); see also: D. L. Bomgardner, "Amphitheatre on the Fringe," *JRA* 4 (1991): 282–94.

108. Golvin, *L'amphithéâtre romain*, pp. 408–12.

109. Caesarea: A. Reifenberg, "Caesarea, a Study in the Decline of a Town," *IEJ* 1 (1951): 25–26; D. Roller, "The Wilfrid Laurier University Survey of Northeastern Caesarea Maritima," *Levant* 14 (1982): 90–103; Beth Guvrin: Kloner and Hübsch, "The Roman Amphitheater of Bet Guvrin," pp. 85–106; Bostra: R. al—Mougdad, P. M. Blance, and J. M. Dentzer, "Un amphithéâtre à Bosra?", *Syria* 67 (1990): 201–4.

110. Neapolis: Magen, *Neapolis*, pp. 171–84; Scythopolis: G. Foerster and Y. Tsafrir, "The Amphitheater and Its Surroundings," *Excavations and Surveys in Israel* 6 (1987–88): 35–38.

111. For general information, see L. Friedlander, *Roman Life and Manners under the Roman Empire*, vol. 2 (London, 1965), pp. 40–90; J. Pearson, *Arena—The Story of the Colosseum* (New York, 1973); H. Hönle und A. Henze, *Römische amphitheater und stadien* (Atlantis, 1981).

112. For a comprehensive treatment of this form of punishment in the Roman world, see T. Wiedemann, *Emperors & Gladiators* (London, 1992), pp. 68–92; K. M. Coleman, "Fatal Charades: Roman Executions Staged as Mythological Enactments," *JRS* 80 (1990): 44–73.

113. For the Herodian period, see *Ant.* XVI, 137; *War* VII, 23–25.

114. The *ludarius* or *monomachos* appearing in the Talmudic literature is a person who took part in gladiatorial contests; see Genesis Rabba 96 eds. Theodor-Albeck, p. 1200; cf. *Aruch ha-Shalem*, vol. 5, p. 176, Monomachos, and Krauss, *LW*², p. 343. The *kunegos*, on the other hand, was a man who engaged in the baiting and hunting of wild animals within the walls of the amphitheater; see Pesikta de-Rav Kahana 28.3; Seder Eliyyahu Rabba 8; Yalkut Shimoni, Va-Era 182. [See Krauss, *LW*², p. 553; Lieberman, *Greek and Hellenism*, p. 29, n. 52, and his note in Pesikta de-Rav Kahana, ed. Mandelbaum, p. 475 to p. 427. D.S.]

115. Engraved depictions of gladiators were found on the walls of burial caves in Shearim and at Tel Eitun in southern Judaea; see B. Mazar, *Beth Shearim*, vol. 1 (Jerusalem, 1973), pp. 183–84; V. Tzaferis, "A Monumental Roman Tomb on Tel Eitun" [in Hebrew], *Atiqot* 8 (1982): 22–25. One of the walls of the main entrance to the amphitheater in Neapolis features a number of engravings depicting certain animals associated with the spectacles held here; see Magen, *Neapolis*, p. 173.

116. Exotic animals were exhibited by Herod in Jerusalem, and it can be assumed that this was also the case in Caesarea; see *Ant.* XV, 273. Eusebius lists some of the animals exhibited on the occasion of the execution of Christian martyrs in the arena of Caesarea; see Eusebius, *The Ecclesiastica History*, VIII, 7.1.

117. For example, as expressed by Resh Lakish: "If you were to sell yourself to *lanistae* (who purchase men to participate in gladiatorial contests), you would sell yourself for a high price. . . ." (Y. Terumot 8.5, 45d).

118. The deliberations of the third- and fourth-generation Palestinian Sages concerning the redemption of Jews sold as gladiators are explicit proof of this; see Y. Gittin 4 9,46b; B. Gittin 46b–47a. On this phenomenon in general, see Friedlander, *Roman Life and Manners*, vol. 2, pp. 48–51; J. J. S. Gracia, "Gloire et mort dans l'arène, les représentations des gladiateurs dans la Péninsula Ibérique," *Gladiateures et amphithéâtres*, eds. C. Domergue, C. Landes, and J. M. Pailler (Actes du Colloque à Toulouse et à Lattes 26–29. Mai 1987, Lattes 1990), pp. 185–95.

119. Friedlander, *Roman Life and Manners*, vol. 2, pp. 46–47, 52–54.

120. Ibid., pp. 59–60. This meal, where each gladiator was served the food he had requested, is also mentioned by Resh Lakish; see B. Gittin 47a. On the *cena libra* in light of Resh Lakish's words, see M. Z. Brettler and M. Poliakoff, "Rabbi Simeon ben Lakish at the Gladiators' Banquet: Rabbinic Observations on the Roman Arena," *HTR* 83 (1990): 93–98.

7

Roads and Backstreets

Road Widths

Let us now look at the roads and side streets[1] in the Roman Palestinian town. The literary evidence about the width of such streets is somewhat problematic. In the baraita in B. Baba Batra 99ab we read as follows:

> A private path is four cubits wide, a path from one town to another is eight cubits, a public path 16 cubits, and a path to the cities of refuge[2] 32 cubits wide.

Likewise, M. Baba Kama .5, in the name of Rabbi Eliezer (late first century C.E.), tells us that a standard public path is 16 cubits wide. If we assume the cubit equals approximately 70 cm, we arrive at the following approximate road widths:

private path	2.80 m (=8.5 ft.)
from one town to another	5.60 m (=17 ft.)
public path	11.20 m (=34 ft.)
to cities of refuge	22.40 m (=68 ft.)

This pattern does not correspond to the standard Roman road measurement. Most major Roman roads were about 16 ft. wide (10.5 cubits) and rarely more than 21.5 ft. wide (14 cubits). The narrower streets (*angipontus* or *semitae*) had to be at least 9.57 ft. (2.9 m) wide (a little more than 4 cubits) to allow for projecting balconies.[3] The great trunk roads through Gaul or Italy or along the Euphrates frontier in Syria might be 24 ft. wide (16 cubits).[4] Apparently, some roads were even broader than this, since the Pergamene law[5] states that the minimum width of a main country road must be 30 ft. and that of a byroad 12 ft.[6]

Krauss noted these discrepancies,[7] writing that "ordinary Roman *stratae* were about 5 m wide, making the Rabbinic *stratae* some 3 m broader, and we do not know wherefore there was this great difference between them." He adds that in the "Palestinian town of Petra there are remains of the Roman road, which is only 2.8 m wide, and must therefore be considered as a *via secundaria,* but we cannot determine what is its equivalence in Rabbinic parlance."[8]

The whole system of measures described in the Baba Batra baraita is based on multiples of the fathom (orguia = 4 cubits), which is primarily a Greek measure and not a part of the Roman linear system.[9] Hence, these *shiurim* (legal measures) echo the original linear context of their Greek equivalents, which were probably adopted into Jewish law at an early date. In our specific case, these measures seem to have been arrived at by taking into account existing norms for road widths and reducing them to multiples of the fathom. Thus, these Tannaitic texts, which refer to standard road widths of 4, 8, 16, and 32 cubits, should not necessarily be read as accurately reflecting contemporary Palestinian Roman road standards, and should be interpreted as largely theoretical.

Main Streets and Backstreets

The main streets of the town, like the *cardo* and *decumanus maximus* running roughly at right angles to one another and usually crossing at the forum, may have been quite broad, certainly with enough space to admit wagons and carts.[10] However, the side streets, often called סימטאות, *simtaot,* from the Latin *semita,*[11] were certainly narrow. Nonetheless, in these passageways commercial activities took place, as we can deduce from the phrase in T. Bikkurim ad fin., תגרי סימטא, *tagarei simta,* meaning the *semita*—traders (or hucksters).[12] Indeed, the rabbis regarded these traders in a rather negative light,[13] perhaps, among other reasons, because they blocked up these narrow streets. This would certainly seem to be the case reflected in the Sifre to Leviticus 25:42 (Be-Har Perek, 109d):

> . . . that he should not stand (the slave) up in the סמטא—*semita*—to sell him on the "selling stone" (אבן המקח—the auctioneer's platform, on which the object to be sold was also placed).[14]

These *semitae* were probably just off the main market area; hence, the comparison in Rabbinic sources between סימטא—*semita*—and פלטיא—*platea.*[15] This would also explain how at times they came to be positioned between columns.[16] Since the *semita* branched off at an angle to the street (*platea*), a portion of it was covered by the *platea's* portico, and hence it was partially between the portico's columns.[17]

Traffic and Traffic Accidents

Much traffic had to pass through these narrow streets, and people who shopped in the market had to bring home their purchases. They transported jars of wine and oil, as well as other foodstuffs, and carried water from a public well (see also the discussion in chapters 1 and 9). Building contractors had to bring their materials through these streets to the construction site,[18] probably transporting stones and sand on wagons.[19] In T. Baba Meẓia 12.5 we read:

> A person brings his stones and unloads them at the entrance of his house in the public area (i.e., the street) to raise them up to the top of the wall[20] he is building. But he is not permitted to leave them there for

> any length of time, and if someone was hurt on them, he is culpable. If he gave them over into the hands of the camel driver, the camel driver is culpable; to the mason, the mason is culpable; to the porter, the porter is culpable.

Likewise, in T. Baba Meẓia 11.6 we read:

> A person may bring his sand (or mortar—עפר) to the entrance of his house to soak it to make of it plaster . . . , but he should not mix it up on one side and build on the other, but mix it up on the spot where he is building.

Beams for roofs might at times be transported by hand. The streets, as already described, were narrow, perhaps little more than a meter wide and, furthermore, often had sharp bends. An average roofbeam, on the other hand, was 2.5 to 3 m long or even longer.[21] One can well imagine how difficult it was to negotiate these long heavy beams through these narrow, twisting alleys. Small wonder that in M. Baba Kama 3.5 we read:

> The one came with his jar and the other with his beam, [and they collided so that] the jar of the one was broken on the beam of the other, the latter is not culpable, since each alike had the right of passage. If the man with the beam came first, and the man with the jar came after, and the jar broke against the beam, the man with the beam is not culpable. If the man with the beam stopped suddenly, he is culpable, but if he said "Stop" to the man with the jar, he is not culpable. . . .

These narrow twisting streets were also dirty[22] and dim,[23] often with piles of sand or stones or pocked with deep holes and ruts.[24] Accidents and collisions were common, as we see from M. Baba Kama 3.4:

> If two pot sellers were walking one behind the other, and the first one stumbled and fell, and the second stumbled over the first, the first one is liable for the injury suffered by the second.[25]

How similar this picture is to that sketched by Carcopino, based on Juvenal's description of Rome:

> The herd of people which sweeps the poet along proceeds on foot through a scrimmage that is constantly renewed. The crowd behind threaten to crush his loins. One man jostles him with his elbow, *another with a beam he is carrying, a third bangs his head with a wine cask.* A mighty boot tramps on his foot, a military nail embeds itself in his toe,[26] and his newly-mended tunic is torn. Then, of a sudden, panic ensues: a wagon appears, on top of which a huge log is swaying, another follows loaded with a whole pine tree, yet a third carrying a cargo of Ligurian marble. "If the axle breaks and pours its contents on the crowd, what will be left of the bodies?"[27]

Of course, no town in Palestine was as big and as densely populated as Rome. Nonetheless, on a much smaller scale, the same kinds of activities took place in Palestine urban centers, so that the similarity between the sources, although it should not be overemphasized, is legitimate and meaningful.

Streets Not Straight

We have already mentioned in passing that one of the dangers in transporting breakable goods along the narrow alleyways was the often sharp and sudden turns and corners around which one could not see. This we learn from a passage in Y. Berachot 9.1 ad fin., 13b:

> It once happened that Rabban Gamliel (end of the first century C.E.) saw a beautiful gentile woman and made a benediction over her (one that one makes when seeing a beautiful person). . . . And was it then the habit of Rabban Gamliel to stare at women? [No,] but [this time] he did so [as he came] around a sudden turn (דרך עקמימיתה) [in the road], as in this פופסדוס, and he [came upon her and] looked at her unwittingly.

Lieberman[28] identified the word פופסדוס (*popsdos*) on the basis of variant reading, parallels, and other occurrences in Rabbinic literature[29] with the Greek πρόσοδος,[30] an approach road. He explains that it went off the סטרטיאה, *strata*—main road,[31] at a sharp angle, so that whoever came out of the *strata* onto it would be liable suddenly to come up against people standing there without his foreknowledge or intention.[32] Indeed, the Sifre to Deuteronomy 5:10 (sec. 20, ed. Finkelstein p. 32) says explicitly: There is no road that has no sharp bend (עקימות or עקמומיות).[33]

State of Roads—Paved or Rutted

The main roads were almost all well paved with large flat stones, as we know from numerous archeological findings. Indeed, Roman law determined that "Every person must construct the public street in front of his own house, clean the gutters which are exposed, that is to say, open to the sky, and keep the streets in such a condition that a vehicle will not be prevented from traversing it. Those who rent the houses must build the street, if the owner does not do so, and they can deduct the expense from the rent."[34] However, A. H. M. Jones points out that "It is difficult to believe, however, that the magnificent and uniform paving which we see today in the principal streets of excavated cities was maintained by this system, and it seems likely that the householders regularly commuted their obligations for a cash payment, and that the city undertook the work; we know that cities maintained gangs of public slaves for street paving" (see Pliny, Ep. 20.32).[35]

In third-century Palestine we find evidence that roads were paved with stones taken from pagan temples. In B. Avoda Zara 50a we read:

The palace of King Yannai was in ruins. Gentiles came and set up Mercurius there. Subsequently other gentiles, who did not worship Mercurius, came and removed them, and paved the roads and streets with them. Some Rabbis refrained from walking on them (i.e., not to benefit in any way from what was once idolatry), while others did not. R. Yoḥanan (d. 279 C.E. in Tiberias) said: [If] the son of the holy ones (a very pious Rabbi) walks on them, shall we abstain [from doing so]?[36]

There may be another specific reference to the paving of streets in Sifre Zuta to Numbers 11:31:[37]

יכול שיהיו אסתרסיאות מקולקלות? ת"ל. "וכאמתיים על פני הארץ"-על הפנוי שבארץ. Were they perhaps like spoiled *astrase'ot?* [No] for they were, as it were, 2 cubits high upon the face (*pnei*) of the earth" (Numbers 11:31)—On what was flat and unencumbered (*panui*) on the face of the earth.

The word אסתרסיאות has been explained by Krauss[38] on the basis of the parallel in the Mechilta to Exodus 16:13[39] אסטרטאות as (a corrupt) form of *strata*. However, that great philologist and Krauss' mentor, Immanuel Löw, suggested to Krauss[40] that we have here the Greek word στρῶσις, meaning paving.[41] The whole passage is saying that the quails were laid out in the Israelite camp, not like a street in disrepair, but like one that is well paved.[42]

Although the main streets might have been well kept, the back streets were far less likely to have been properly paved—hence the possibility of digging holes and ditches—and probably they became very muddy in the winter rains.[43] On the other hand, some streets may have had pavement,[44] drains, and perhaps even canals with running water (see discussion on channels in chapter 9).

Front Doors Look onto the Street

The front doors of houses often opened directly into the streets (when they did not open into internal courtyards, as in the Roman *insulae*). The door shut from the inside against an external stone threshold, called an אסקופא תחתונה[45], in Hebrew and *limen inferum* in Latin. People would leave their shopping purchases on this doorstep, as is perhaps reflected in M. Shabbat 10.20: A basket full of fruit placed on the outer threshold. . . . People sat and read on these doorsteps (M. Eruvin 10.3), even lay on them (M. Ohalot 11.5), perhaps chatting with their neighbours across the street or at times cursing them. In Derech Ereẓ Zuta 3.11[46] we read:

Be not like the uppermost threshold, which trips people up and will soon be damaged, or the middle one on which people sit [glowering] in anger, but like the lowest threshold, which most people tread on, and which, even when all the house has collapsed in ruins, remains in place forever.[47]

Evidence of such a "multiple threshold" consisting of three doorsteps, the lowest of which led right out into the street, and upon which everyone stepped, has been found in Susia and described by Yizhar Hirschfeld.[48]

Industry on the Streets

We have already mentioned (see chapter 1) that some streets of a city bore the name of an industry, in the customary way of medieval cities and present-day Eastern cities, where a number of small shops producing the same kind of ware concentrated in a certain part of the town create an area bearing the name of the craft. In Rome, for example, we know of the Shoemaker's Street, Harnessmakers' Street, and Carpenters' Street, probably indicating a concentration of petty artisans. Even the location of a house could be designated as situated "among the scythe makers" (*inter falcarios,* Cicero in Cat. 1.8).[49] In Tiberias we know of a building in a market (or street)[50] of carpenters, one of fullers,[51] one of wine salesmen,[52] and one of basket makers.[53] Clearly, these "concentrations" of petty artisans added to the problems of traffic congestion. Materials had to be delivered to these artisans, and customers came and bought from them directly or through middlemen who came to distribute the artisans' wares. One can well imagine porters stumbling along the dark rutted alleys, bent under the heavy burden of a wooden cupboard[54] or other items of furniture[55] that were being delivered, while hand-draw wagons transported heavy storage jars of wine and women jostled one another to buy clothing or toilet articles.[56]

Balconies Overlooking the Streets

I have already alluded to the darkness of the streets.[57] It has been suggested that this was, at least in part, due to the fact that often they were covered over with projecting balconies. Thus, in M. Shabbat 11.2 we read that:

> Two balconies opposite one another on both sides of the public area (i.e., road),[58] he who passes over, or throws, an object from one to the other is not culpable (on Shabbat).

Apparently, balconies could be close enough for a person to hand something to his neighbor on the opposite side of the street. In Roman law we find rules determining the minimum distance required between closely placed balconies,[59] but we know of no evidence for such constraint in Roman Palestine.[60]

Stepping Stones on the Streets

There seems to be some literary evidence[61] suggesting the existence of stepping stones on streets in towns, much like the kind we are so familiar with in Pompeii. Pompeii had, of course, one special topographic characteristic, occupying, as it did, the summit and slopes of a small hill. Hence the lower streets, according to the drainage level of the ground, received the rainwater and refuse of the upper streets. In times of heavy rain the lower streets, in Dyer's words, "must have flowed like a torrent or a Welsh crossroad."[62] No sewage system could have contained the downward rush of water. Indeed, a similar sight may now be witnessed during the winter rains in the heavily paved streets of Florence, where stepping stones of the largest size would not be out of place. At Pompeii, where the lie of the ground together with the close-set stone surfaces and sides of the streets provided a ready-made watercourse, sidewalks of substantial height were absolutely necessary for pedestrians. The means of crossing from one sidewalk to another in any weather was naturally provided by stepping stones of corresponding size.[63]

These stepping stones had to be lower than the height of a wagon's axle and narrower than the distance between its wheels, so that carriages would not be obstructed by them.[64] Similarly, such stepping stones might well have been required in Galilean hill towns. It is certainly true that in present-day Jerusalem and Tel Aviv during the torrential winter downpours, such stepping stones would be most convenient for pedestrians.

Now in B. Shabbat 8a[65] we find a brief halachic discussion on the status of columns found in a public place:

> Ulla (Palestinian authority of the later third century C.E.) said: A stone block (or column—עמוד) nine [handbreadths] high in a public place, and many people (רבים—porters?)[67] lean their loads (מכתפין) on it, and a person threw [an object] onto it and it landed on it, he is culpable. Why [is he culpable]?[68] [If it is] less than three [handbreadths high] people step on it. From three to nine [handbreadths high] people do not step on it, neither do they set their loads on it (presumably because it is too low). Nine [handbreadths high] people rest their loads on it.

A handbreadth is about 11.5 cm (or a little over 4 in.), and people apparently would step on stones up to 3 handbreadths, about 34.5 cm (or 13.5 in.).

We shall not elaborate on the halachic meaning of this passage. For our purposes, it suffices to point out that Pompeiian stepping stones were between 12 and 18 in. high,[69] a height roughly comparable with that mentioned in our Talmudic discussion. It seems plausible to suggest that these stones, rather than being simply blocks scattered in the middle of a public pathway, were specially placed to facilitate crossing the road during the winter rains. Such an interpretation is further supported by the use of the word עמוד (*amud*), column, rather than אבן (*even*), stone, suggesting something purposely placed rather than random debris.[70] Winter rains were at times very severe and could even flood or wash away public platforms built of stone.[71]

Our explanation is borne out by two facts: Streets having stepping stones also had raised pavements—as indeed was the case in Pompeii and as we find in Beit Shean (see chapter 10 by Schwartz), and at least the lower level of front doors opening onto the street was higher than the level of the street itself. Without this barrier, rainwater would have entered the house through the doorway and flooded the interior. Indeed, we have seen that there were at times as many as three thresholds: the *lowest* communicated directly with the street; the *highest* provided a stop against which the door shut tightly. This top threshold was much higher than street level and hence would serve to keep out the rain.

Administrative Upkeep of Roads

We have some indirect information on the administrative aspects of the building and upkeep of the city street system in Roman Palestine. It is not clear whether it was organized in accordance with the main guidelines of Roman law or in some other manner. When speaking of Jerusalem in the first century C.E. prior to the destruction of the Second Temple in 70 C.E., the Mishna in Shekalim 1.1[72] gives the month of Adar (February–March) as the time for repairing the roads (דרכים) and thoroughfares (רחובות), which presumably had been damaged during the winter rains. These repairs were paid for out of funds drawn from the Temple treasury. The Mishna in Sota 8.2 also mentions the mending of streets as being the obligation of the members of the city, and even those who return from the battlefield, for some reason or another, must participate in roads repair (ומתקנין את הדרכים). There is, however, a class of individuals, such as newlyweds or persons who have just built houses (see Deuteronomy 20:5–8), that does not participate in battle; but neither are these type of people in the "home guard." They do not provide water for the soldiers and are not required to mend the roads (Deuteronomy 20:3; T. Sota 7.23, ed. Lieberman p. 201; Y. Sota 8.8, 23a). However, these appear to be ancient texts, and may refer to special events during time of warfare.

On the other hand, the same Tosefta in Sota also mentions a general tax, called פסי העיר, or פיסי העיר, to be paid to the town authorities. This tax is also mentioned in accurate readings of the Yerushalmi in Sota 8.8, 23a, although it is absent in our printed texts. Lieberman argues convincingly that these *fisim* (taxes) have nothing to do with the defense expenditures of the city but are a general tax,[73] and this certainly seems to be the understanding of Rabbi Yoḥanan in Baba Batra 8a, who explains that when the Mishna (Sota. 1.5) rules that after a person has lived in a town for 12 months, he is considered as one of its citizens, it is referring to his obligation to pay לפסי העיר, the city taxes.[74] However, we have no other clear information on how this tax burden was allotted—either in frequency or in specific fashion.

We also know from B. Baba Batra 7b that there were communal

taxes levied on local townsfolk to finance the building and renovation of city walls (see discussion in chapter 7). During the third century C.E. we are witness to a lively discussion over how these tax burdens should be more equitably allocated: in accordance with wealth and income (tax bracket), size of family, or relative proximity to the walls? However, no similar discussion is to be found concerning the upkeep of streets, nor is the issue even incidentally mentioned in the texts that deal with wall building. One must therefore assume that this was part of the responsibility of the local city council, the *boule,* which would try to reclaim these costs from the citizens; failing that, street maintenance formed one of the various burdensome monetary obligations placed upon the richer members of the council, at times against their will. (see discussion in chapter 8).[75] Several inscriptions record the building or repair of roads, arcades, and decorations such as mosaics on the part of wealthy individuals, often highly placed officials in the local administration.[76]

Notes

1. On the typology on Roman roads, see W. L. MacDonald, "Connective Architecture," chap. 3 in *The Architecture of the Roman Empire,* vol. 2, An Urban Appraisal (New Haven and London, 1986), pp. 32–51, especially p. 33. See also S. Anderson, ed., *On Streets* (Cambridge, 1978).

2. Cf. Numbers 35:11–30.

3. See J. Carcopino, *Daily Life in Ancient Rome* (London, 1941), p. 58, and G. Dalman, *Palästinajahrbuch,* vol. 12 (1916), p. 39. Cf. Cod. Just. 8.10.11–12 on balconies and see discussion in section Balconies Overlooking the Streets in this chapter.

4. M. P. Charlesworth, *The Roman Empire* (London, 1968), p. 33. See P. Louis, *Ancient Rome at Work* (London, 1927), p. 202, for the statement that the *Via Sacra* in Rome, the Appian Way, and the Valerian Way are between 21 and 24 ft. wide. See also S. B. Platner, *A Topographical Dictionary of Ancient Rome* (Oxford, 1929), pp. 45–48. Ivan D. Margary, in his classic *Roman Roads in Britain* (London, 1955), p. 15, says of "important roads" that they were found to be "24 feet or so." For Bostra, see Y. Tsafrir, *Erez-Yisrael from the Destruction of the Second Temple to the Muslim Conquest,* vol. 2 (Jerusalem, 1984), p. 81: 8 m for the road itself and about 19 m with the pavement. For a comparative survey of the widths of thoroughfares, see MacDonald, *Architecture,* vol. 2, pp. 41–42. And for Roman Palestine see S. Dar, Z. Safrai, and Y. Tepper, *Um Rihan: A Village of the Mishnah* (Tel-Aviv, 1986) [in Hebrew], pp. 22–26.

5. Dittenberger, *OG1* 483, lines 27–28.

6. M. Rostovtzeff, *The Social and Economic History of the Hellenistic World* [*SEHHW*], vol. 3 (Oxford, 1941), p. 1583, n. 4; A. H. M. Jones, *The Greek City* (Oxford, 1967), p. 213; J. E. Stambaugh, *The Ancient Roman City* (Baltimore and London, 1988), p. 188. For roads of these breadths, see Kuhl, *Palästinajahrbuch* 24 (1928): 129. See also Varro, *de Lingua Latina* 7.15, and Y. Tsafrir and Y. Foerster, "From Byzantine Scythopolis to Arab Baysan—Changing Urban Concepts," in *Cathedra* 64 (1992): 8 [in Hebrew]. They state that the main road of Beit Shean was about 8 m wide and about 12 m with the pave-

ments. If we further include the covered arcades on either side of the road, its total width is between 23.5 and 24 m.

7. S. Krauss, *Kadmoniyyot ha-Talmud,* vol. 2, part 1 (Tel-Aviv, 1929), p. 150. He reckoned the length of the cubit differently. We shall not enter into this issue here. Meanwhile, see my entry in the *Encyclopaedia Judaica* (Jerusalem, 1972), vol. 16, p. 389, bibliography p. 392.

8. He refers us to G. Dalman, *Neue Petra-Forschungen* (Leipzig, 1912), p. 11. He further adds that the Romans limited a public roadway to a breadth of 8 ft., which would allow two carriages to pass by one another, and that hence such a road was called *viae,* in the plural (i.e., having two "lanes"). In addition, there was an *iter,* which was narrower, and a *semita,* which was half an *iter,* that is, 1.5 ft. (referring to C. Merckle, *Engineeurtechnik* [Berlin, 1989], p. 230). Cf. also ibid. pp. 153–54.

9. D. Sperber, "A Note on Some Shiurim and Graeco-Roman Measurements," *JJS* 20 (1969): 81–86.

10. See Canticles Rabba 5.2. The degree to which they were laid out orthogonally generally depended to a great extent on the local topographic conditions. See Tsafrir and Foerster, "Byzantine Scythopolis," pp. 8, 18.

11. See S. Krauss, *Griechische und Lateinische Lehnwörter im Talmud, Midrasch, und Targum,* vol. 2 [*LW*²] (Berlin, 1899; reprint, Hildesheim, 1964), p. 385a s.v. סימטא. However, see Lieberman, *Tosefta ki-fshuṭah,* vol. 2 (New York, 1955), p. 854, n. 99, where he expresses uncertainty about the etymological source for this word. He refers us to Perles, *MDWJ* 37 (1893): 37 (already referred to by Krauss in *LW*², p. 385a).

12. See also B. Pesaḥim 50b; Derech Ereẓ Rabba chapter 11, ed. Higger, p. 309.

13. For the reasons behind this negative attitude, see Lieberman, *Tosefta,* vol. 2., p. 854, citing early authorities. However, they are not altogether convincing. Note that some authorities (Kaftor ve-Feraḥ, of Esthori ha-Farḥi, chapter 47) read: תגרי שמטה, meaning those that trade on the Sabbatical year. Clearly, this is an emendation that serves to explain the otherwise somewhat surprising attitude of the rabbis to these petty traders.

14. Noted by Lieberman, *Tosefta,* vol. 2, p. 854. Perhaps this is why he had his doubts about the derivation of the word (see above note 11), since a *semita* does not seem to be the sort of place where one would set up a slave platform for selling slaves.

15. See Y. Baba Meẓia 1.2, 8b. On the *platea,* see chapter 1.

16. See Y. Shabbat 1.1, 2d; סימטאות שבין העומדים נידונים ככרמלית. However, Liebermann, *Hayerushalmi Kiphshuto,* vol. 1 (Jerusalem, 1934), p. 16, reads מיסטויות, comparing with Y. Pesaḥim 5.8, 32c: מסטויות היו עושין להן, which he equates with אצטבי or *stoa* in B. Pesaḥim 65b. He explains our text with reference to B. Berachot 7a: Said Rabbi Zeira in the name of Rav Judah: A *stoa* which is before the columns (אצטבא שלפני העמודים) is considered a *carmelit.* He notes the difference between the phrase "*between* the columns" and "*before* (i.e., in front of) the columns," and further refers us to J. N. Epstein, *Tarbiẓ* 1/2 (1930): "Le-Ketovot Khorazim" (article by A. L. Sukenik) 135, n. 2. However, I am not altogether convinced that there is a need for this emendation (see chapter 1, note 16.)

17. On the portico and its columns, see chapter 1.

18. On building materials, see Krauss, *Kadmoniyyot,* vol. 1, part 2,

pp. 249–72; on builders and contractors (קבלנים), see ibid., pp. 272–83. See also A. K. Orleandos, *Les Matériaux de Construction* (Paris, 1968).

19. On wagons and draught animals, see Krauss, *Kadmoniyyot,* vol. 1, part 1, pp. 170–86, and cf. ibid., vol. 1, part 2, p. 277. Already Plautus (d. 184 B.C.E.) complained (Auluraria 505): wherever you go these days, you get more carts in front of the city houses than you ever would on a farm. Juvenal (d. 130 C.E.), Satires 3.254, tells how wagons carried firewood timber and pine for building. Such vehicles were allowed in Rome during daylight hours and exceptions to the rule were made by Julius Caesar for litters carried by slaves. See J. A. Shelton, *As the Romans Did* (New York, 1988), pp. 69–70, nn. 43, 45.

20. דימוס-δόμος, a row of layers of bricks or stones.

21. See Y. Hirschfeld, *Dwelling Houses in Roman and Byzantine Palestine* (Jerusalem, 1987) [in Hebrew], p. 65.

22. B. Berachot 24b, Rabbi Yoḥanan, Rabbi Joshua b. Levi, both mid-third century Palestinian authorities; B. Sukka 28a. Rabbi Yoḥanan b. Zakkai, second half of the first century C.E.; B. Rosh ha-Shana 34b, Rabbi Abbahu, Rabbi Yoḥanan. All these sources speak of dirty back streets מבואות המטונפים. I have not cited all the references to this phrase, only the Palestinian ones. Perhaps this may explain the puzzling passage in T. Tehorot 7.11, p. 668: גנות העיר שדרך הרבים מהלכת עליהן, city gardens over which public pathways pass. Liebermann, in *Tosefeth Rishonim,* vol. 4 (Jerusalem, 1939), p. 79, convincingly emends to גגות העיר, the city *roofs,* over which these public pathways go. May we suggest that people commonly took shortcuts across the connected roofs, rather than negotiate the narrow, rutted twisting streets.

23. מבואות האפלים, dark backstreets: M. Terumot 11.10; M. Pesaḥim 4.4; T. Taanit 3.13; Y. Taanit 4.4, and see Liebermann's comment in *Hayerushalmi* (p. 370) to Y. Pesaḥim 1.1, referring us to Y. Sota 5.2, 16c, that those *mevo'ot,* backstreets, were very dark, often because they were covered like the covered markets in the Old City of Jerusalem (or the covered bazaar in Istanbul). See also Stanbaugh, *Ancient,* p. 188, citing Tacitus Annales 15.93, and see below. On *mevo'ot,* see Dar, Safrai, and Tepper, *Um Rihan,* pp. 23–24.

24. See M. Baba Kama 5.5, on בור שיח מערה and also חציצין ונעיצין, in the public places; all these terms refer to different kinds of pits, ditches, and ruts. See further M. Baba Batra 3.8; B. Baba Batra 27b, 60a, and Krauss, *Kadmoniyyot,* vol. 1, part 1, pp. 153–54.

25. Of course, cases cited in a legal codex do not necessarily indicate the frequency of actual occurrences. However, these cases do seem to reflect a "real life" background situation.

26. On Roman military hob-nailed sandals (סנדל המסומר), see my note in my article, "Al Sandal ha-Mesumar," *Sinai* 61 (1967): 69–73, and see most recently H. Eshel's note in his article, "Sandalim Mesumarim bi-Mekorot ha-Yehudim, u-Mimẓa Ḥadash mi-Mearah be-Ketef Yericho," *Zion* 53 (1988): 191–98.

27. Juvenal 3.2 36–259; Carcopino, *Daily Life,* p. 63. Cf. Martial 12.57.

28. Liebermann, in *Hayerushalmi,* pp. 346–47, to Y. Eruvin 8.8, and earlier in *Yediot ha-Ḥevra ha-Ivrit le-Ḥeker Ereẓ-Yisrael ve-Atikoteha,* vol. 4 (Jerusalem, 1934), p. 23 et seq. (reprinted in his *Studies in Palestinian Talmudic Literature* [Jerusalem, 1991] [in Hebrew], pp. 454–56).

29. Y. Berachot 8.8 25b, Y. Terumot 8.4, 46b, Y. Shekalim 7.2, 40c.

30. Earlier interpretations were patently unacceptable. See Krauss, *LW*²,

p. 423b s.v. פוורסוס; idem, *Additamenta ad librum Aruch Completum Alexandri Kohut* (Vienna, 1937), p. 321; ἐπιφύριος—half moon; idem, *Kadmoniyyot* vol. 1, part 1, p. 58; ἄμφοδος, street, or block of houses surrounded by streets.

31. See chapter 1.

32. Cf. Y. Baba Kama 3.6: כיון שעמד, נצשה כקרן זוית, and also T. Baba Kama 1.1 and B. Shabbat 7b (Rabbi Yoḥanan). See also Y. Dan, *The City in Ereẓ-Yisrael during the Late Roman and Byzantine Periods* (Jerusalem, 1989), p. 62, on the twisting streets of Byzantine Shivta in the Negev. These were built for strategic reasons to make it more difficult for an enemy to break into the city. See also Liebermann, *Hayerushalmi,* pp. 346–47.

33. Although the context of the passage suggests that it is talking of long cross-country highways.

34. *Digesta* 43.10.3, Papinianus.

35. Jones, *Greek City,* pp. 213, 349, n. 5, and Stanbaugh, *Ancient,* pp. 181–89. On repairing streets, see *Digesta* 43.11.1.3.

36. Cf. T. Avoda Zara 3.13. This passage has been examined in detail by Lieberman in his article, "Palestine in the Third and Fourth Centuries," *JQR* 36 (1946): 366–69. He identifies the location as Tiberias and the second set of gentiles as Christians. He points out that the utilization of material taken from heathen temples for building purposes was a common practice among Christians under Constantius (referring to Libanius Oration 18.126) but is surprising for the mid-third century C.E. See further my comments in my article "*Raeda-Rheda* and its Wheels," chap. 23 in *Material Culture in Ereẓ-Yisrael during the Talmudic Period* (Jerusalem, 1993) [in Hebrew], pp. 154–55.

37. Ed. Horowitz, p. 273 (1st ed. [Breslau, 1910], p. 81). M. Oholot 18.5 is not relevant to this issue.

38. Krauss, *LW*[2], p. 836.

39. Ed. Horowitz-Rabin, p. 164.

40. Cited in Krauss, *Kadmoniyyot,* vol. 1, part 1, p. 154, n. 3.

41. *LSJ*9 p. 1656b s.v. στρῶσις II, citing Ephesos 3, p. 100 no. 8 (first century C.E.).

42. See above note 24.

43. Krauss, *Kadmoniyyot,* vol. 1, part 1, p. 154; cf. Martial 5.22. On the unpaved twisting street of Shivta, see A. Segal, *Shivta: Man and Architecture of a Byzantine Town in the Negev* (Beer-Sheva, 1981), p. 25. See further E. J. Owen, *The City in the Greek and Roman World* (London and New York, 1992), pp. 11–12, 157. In Tanḥuma Genesis, Ḥayye 3, we read that: A king of flesh and blood when confronted with a deeply rutted path (דרך של שקיעה) walks on stones which are hard (i.e., one does not sink into them). I understand this passage to be talking about interurban routes.

44. This seems to be suggested by the term צידי רשות הרבים, which appears in B. Shabbat 6a, B. Eruvin 94a, B. Ketubot 31b, B. Ketubot 86b, B. Kiddushin 73b, and B. Baba Meẓia 10b.

45. Derech Ereẓ Zuta 1.2, ed. Sperber p. 14; Avot de-Rabbi Nathan 1, chapter 26 ad fin.

46. Ed. Sperber, p. 36.

47. On the subject of doorsteps, see my "The Doorway and the Threshold," chap 6 in *Material Culture,* pp. 46–48, and in my Hebrew edition of *Derech Ereẓ Zuta*[2] (Jerusalem, 1982), pp. 85–87, 116.

48. See A. Peniel, ed., *Susia—Ha-Ir ha-Ivrit ha-Kedumah: Leket Ma'amarim* (Susia, 1990), p. 48.

49. See T. Frank, *An Economic Survey of Ancient Rome* vol. 5, *Rome and Italy of the Empire* (Baltimore, 1953), pp. 223–24.

50. כפתה דשקקא דגזורי. This is the correct reading in Y. Eruvin 5.7, 22d according to the Meiri. See Liebermann, *Hayerushalmi,* p. 302, and *Sefer ha-Yishuv* 1/1, ed. S. Klein (Jerusalem, 1939), p. 50, n. 13.

51. B. Ḥulin 86b: שוקא דקסרי, read: דקימרי, with Ms. See Sefer, *ha-Yishuv,* p. 50, n. 8.

52. Eccles. Rab. 10.8: שוקא גריבא. See S. Klein, *Ereẓ ha-Galil* (Jerusalem, 1967), p. 97.

53. Genesis Rabba 79.6, ed. Theodor-Albeck p. 943. The reading is problematic, and this translation is suggested by Klein in *Ereẓ ha-Galil,* p. 97, n. 38, basing himself on Albeck's discussion to line 3.

54. In rabbinic parlance שידה תיבה ומגדל; see Krauss, *Kadmoniyyot,* vol. 2, part 1, pp. 51–56.

55. On furniture in general use see Krauss, *Kadmoniyyot,* vol. 2, part 1, pp. 5–58.

56. But cf. Genesis Rabba 18.1, that women did not go to the market, rather their husbands went. However, this would seem to be an idealized statement, which probably did not reflect common practice.

57. See above note 23.

58. So too in M. Eruvin 7.4, and in Tosefta ibid. 12.B. See Krauss, *Kadmoniyyot,* vol. 1, part 2, p. 436, n. 5; Y. Hirschfeld, *Dwelling Houses* (Jerusalem, 1987), p. 170. Special regulations forbade the building of balconies, or indeed any projecting beams or balustrades, in Second Temple period Jerusalem for reasons connected with the laws of impurity. See B. Baba Kama 82b, and Krauss, *Kadmoniyyot,* vol. 1, part 1, pp. 100–102. See my discussion in *Yedion Yad Ben-Ẓvi,* 3(1975): 26–28.

59. Cf. above note 1 referring to Cod. Just 8.10.11–12; Leo's New Constitution 113—10 ft. between balconies. In Roman law on the problem of blocking out a neighbor's daylight, see G. Hermansen, *Ostia: Aspects of City Life* (Edmonton, 1982), p. 94, and *Digesta* 488.2.14.

60. Neither from Rabbinic literature nor from external sources, such as Julian of Ashkelon. On the latter and on his information on rules of building, see S. Lieberman, *Studies in Palestinian Talmudic Literature* (Jerusalem, 1991), pp. 339–417 (first published in *Tarbiẓ* 40 [1971]: 409–17).

61. So far I have not found any clear archeological evidence of this phenomenon in Roman Palestine, although there are steps to climb along the streets of Beit Shean. See Schwartz's discussion in chapter 10 on streets.

62. T. H. Dyer, *Pompeii: Its History, Buildings and Antiquities*[3] (London, 1871), pp. 71, 81–82.

63. W. Smith, W. Wayte, and G. E. Marindin, *A Dictionary of Greek and Roman Antiquities*[3] (London, 1891), p. 953a.

64. Ibid., pp. 952–53. On wheels and axles and ancient carriages in general, see S. Piggott, *The Earliest Wheeled Transport from the Atlantic Coast to the Caspian Sea* (Ithaca, 1983), and Krauss, *Kadmoniyyot,* vol. 1, part 1, pp. 179–86.

65. Partial parallel in B. Eruvin 33a and cf. B. Shabbat 9a.

66. Cf. chapter 1 in which I mentioned special blocks of stone on which the porters loaded and unloaded their heavy burdens.

67. Text from this point onward is missing in the parallel in B. Eruvin 33a (see above note 54).

68. Cf. above note 64.

69. Cf. for example M. Oholot 18.6.

70. See M. Taanit 3.8 and my article on this subject in *Sinai* 97 (1983): 39–42 and again in my book *Material Culture,* chap. 1.

71. M. Taanit 3.8, Y. Taanit, ibid., 66d.

72. Cf. M. Moed Katan 1.2.

73. Lieberman, *Tosefta,* vol. 8, p. 695, on Y. Sota 8.8, 23a.

74. The etymology of the word is as yet unclear. Krauss, *LW*², p. 450a s.v. פיסין, explains it as being derived from the Greek λοιπάς, which he translates Steuer-tax. However, I do not find this meaning attested for by λοιπάς. Presumably, he thought the *lamed* in לפסין, or לפסי העיר, is a part of the word itself. This is by no means clear, since good readings have נותנין פיסי העיר (Lieberman, *Tosefta,* to Sota, ibid.). Likewise, we find הפיסין (Krauss, *LW*², p. 450a). Perles (cited by Krauss, ibid.) did not suggest *pensio,* as Krauss stated, but *pensa* (*pensa, peisa, pisa*). Brockelmann, in his *Lexicon Syriacum,*² (Malis Saxonum, 1928), p. 580b s.v. פסא, states that פיסא gleba is from נפס (referring to Noeldeke). Cf. Fraenkel, *Die Arämaischen Frendwörter* im *Arabischen* (Leiden, 1886), p. 60. The Syriac etymology was already suggested by Löw, apud Krauss, *LW*2, p. 450a, and followed by J. N. Epstein, *Mavo le-Sifrut ha-Amoraim* (Jerusalem, 1962), p. 216. E. Y. Kutscher, *Erchei* 1 (1972): 100–102, wished to relate the word to the Latin *fossa,* ditch, moat, hence linking it up with the expenses of defending the city, that is, building walls and moats (see discussion in chapter 8). However, we have already noted that Lieberman argued that this was a general city tax, and not specifically a "war tax." Thus, the etymology remains as yet unsolved, unless we accept the Syriac approach.

75. See Dan, *City in Erez̧-Yisrael,* pp. 115–17. Cf. Z. Yeivin, "Demutah shel ha-lr ha-Yehudit," *Etmol* 3, no. 6 (1978): 6–7 (cited by Dan).

76. See Tsafrir and Foerster, "Byzantine Scythopolis," pp. 14–15 (citing G. Mazor, "Mercaz Beit Shean ha-Kedumah—Darom," *Preliminary Archeological Reports* 81 [1988]: 8; ibid., 83 [1988]: 44–47).

8

City Walls

References to a variety of topics relating to city walls appear not infrequently in Rabbinic sources. This is by no means surprising, since quite a number of Palestinian Roman (and Byzantine) cities were walled. Such was the case with Caesarea, Beit Shean, Jerusalem, Gaza, Ashkelon, Akko, Neopolis, Tiberias, Emmaus, Beit Guvrin, and Ashdod.[1] The importance attributed to such walls is clearly expressed in the following parable in Mechilta Yitro, 5, ed. Horowitz-Rabin p. 219:

> A certain person entered the city. He said to them (the citizens): I will rule over you. They said to him: Have you done anything for our good that you should rule over us? (i.e., that we should accept you as our ruler)? What did he do? He built them a wall, and brought them water [into the city] (See discussion below).

Some of these walled cities are portrayed in the mosaic Medva (Medeba) map[2] of the late sixth century C.E.[3] We shall begin our survey with what is known about financing the building and upkeep of city walls.

Financing the Building of Walls

We ended the last chapter with a reference to the discussion in Baba Batra on walls and their upkeep. The Mishna there (1.5) states that one—presumably the city council—may force residents of a city to share in the cost of building the city walls with its double doors and (a massive) bolt (חומה ודלתיים ובריח). To this Rabban Simon ben Gamliel (fl. ca. 135–70 C.E.) remarks that "not all cities require a wall." The Talmud (B. Baba Batra 7b) explains Rabban Simon ben Gamliel's view as follows:

> Not all cities require a wall—only one which is close to the border requires one, while one which is not close to the border does not.

This is the view of Rabban Simon ben Gamliel, while the anonymous view of the Mishna, which makes no mention of any distinction between different types of cities according to their location, assumes, according to the Talmud, that even cities of the interior are occasionally subject to attacks by גייסא—marauding bands. This was certainly true of the third century C.E.,[4] in which problems of defense and security were not limited to border towns. There is ample evidence that throughout the third century Palestine entered into direct military engagement in addition to being in the main area of contention and battle along the Romano-Persian border. Likewise, in the fourth century there were a number of Palestinian Jewish insurrections which brought in their wake widespread bloodshed and destruction of property.[5] Furthermore, there was a plague of brigandage throughout the third century, and Palestinian cities whose walls had fallen into disuse and decay were taking pains to repair them for fear of incursions of barbarian armies and as protection against savage marauders that roamed the countryside at will.[6,7]

This is reflected in the legal discussion recorded in B. Baba Batra 7b:

> R. Eleazar asked R. Yoḥanan (Tiberias, ca. 250–279 C.E.): [When forcing citizens of a city to pay for the construction or repairs of its walls] does one collect according to the number of souls [in a family] or according to the distribution of wealth? And he replied: According to wealth and Eleazar, my son (i.e., disciple), fix [this ruling] with nails (i.e., be certain to keep to it). Others say: he asked him whether one collects according to wealth or proximity of houses [to the walls] and he replied: According to proximity of houses, and Eleazar, my son, fix [this ruling] with nails.

Elsewhere we have pointed out the fact that Rabbi Yoḥanan stressed so forcefully that Rabbi Eleazar should follow his ruling in itself demonstrates that this was no abstruse and abstract legal debate but something of real and topical significance. Indeed, this conclusion is born out by the continuation of the same Talmudic passage, which relates that:

> R. Judah Nesiah (fl. ca. 250–285 C.E.) placed the expenses of (mending Tiberias') walls (דשורא) upon the Rabbis [too]. Resh Lakish (died ca. 275) said to him: Rabbis do not require protection (i.e., the Torah which they study protects them; hence they do not need to participate in these expenses).

Probably the main source of financing for these projects came from wealthy members of the municipality and from state-supplied funds.[8]

The Walls of Tiberias

There seems to be some evidence that the city of Tiberias, which according to Josephus, had been surrounded by a wall built by its founder, Herod Antipas, had an additional wall built around it during the third century C.E. (It was surrounded on three sides by a wall, and the Sea of Galilee formed the fourth "wall" on the east.[9]) In the winter rains of the year 1945 a portion of the southern wall of the city was uncovered. Close to the ruins of the wall a slab of basalt was found engraved with the following inscription:

> Pompeius
> . . . ullus (centurio) leg(ionis)
> Vl ferr(atae) dom(o)
> Europo[10]

M. Avi-Yonah, who published this find,[11] believed that it came from a Roman soldier's funerary monument, the stones of which were later used to build the city walls. Since the inscription mentions the sixth legion, without its epithet "*fidelis et constans*" granted by Septimus Severus (193–211 C.E.), Avi-Yonah dated it to the later second century. Hence, the wall into which he believed it to have been built (in secondary use) must be later than that date. An additional funerary inscription, which he dated to the late second or early third centuries, was similarly used in the city wall. On the basis of this he argued that the walls, which must be later than the inscriptions, were probably built during the early to middle third century.[12]

However, M. Schwabe[13] cast some doubts on the validity of those conclusions. He does not contest the secondary use of these inscriptions in the third-century city walls. Indeed, he notes that these funerary monuments must have been *torn down* to supply the building materials. For in such a short time, from the late second to the early third century, not enough time would have elapsed for their natural decay. He argues that when Tiberias and the neighboring Ḥamat were united, and the city wall had to be extended to surround both of these areas, the funerary monuments standing at that time on two sides of what had become an internal road, had to be pulled down, and their stones would naturally serve to repair the *additional* sections of the city walls added during the third century. However, the *original* wall may well have been constructed much earlier, perhaps already in the time of Herod Antipas, who founded the city in Tiberias' honor.[14] (For a further discussion on this issue and an up-to-date description of the archeological evidence bearing upon it, see the section on Urban Security in chapter 10.)

Be that as it may, it is clear from the Rabbinic sources that during the third century, leading Jewish authorities in Tiberias were discussing the building, repairing, or extending of the city walls and the possible sources of funding for these activities. Thus, the two sets of evidence support one another in that both point to a renewed involvement with the city walls of Tiberias around the mid-third century.

The Walls of Caesarea

Similarly, Avi-Yonah contended that the (outer) city wall of Caesarea was built toward the end of the third century when the Empire was threatened by anarchy, war, and possible dissolution.[15] Recently scholars, using aerial photography as well as additional excavation, have concluded that this outer wall is of Byzantine pedigree,[16] a view that has for the most part been accepted.

Further Evidence for Third-Fourth Century Wall Building

Further evidence of late third- or early fourth-century concern with the building or repair of walls may be found in a (difficult) passage in Deuteronomy Rabba, ed. Liebermann[2] (Jerusalem, 1965), p. 19:

R. Judah b. R. Simon (fl. ca. 290–350 C.E.) began: "Who will bring me into a strong city (עיר מצור—*ir maẓor*)? (Psalms 60:11)—And have I not other fortified towns (מבצרות—*mivẓarot*, a play on מבצר—מצור, *mivẓar—maẓor*)?[17] In any case, there is no city (מדינה) that has no טיחוסים—τείχισις—wall building,[18] a city which all are fortifying.[19]

Whatever this passage means, it is clear that it speaks of the fortification of city walls during the late third or early fourth centuries.

Repair of Walls

A passage in *Codex Justinianus* (11.4.1.1) at about the same time (Diocletian, 284–305 C.E.) also refers to this repair of decaying city walls:

> As you say that the Governor of the province has applied the funds which were intended for public exhibitions to the repair of the walls of the city, what has been done for the general welfare cannot be revoked by us, but the regular performances in the arena shall take place in accordance with the ancient custom, after the repairs of the walls have been completed. For in this way, by strengthening the wall, provision made for the defense of the city and those matters which have reference to the public safety having been accomplished, the games can be celebrated afterwards.

The order of priorities here expressed is most revealing. Public safety is, apparently, only marginally more important than public entertainment.[20]

Gateways

The actual physical aspects of the walls, their breadth, height, shape, and number of gates, depended largely on local topography and geological characteristics.[21] The type of stone with which they were built would be posited by the local material. The line of the wall would have to take into account the contour of the terrain, and in some cases the variation of the coast. Similarly, the number of gates would be dependent on these factors, which would also determine the courses of the major interurban routes (see chapter 10).

Tiberias, which was surrounded on three sides by a wall, with the sea as her fourth east wall (see note 9), had three (main) gateways,[22] which are mentioned in Rabbinic literature. Thus, in Tanḥuma Genesis Buber Va-Yishlaḥ 2.166 (= B. Sanhedrin 98a) Rabbi Yose b. Kisma (fl. ca. 110–135 C.E.), when strolling about with his disciples in Tiberias, was asked: When will the Messiah come? His answer was: This gateway (השער הזה) will be built and fall down [re]built and fall down, and there will not be time to rebuild it till the Son of David comes. It would appear that in this cryptic statement he was referring to a major gateway, probably opening the city wall.[23] Another reference appears in the early third century. We find Rabbi Yannai and Rabbi Yoḥanan sitting by (על) the gate of Tiberias (פיילי של טבריה—πύλη),[24] also called (ibid.)

פתח המדינה, the gateway of the city (Tanḥuma Deuteronomy Shoftim 10).[25] The main roads that crossed the city from end to end terminated in these main gates and consequently are called in Rabbinic literature מבואות הפולשים, open-ended roads (or alley).[26] In the case of Tiberias, which was open to the sea on the east side, some of the roads apparently went straight down to the sea. This seems to be the meaning of the passage in B. Eruvin 8a, in which the Tiberian Rabbi Isaac [Nappaḥa] (fl. ca. 250–32 C.E.) speaks of an alleyway (מבוי), one end of which ends at the sea (כלה לים). The other end went to the municipal rubbish dump (וצדו אחר כלה לאשפה), which must surely have been outside the city.[27]

As to the detailed appearance of these gates, we have relatively little Rabbinic evidence. They had a threshold (called a שקוף), against which the gates would swing shut.[28] Sometimes the cities locked their gates at night.[29] The Medva (Medeba) map has several portrayals of (Byzantine) city gates, such as the east gate of Ashkelon,[30] and the east gate of Neopolis.[31] They are major monuments, from which the main street, often colonnaded, traversed the town (westward), sometimes meeting its crossroad partner at a key point in the town.[32] Archeological evidence has uncovered several fine preserved examples of city gates in Tiberias (the round gate) and similarly in Gadara and the Northern Gate of Beit Shean (See chapter 10, section on Urban Security and also chapter 1, on the market.)

Projection in the Walls and Towers

It would seem that the city walls of Tiberias were not straight but had at intervals projecting sections called פיגום, *pigum,* or פיגמא (Aramaic), *pigma.*[33] Such projections would also appear to be mentioned in T. Eruvin 4.7, ed. Lieberman p. 106: כתליה וחזיזיה—the city wall and its projecting sections.[34] Krauss[35] convincingly relates these projecting sections to the well-known technique of building city walls with projecting towers at regular intervals, so as to permit the defenders on the wall to attack their enemies from three sides. As Tacitus (Hist. 5.11) formulates it regarding Jerusalem's city wall: ". . . muri per artem obliqui aut introrsus sinuati, ut latera obpugnantium ad ictus patescerunt"—walls that had been skillfully built, projecting out or bending in so as to put the flanks of an assailing body under fire.[36] Needless to say, there were towers in the city walls, such as the remains of which were found in Caesarea[37] and, of course, the famous towers of Second Temple Jerusalem.

Ramparts

I have already noted the relative dearth of Rabbinic information on the detailed structure of the city wall, its thickness, how the upper ramparts were designed, and so forth. One piece of evidence we do have comes from the Byzantine period (?) and refers to the latter days of the Second

Temple. It is by no means clear what period it really reflects, whether the late first century C.E. or the Byzantine period. It concerns the heroic tale of Geviha ben Pesisa, related in Pesikta Rabbati[38] chapters 29 to 30, ed. Ish Shalom, pp. 139b–40b. In his aggressive defense of the beleaguered city of Jerusalem, shortly before its destruction in 70 C.E., we are told that this legendary warrior climbed atop the wall of Jerusalem. When he saw the Romans hurl a *ballista* toward the city, he gathered his strength and kicked the hurtling projectile back into the enemy camp. We are informed that there were two walls[39] surrounding the city, an outer and an inner one, and on one occasion out of exhaustion he fell between the two walls; the people of Jerusalem feared he had been killed. But he soon rose up, assuring them he had collapsed only because of hunger. They fed him a hearty meal and he returned to his deeds of valor.[40]

According to this passage, the walls must have been sufficiently broad to allow him to step on top of them. Furthermore, they must have been built with a protective rampart, so that he would not be exposed to enemy arrows and missiles. This, indeed, is the standard form of a heavily fortified city wall, and hence such a description is by no means unexpected. Although it is not clear which historical reality this passage truly reflects, the author-editor, whether late Roman or Byzantine, is describing something reasonably realistic and probably reflecting conditions of his age.

Alternative Fortification Systems

It would be incorrect to think that all cities had walls. Shivta, for example, had no city walls, and apparently none of the Negev cities had them, with the possible exception of Mamshsit-Kurnub.[41] However, the houses on the outer perimeter of Mamshsit-Kurnub had their exterior walls built one against the other, so that in effect they formed a continuous barrier as effective as a wall. This barrier was interrupted by only the many entrances to the city, which were positioned at the end of the main street and served as city gates.[42] We are reminded of the Mishna in Arachin 9.6: A city whose roofs form its wall.[43]

Outside the Walls

Of course, the buildings in walled cities were not necessarily circumscribed by the perimeter of the walls. Indeed, according to Roman law, a city was defined by the *pomerium,* and Caesar's legislation concerning Rome indicates that its laws were operative within one mile of continuous habitation of the city.[44] Along the main roads approaching the city gates there were many different kinds of structures: shops, taverns, and travelers' shelters, *burgi,* which also served caravanserais[45] (see chapter 2, note 16). In Caesarea, the theater, amphitheater, hippodrome, and probably other as yet undiscovered buildings are found outside the city walls.[46] Similarly, we have already mentioned that outside Tiberias's city walls were factories (pottery works, glassworks) and the stadium.[47] This is also the case at the Port of Ostia, where a whole complex of buildings was found outside the northeastern part of the city. Likewise, at Gerasa the hippodrome is located south of the city and the festival theater and the temple to Nemesis to the north.[48] One reason why certain kinds of buildings, especially those dedicated to different forms of entertainment, might not have been built within the city is municipal officials may have wanted to keep possible rioting, often occurring in large restless crowds, outside the city, thus reducing potential dangers to the security of the city[49] (see also chapter 1 on the dangers of fire). An additional edifice often found close to the walls, inside or outside the city, is the *castellum*, or water tower. The location of the *castellum* of Tiberias, specifically mentioned in Y. Avoda Zara 3.1, 42a, has not yet been identified.[50] We shall discuss this issue in the following chapter. (See also Schwartz's discussion in chapter 10 on building outside the walls.)

Notes

1. See Y. Dan, *The City in Ereẓ-Yisrael during the Late Roman and Byzantine Periods* (Jerusalem, 1984) [in Hebrew], p. 59.

2. See M. Avi-Yonah, ed. *Mapat Medva* (Jerusalem, 1943), pass., Ashkelon, Neopolis.

3. See Avi-Yonah, *Mapat Medva,* p. 5, on the dating of the map, and recently in the mosaics at Umm el Rasas, Jordan. Piccirilo, L.A. (J. Schwartz's note).

4. The situation throughout the rest of the Empire has been succinctly summarized by R. MacMullen in his classic *Soldier and Civilian in the Later Roman Empire* (Cambridge, 1963), p. 35. See also E. J. Owens, *The City in the Greek and Roman World*[2] (London, 1992), pp. 148, 151, and S. Frere, *Britannia*[3] (Oxford, 1987), p. 242.

5. See D. Sperber, *Roman Palestine 200–400: The Land* (Ramat-Gan, 1978), p. 48 et seq. See also L. I. Levine, *Roman Caesarea: An Archeological-Topographical Study,* Qedem 2 (Jerusalem, 1975), p. 9, n. 41, with additional bibliography.

6. Sperber, *The Land,* p. 54; R. MacMullen, *Enemies of the Roman Order* (Cambridge, 1967), pp. 255–69.

7. Sperber, *The Land,* p. 55.

8. MacMullen, *Soldier and Civilian,* p. 35, n. 43; Owens, *City,* p. 151, referring to *CIL* II. 3270. See also H. de la Croix, *Military Considerations in City Planning: Fortifications* (New York, 1972). From the late fourth century there is a constitution of Arcadius and Honorius referring to one-third of the revenues from the *fundi rei publicae* to the cities for the repair of their walls (Cod. Theod. 15.1.33,395). See F. F. Abbott and A. C. Johnson, *Municipal Administration in the Roman Empire* (Princeton, 1926), p. 502.

9. See S. Klein, *Ereẓ ha-Galil*[2] (Jerusalem, 1967), p. 97. See Y. Megila 1.1, 70c, B. Megila 56, B. Erachin 32a. There seems to be evidence of a wall covering part of the east side, but it was probably built during the Byzantine period. See Klein, *Ereẓ,* p. 4. (This view is rejected by Schwartz; see his section on Urban Security in chapter 10.)

10. See also L. Di Segni, "Ketovot Tiveriya," *Idan* II (1988): 80. J. Schwartz suggests: [Cat]ullus.

11. M. Avi-Yonah, "Newly Discovered Latin and Greek Inscriptions," *QDAP* 12 (1946): 88–91.

12. See M. Avi-Yonah, *Biyemei Romi u-Bizantiyon* (Jerusalem, 1946), p. 75, p. 217, n. 3, and cf. pp. 81–82. However, now modern scholars (Foerster and Hirschfeld) regard these as sixth-century walls. See Schwartz in his section on Urban Security in chapter 10. Hirschfeld, who is currently excavating at Tiberias, writes in a private communication (of 3.2.94) that there are three walls at Tiberias: the Wall of Antipas, the Wall of Rabbi Judah Nesiah, and the Wall of Justinian. Of these, only the latter wall is really known to us. The other two "seem to elude us." There are additional lines of fortification on Mt. Berenike, which protect the lower city. Perhaps the present excavations will further clarify some of these issues.

13. M. Schwabe, *Le-Toldot Tiveriah* (Jerusalem, 1949), pp. 46–47.

14. The exact date of the founding of Tiberias is as yet unknown, but ancient literary sources, such as Josephus and Eusebius, when compared with numismatic evidence, indicate that it must have been inaugurated between 17 and 21 C.E. See Avi-Yonah apud *Erez Kinnarot* (Jerusalem, 1951) [in Hebrew], pp. 44–45, and A. Kindler, *The Coins of Tiberias* (Tiberias, 1961), p. 15.

15. See Avi-Yonah, *Jerusalem and Caesarea, in Judea and Jerusalem—The Twelfth Archeological Convention* (Jerusalem, 1967) [in Hebrew], p. 80, cited by Levine, *Roman Caesarea*, p. 7.

16. Levine, *Roman Caesarea*, p. 9, n. 42, citing Adamesteanu, in *Scavi di Caesarea Maritima*, ed. A. Frova (Rome, 1966), pp. 45–53.

17. Ibid. See editor's note 9.

18. H. G. Liddell, R. Scott, and H. S. Jones, *A Greek-English Lexicon*, 9th ed. [*LSJ*] (Oxford, 1940), p. 1764a s.v.

19. See editor's note 10 on the correction of the reading ניחוסים to טחוסים. The *tet* was split up into two letters, *nun* and *yod*. See my *A Dictionary of Greek and Latin Legal Terms in Rabbinic Literature* (Jerusalem, 1984), pp. 94, 146, for similar examples of this phenomenon. For the identification of the word, he refers us to Brüll, *Jahrbücher* 8, p. 147, n. 1. However, in the second edition of Deuteronomy Rabba he added, note 13, that perhaps we should read טיחוסים, which is the plural of τεῖχος, wall. That is to say, there are no cities without walls. For our purpose there is little difference between these two etymologies, since they both relate to walls. For the phrase כטיכוס וכחומה, see Pesikta Rabbati chapter 14, ed. Friedman—Ish Shalom 59 (It looks as though this phrase may have started off as a single Greek loanword with its Hebrew gloss.) For טיכסא דמדינתא, see Genesis Rabba 63.8, ed. Albeck p. 690. See further S. Krauss, *Griechische und Lateinische Lehnwörter im Talmud, Midrasch und Targum*, vol. 2, [LW^2] (Berlin, 1899: reprint Hildesheim, 1964), p. 263 s.v. טיכוס.

20. See M. Grant, *Gladiators* (Harmondsworth, 1971).

21. On the typology of gates, see W. L. MacDonald, *The Architecture of the Roman Empire*, vol. 2, *An Urban Appraisal* (New Haven and London, 1986), p. 80; A. Johnson, *Late Roman Fortifications* (London, 1983), and S. Krauss, *Kadmoniyyot ha-Talmud*, vol. 1, part 1 (Tel-Aviv, 1929), p. 61.

22. See Schwabe, *Le-Toldot Tiveriah*, p. 42.

23. This, of course, posits an earlier date for the building of the walls of

Tiberias, supporting Schwabe's view and contradicting Avi-Yonah's, as cited above. However, Rashi in B. Sanhedrin 98a explains that he was referring to the Gate of Rome. See B. Z. Bacher, *Aggadot ha-Tannaim,* vol. 1, part 2 (Yaffo, 1921), pp. 118–19 (and especially p. 119, n. 1).

24. In Tanḥuma Lev., Emor 9, and Pesikta de-Rav Kahana ed. Buber 74b we find תרע פילי, where the one is an Aramaic gloss on the Greek πύλη (Krauss, *LW*[2], p. 64). (See Pesikta de-Rav Kahana ed. Mandlebaum p. 148, line 14.)

25. At first I thought these gateways may have had an official gatekeeper, called a פיילן (= πυλωφύλαξ, BGU 14v2, third century C.E.). In Ecclesiastes Rabba to Eccles. 7.9 we read that Rabbi Simon b. Lakish (d. Tiberias ca. 275 C.E.) used to study in the אלסים (= ὑάλωσις—glass factory) (see S. Liebermann, "Tikkunei Yerushalmi," *Tarbiẓ* 3, no. 2 [1932]: 208, n. 7; Schwabe, *Le-Toldot Tiveriah,* p. 45, n. 125) of Tiberias, which was outside the city and close to the city gate. A פיילן would bring him water to drink every day. He studied regularly at this spot. See Genesis Rabba 34 ad fin., p. 327; S. Klein, *Sefer ha-Yishuv,* vol. 1 (Jerusalem, 1939), p. 49 n. 4; and idem, *Ereẓ ha-Galil,*[2] p. 97. However, this point is somewhat unclear. For in the parallels, Resh Lakish is to be found in the פילון of Tiberias, or פילי שחוץ לטבריה, the *pili* (or *pile*) outside Tiberias. Liebermann equates this with the glass factory mentioned above. Furthermore, he points out that the parallel in Midrash ha-Gaddol to Genesis 25:8, ed. Margulies p. 421, is חד פחר, a *potter,* who brings him water, and indeed he is studying in a פחארא, a potter's workshop (see Sokoloff, *Dictionary,* p. 427b s.v. פחורה.) Liebermann sees the potter's workshop as adjacent to the aforementioned glassworks. Hence, פילון may be a workshop for producing פיילות, dishes, drinking bowls—from Greek φαίλη, a maker of such dishes (Lieberman, "Tikkunei Yerushalmi," p. 208, n. 7). Perhaps we should read פיילר, potter (Sokoloff, *Dictionary,* p. 430b s.v.), as already suggested by Krauss (and Löw) in *LW*[2], p. 444a s.v. פיילן.

26. See for example B. Shabbat 6a, in which the roads are archetypal "public domain," *reshut ha-rabbim,* and explained by Rashi to be open ended at *both* ends. However, Rashi also explains that they open onto the *plateia,* in which case they may be alleyways opening onto the marketplace. See M. Jastrow, *A Dictionary of the Targumim, the Talmud Babli and Yerushalmi, and the Midrashic Literature* (Philadelphia, 1903), p. 1185 s.v. פלש, "an alley opening onto a street, not closed by a legally required fictitious partition."

27. J. Schwartz points out to me that if the road goes from east to west that brings us to Mt. Berenike, then it is not a good idea to put a rubbish dump onto the slope of a mountain.

28. See Y. Eruvin 5.1, 22b.

29. B. Eruvin 6b, referring to Jerusalem. If the פיילן was a gatekeeper (see above note 25), then presumably it was also his duty to lock the gates at night.

30. Avi-Yonah, *Mapat,* p. 24, n. 94.

31. Ibid., p. 15, n. 32.

32. It may be apropos at this point to mention another kind of gate that was unrelated to the city walls and was wholly of a monumental nature, that is, the *tetrapylon,* a quadrupal arch. On this monument in general, see MacDonald, *Architecture,* vol 2, pp. 87–92. It was usually located on a main thoroughfare, though not necessarily in the center of the city. Some cities had more than one, such as Gerasa, which boasts the best-preserved remains in the area. The *tetrapylon* of Caesarea was a well-known landmark and is mentioned in Rab-

binic as well as external sources. In the Expositio Totius Mundi (of 350 C.E.) sec. 26 we read: "Likewise there is also Caesarea . . . the tetrapylon is famous everywhere, it is a unique sight." Tosefta Ahilot 18.13, p. 617, explaining the Mishna in Oholot 18.9 that states everything east of Caesarea is impure because of graves found there, explains "east of Caesarea" as "from opposite its tetrapylon to opposite its winepress." For a full discussion of this monument, see Levine, *Roman Caesarea,* p. 38. There are as yet no remains of this edifice, and it is still unclear where exactly it was situated. For a discussion of the philological aspects of the occurrence of this word in Rabbinic literature, see my *Essays on Greek and Latin in the Mishna, Talmud, and Midrashic Literature* (Jerusalem, 1982) [English section], pp. 29–39. See further chapter 8 and Krauss, *LW*², p. 262b s.v. טיטרפלין, referring to Y. Kilaim 4.2,296. Y. Eruvin 1,19c, Y. Sukka 1.1, 52a: טטרפליות שבכרמים, should be corrected to שבכרכים, in the towns. And this correction was accepted by Lieberman in *Hayerushalmi Kiphshuto* (Jerusalem, 1934), p 241, to Eruvin, ibid.

33. Y. Eruvin 5.1, 22b. See Klein, *Ereẓ ha-Galil,* p. 96; Krauss, *Kadmoniyyot ha Talmud,* vol. 1, part 1, pp. 61–63. Cf. M. Eruvin 5.1, which speaks of irregular projecting and inset sections (פיגום נכנס פגום יוצא). See Albeck's commentary ad loc. However, Liebermann, *Hayerushalmi,* vol. 1, p. 202 (and "Tikkunei Yershalmi," pp. 208–9) prefers to interpret the words as being of Greek origin, πῆγμα, a platform (or scaffold), which he believed was a raised platform placed near the stadium (אצטדיון, Eruvin, ibid.) to enable onlookers to view the games within the stadium. This interpretation does not, however, suit the Mishna Eruvin text. See also T. Eruvin 4.5–6, ed. Lieberman, p. 105; idem, *Tosefta ki-fshuṭah,* vol. 3 (New York, 1962), ad loc., p. 369; and cf. ibid., p. 354, n. 55.

34. See Lieberman, *Tosefta,* vol. 3, ad loc., p. 371. The term בדודיות in M. Eruvin 5.1, explained by the Aruch (*Aruch Completum,* ed. A. Kohut, vol. 2, pp. 237b–38a) as bits of the wall, may well refer to ruined parts of the walls of *a house,* rather than of the city walls (contra Krauss, *Kadmoniyyot ha-Talmud,* vol. 1, part 1, p. 62).

35. Krauss, *Kadmoniyyot ha-Talmud,* vol. 1, part 1, p. 62.

36. Cf. Vitruvius 1.5, 2, 4–5. See also E. W. Marsden, *Greek and Roman Artillery: Historical Development* (Oxford, 1969), p. 126 et seq. On Caesarea's city walls, with their towers and adjacent buildings, see Levine, *Roman Caesarea,* pp. 9–13.

37. Levine, *Roman Caesarea,* p. 10.

38. For the dating of this text, see my article in *Encyclopaedia Judaica,* vol. 13 (Jerusalem, 1971), columns 335–36.

39. But J. Schwartz suggests to me that the text may be speaking of a double wall with a space in between, much like the walls of Herodion.

40. Cf. Lamentations Zuta, ed. Buber, p. 54.

41. Y. Dan, *City,* p. 59.

42. See A. Segal, *Shivta: Plan and Architecture of a Byzantine Town in the Negev* (Beer Sheva, 1981), p. 29 et seq., and the plan on p. 18.

43. And cf. B. Erachin 32a, Megilah 5b: שור איגר; see Dan, *City,* p. 60.

44. See M. Schwabe, "Ketovet ha-Burgos mi-Kesaria she-be-Ereẓ-Yisrael," *Tarbiẓ* 20 (1950): 272 et seq., on a Byzantine inscription commemorating the erection of a *burgus* out or on the east wall of Caesarea. See further S. Safrai, apud *Roman Frontier Studies 1967: The Proceedings of the Seventh Interna-*

tional Congress Held at Tel-Aviv, ed. M. Gichon and S. Applebaum (Tel-Aviv, 1971), pp. 227–28, 307, on second-century *burgi* from Mechilta, ed. Horowitz-Rabin, p. 307, etc. and additional note later on pp. 229–30 by Safrai and S. Applebaum.

45. See Owens, *City,* p. 184, n. 21, referring to Tabula Heracleensis, and also Abbott and Johnson, *Municipal,* pp. 289–90, lines 20–23, 56–58.

46. Levine, *Roman Caesarea,* p. 11.

47. Y. Eruvin 5.1, 22b; Liebermann, "Tikkunei Yerushalmi," pp. 207–9; idem, *Hayerushalmi,* vol. 1, pp. 292–93. Indeed, this was true of many Roman cities, where stadia, amphitheaters, and circuses, all of which made considerable demands on urban space, were often found outside the city proper. Sometimes it was the suitability of the location and of the natural geography of the site rather than the actual availability of land that determined the position of these buildings. See Owens, *City,* p. 152, and cf. p. 125 et seq.

48. Levine, *Roman Caesarea,* p. 11, who adds that in some of these cases the buildings were added after the original foundation of the city was built and were thus placed outside the walls, whereas at Caesarea they were placed outside the city at the time the city was founded. Indeed, a lot of industry and "entertainment" automatically goes outside the city. See Schwartz's discussion on Industrial Areas in chapter 10.

49. Cf. R. MacMullen, "Urban Unrest," chap. 5 in *Enemies,* p. 163 et seq.

50. See Klein, *Ereẓ ha-Galil,* pp. 96–97.

9

Water Supply, Sewage, and Drainage

It is well known that Ereẓ Yisrael was not blessed with a plentiful supply of water. Other than the narrow winding Jordan, there are few rivers in the country and hardly any fresh water lakes, other than the Sea (!) of Galilee and Huleh Lake (which virtually no longer exists). Consequently, the cities, which required an abundant and regular flow of water, relied mostly on wells and on rainwater trapped in numerous small private and public cisterns. Fountains (springs) might have been situated at considerable distances from the city, and water would have been transported via an open canal (such as in present-day Wadi Kelt between Jerusalem and Jericho),[1] through a closed piping system, which sometimes spanned hills and valleys for many miles, or by aqueducts (such as those near Caesarea).[2] There were also large underground water systems with vent pipes surfacing at regular intervals to relieve water and air pressure and to enable workers to inspect and clear out the silt deposits and other obstructions[3] (witness the magnificent complex bringing water to Jerusalem through the adjacent Armon ha-Naẓiv[4]). There were also overhead pipes made of lead, earthenware, or at times even wood that were laid out carefully above ground, taking advantage of the lay of the land and using gravitational force to transport water over a great distance from a source high in the hills to a city situated low on the plains. Such piping systems required considerable sophistication in planning[5] and construction, not only in choosing optimal routes but also in calculating water pressures and the strengths and diameters of piping units, in placing air vents to relieve excessive pressure, and in installing sludgecocks for removing silt deposits and for filtering the water.

Vitruvius's Description of Water-Supply Systems

A detailed description of different water-supply systems can be found in the work of the great first century C.E. Roman architect Vitruvius in his *De Architectura*. In book 8, chapter 6, sections 6 to 9 he writes as follows:[6]

> *On Aqueducts, Leaden and Earthen Pipes*
> 1. The supply of water is made by three methods: by conduits along artificial channels, or by lead pipes, or by earthenware tubes. And they are arranged as follows. In the case of channels, the structure must be on a very solid foundation; the bed of the current must be leveled with

a fall of not less than 6 inches in 100 feet. The channels are to be arched over to protect the water from the sun. When they come to the city walls, a reservoir is to be made. To this a triple receptacle is to be joined, to receive the water; and three pipes of equal size are to be put in the reservoir, leading to the adjoining receptacles, so that when there is an overflow from the two outer receptacles, it may deliver into the middle receptacle.

2. From the middle receptacle pipes will be taken to all pools and fountains;[7] from the second receptacle to the baths,[8] in order to furnish a public revenue; to avoid a deficiency in the public supply, private houses are to be supplied from the third: for private persons will not be able to draw off the water, since they have their own limited supply from their receptacle. The reason why I have made this division is in order that those who take private supplies into their houses may contribute by the water rate to the maintenance of the aqueducts.

3. If there are hills between the city and the fountain head, we must proceed as follows. Tunnels are to be dug underground and leveled to the fall already described. If the formation of the earth is of tufa or stone, the channel may be cut in its own bed; but if it is of soil or sand the bed and the walls with the vaulting are to be constructed in the tunnel through which the water is to be brought. Air shafts are to be at the distance of one *actus* (120 feet) apart.

4. But if the supply is to be by lead pipes, first of all a reservoir is to be built at the fountain head. Then the section of the pipe is to be determined for the supply of water, and the pipes are to be laid from the reservoir in the city. . . .

5. When, however, an aqueduct is made with lead pipes, it is to have the following arrangement. If from the fountain head there is a fall to the city, and the intervening hills are not so high as to interrupt the supply, and if there are valleys, we must build up the pipes to a level as in the case of open channels. If the way round the hills is not long, a circuit to be used; if the valleys are wide spreading, the course will be down the hill, and when it reaches the bottom, it is carried on a low substructure so that it may be leveled as far as possible. This will form a U-shaped bend which the Greeks call *koilia.* When the bend comes uphill after a gentle swelling spread over the long space of the bend, the water is to be forced to the height of the top of the hill.

6. But if the bend is not made use of in the valleys, or if the pipe is not brought up to a level, and there is an elbow, the water will burst through and break the joints of the pipes. Further, standpipes[9] are to be made in the bend, by which the force of the air may be relaxed.[10] In this way, the supply of water by lead pipes may be carried out in the best manner, because the descent, the circuit, the bend, the compression of the air can be thus managed when there is a regular fall from the fountain head to the city.

8. But if we wish to employ a less expensive method, we must proceed as follows. Earthenware pipes are to be made not less than two inches thick, and so tongued that they may enter into and fit one another. The joints are to be coated with quicklime worked up with oil. At the descents to the bend, a block of red stone is to be placed at the actual

> elbow, and pierced so that the last pipe[11] on the incline, and the first from the level of the bend, may be jointed in the stone. In the same way uphill: the last from the level of the bend, and the first of the ascent, are to be jointed in the same way in the hollow of the red stone. 9. Thus, by adjusting the level of the tubes, the work will not be forced out of its place in the downward inclines and the ascents. For a strong current of air usually arises in the passage of water, so that it even breaks through rocks, unless, to begin with, the water is evenly and sparingly admitted from the fountain head, and controlled at the elbows and turns by bonding joints or a weight of ballast. Everything else is to be fixed as for the lead pipes. Further, when the water is first sent from the fountain head, ashes are to be put in first, so that if any joints are not sufficiently coated, they may be grouted with the ashes.

These passages have been examined in detail by a number of scholars,[12] and we also have discussed certain aspects that relate to Rabbinic sources.[13] The general picture that emerges from these descriptions is of water being transferred from a distant water source—a fountain head—by a variety of methods, aqueducts, tunnels, and overland piping systems, to a reservoir called a *castellum,* from which it is distributed throughout the city to pools, fountains, public baths, and (some) private homes. The revenues from the baths and the private recipients help cover the costs of the upkeep of the whole system.

Thalame—the Siphon System

Many elements of this system are familiar to us from descriptions in the Rabbinic sources. The passage of water from the fountain head to *castellum* (water cistern, water tower) via a valley is described in T. Mikvaot 4.8, ed. Zuckermandel p. 656:

> [The water from] a spring leading out to a *thalame* and from the *thalame* to a reservoir is unfit [for ritual ablution] because it is "drawn." What can one do [to remedy this situation]? One can make a small hole [in the pipe system], and the waters become ritually fit.[14]

The general principle is that one may not use water for ritual ablution that has been contained ("drawn"—*mayyim she'uvim*) in a vessel or receptacle (*keli*). Water transported from a spring (fountain head) via a *thalame* system is automatically disqualified, presumably because it has passed through something that is halachically considered a "vessel" and has caused the water to be "drawn." The *thalame,* some kind of a pipe, corresponds to Vitruvius's *venter,* also a kind of bent pipe, called *coellia,* κοιλία, (see his description in section 5) by the Greeks. (All of these words have the same generic meaning of a cavity of some sort, an intestine or a cavity in the ground, and in this context refer to a kind of pipe.) Vitruvius is talking of piped water flowing from a fountain head via a valley to a *castellum,* city reservoir (above the valley but lower than the source), that is, a siphon. In such a system the water goes through a U-shaped pipe–system (siphon in effect) that contains *colluviaria,* standpipes (that is, sludgecocks), which collect the dirt and relieve the mounting air and water pressures[15] (see Vitruvius's description in section 6). These are sections of piping with a "belly" serving as silt traps. Silt, pebbles, and lime deposits constantly had to be cleared from the system.[16] In some cases a large *pithos,* or some other kind of jar, was installed. A terra-cotta pipeline entered the jar through a hole on one side and emptied from it by a pipe cemented to its opposite side. If the pipeline had to negotiate a sharp bend, the offtake pipe was connected to the *pithos* at a right angle. The jar thus served to eliminate inertial thrust as well as to reduce the current built up on the downslope or when rounding the bend of the system. The jar also served as a silt trap, the accumulated debris being removed through its open mouth.[17] Hence, the water passing through this siphon system automatically went through what halachically was considered a "container" (*keli*), causing it to be "drawn." As a result, all water coming from this major source was unfit for use in a *mikveh,* a ritual pool.

The solution was to make a small hole in the bottom of the sludgecock, *colluviaria,* so that it was no longer considered a "container" from a halachic point of view.[18]

In this Tosefta text we have references, direct or oblique, to Vitruvius' fountain head: *venter—thalame* (siphon) system, *colluviaria,* and *castellum.*

The Castellum

The *castellum* distribution system described so carefully by Vitruvius (see sections 1 to 2), an example of which was found at Pompeii,[19] is also referred to in Rabbinic sources. In Tosefta Mikvaot 4.6, ed. Zuckermandel p. 656, we read:

> A *castellum* which distributes its waters into [separate] reservoirs,[20] if it has a hole the size of a wine-skin stopper does not disqualify [its waters for serving for ritual ablution]. But if [there is] not [such a hole, it does] disqualify the *mikveh.* This issue on three separate occasions was brought by the inhabitants of Asia before [the members of the Academy of] Yavneh, and on the third [occasion] they permitted it, even if the hole was [only] the size of a needle.

Here again we see that the *castellum,* distributing the water supply into secondary reservoirs, constitutes a container, thus disqualifying the water for ritual use. This was obviously a serious obstacle to the people of Asia, who probably had no other viable water source for their *mikveh.* It is understandable that they were willing to travel from southern Asia, perhaps present-day Eilath,[21] to Yavneh in Judaea three times to find a suitable solution.

The *castellum* was frequently built on pillars, like a modern water tower,[22] and was situated close to the city walls, either on the inside or on the outside. Thus, it constituted one of the familiar landmarks on the outskirts of the city. Many such water towers were built in the first century B.C.E., and Agrippa, as *aedile,* is credited with having constructed 130 of them, many highly decorated, all in a single year (19 B.C.E.).[23] By the third and fourth centuries C.E. for the most part they were in a state of decay. Thus, Rabbi Levi (mid-third century C.E.) gives a parable[24] of a *castellum* that has a hole in it. Laborers are hired to fill it up with water. The foolish man says: What is the point in my filling it up? I pour in water at one end and it empties out at the other.[25] The clever man says: What difference does it make? I'm getting paid for every bucket of water I handle. From a slightly later date (late third century) comes the testimony that when Rabbi Yasa (= Assi) died, the *castellum* of Tiberias collapsed.[26] The continuation of that text, in the name of Rabbi Zeira, informs us that it was embellished with idolatrous decorations.[27] Apparently, these ornate *castella* were cracking and falling down in the third century. In Caesarea remnants of the *castellum* that collected water from the upper aqueduct have survived.[28]

Aqueducts

When mentioning Caesarea, one readily recalls the magnificent upper and lower aqueducts.[29] The aqueduct appears in Rabbinic sources as a Greek loanword, ἀγωγός,[30] meaning, inter alia, aqueduct, in an Aramaic dialect form: חוגגין, *ḥogegin.* Thus, in Midrash Psalms 42.4, ed. Buber, p. 266, the anonymous homilist interprets the Psalmist's Hebrew חוגג, *ḥogeg:*

> [Like] the Greek word *ḥagogin* (aqueducts) of water.[31] Just as the water-aqueducts have no limit, so when Israel came on the [three] foot-festivals [to Jerusalem] there was no limit [to their numbers] . . . .[32]

And similarly, in Lamentations Rabba 1.16, ed. Buber p. 81, we find Rabbi Levi—the same Rabbi Levi of the later third century who previously mentioned the *castellum!*—saying:

> It is like unto a water-aqueduct (אגוגא דמיא) which does not stop [flowing] either by day or by night. . . .[33]

These indeed are the major characteristics of the aqueduct as formulated by Trevor Hodge:

> First, it operated on the constant offtake principle, and there was usually no water shortage. . . . Normally . . . , the aqueduct was fed by a spring that kept its water coming as fast as it was being used. . . . Second, taps were very little used and all the outlets, in principle, were running 24 hours a day. This meant there were no peak hours, and that accordingly, the quantities of water that passed through the system and thus had to be provided (even if not put to actual use) were truly vast, such as to make modern water engineers gasp.[34]

It has been calculated that between them the aqueducts at Caesarea conveyed about 10,200 m^3 per hour.[35]

Aqueducts required constant attention to ensure a continuous free flow of water. "For nearly all Roman aqueducts used hard water that left a caked deposit which would soon choke the channel if it were not regularly cleaned out; the cleaning process was never-ending, and every extra yard of aqueducts was an extra yard to be kept clean."[36] In some places, surveying the aqueducts was the job of the *officium* of the provincial governor. An inscription from southern Palestine attests to the fact that "a most illustrious elder" of the city was in charge of repairing an irrigation mechanism.[37]

At Caesarea a proconsul was connected with such an operation: "In the time of F[lavius], the most magnificent proconsul, the two aqueducts were renovated from the foundations."[38] However, prolonged neglect could precipitate a crisis in a city. In the early sixth century, Caesarea was brought to the brink of disaster by a series of misfortunes, one of which was the near total breakdown of the water-supply system. Choricius of Gaza, a witness of these events, writes as follows:

> The channel no longer remains unhindered for flowing water as before. Rather the rush of the water was clogged in many places and (the flow was) more sluggish than usual. (The result was) that people came to the (artificial) fountains there in vain, some of which were empty of water, while other people drew less than their needs. . . . Thus, the young and quarrelsome men, wishing to draw water, clash with one another. . . .[39]

Chaotic scenes ensued at wells and cisterns because of the limited availability of water. Finally, the central government intervened, cleared a wide passage, and increased the number of wells and cisterns in the city.

The importance of keeping the canal system clean was recognized by the rabbis. Hence, they permitted certain repairs to be made to the pipes and blockages to be cleaned out even during periods when this kind of work was normally forbidden.[40]

Nymphaea—Fountains

From descriptions of the *castellum* it is clear that water was distributed to furnish various needs, one of which was to supply the public fountains, called *nymphaea* in Rabbinic literature. In Tanḥuma Exodus, Mishpatim 8, 102b, we read:[41]

> It is like unto a *nymphaion*[42] which supplies water to the whole city, and all praise it. One man said to them: Praise the fountain head that supplies it [its water]. . . .

Probably, it is this sort of fountain that is described in T. Avodah Zarah 6.7, which mentions "A fountain head that wells out of a house [temple] of idolatry. . . ." And in B. Avodah Zarah 58b, Resh Lakish (d. in

Tiberias ca. 275 C.E.) speaks of water that was being worshipped by idolators. There was a discussion over whether or not the use of this water became forbidden to the Jews. Rabbi Yoḥanan notes that since it is water owned and used by the public, it cannot be affected by idolatry.[43]

The *nymphaea* were highly decorated buildings, usually placed in a central position in the town, and often terminated the aqueduct supplying water to the general public in the form of a fountain. They were adorned with statuary, and the Roman administrator Agrippa was said to have installed 300 statues on the fountains of Rome in a single year.[44] They could have a massive facade some two or three stories high, with fountains splashing and cascading in all directions, as was the case in Miletos, Aspendos, Sidon, and Perge.[45] One can well imagine that many of the waterspouts protruded from the statues: from the faces, mouths, eyes, and other orifices. T. Avodah Zara 5.6, ed. Zuckermandel, p. 469, teaches that in the case of "faces which spout water in the cities,[46] one should not put one's mouth on the mouth of the face to drink, because it looks as though he is kissing an idolatrous image, but one may catch the water in one's hand and drink it."[47] Excavation of the *nymphaeum* in Gerasa uncovered a stone carved with four dolphins in relief, out of whose eyes flowed forth water.[48] And in a round fountain head, now in the Rockefeller Museum, Jerusalem, the mouth of Phrygian-capped heads, with hair shaped into ringlets, forms the spouts.[49] Heads of fountains were found in Ḥamat Gader in the form of faces out of whose mouths water poured forth.[50]

There is yet another reference to *nymphaea* in a difficult passage of Midrash Psalms 48.4, ed. Buber pp. 275–76:

> "Walk about Zion and go about her; count the towers thereof" (Psalms 48:12). How many *gina'ot*—ג׳ינאות—will there be in Jerusalem. 1184. How many towers will there be in it? 1485. How many *ttpra'ot*—טטפראות? 1496. How many *nitfa'ot*—ניטפאות? 1876. And where (היכן) will the water rise? On 900 *ri'atot*—ריאטות.

The whole passage requires careful analysis to determine the correct reading of the problematic terms, their exact etymologies, and the significance of the numbers. We shall address only some of these issues. One thing is very clear: we are speaking of Jerusalem of the Messianic Age and its wealth of splendid buildings and abundance of water sources. The ניטפאות are surely נימפאות, *nymphaea* (the *mem* and the *tet* are graphically very similar and can easily be interchanged). Further support for such an emendation may be found in the *Aruch*,[51] which preserves a reading: נימסאות, *nimsa'ot,* which should surely be emended to נימפאות. Again, the *peh* and the *samech* look similar graphically and can easily be interchanged. There may even be in the reading ניטפאות,[52] an (unconscious?) play on the Hebrew root *ntf,* נטף, to drop (water), thus relating this word to the *nymphaeum.*[53] טטפראות—*ttpra'ot*—must surely be טטרפ[ל]אות, τετραπυλα, *tetrapula,*[54] archways entered from four sides, notable landmarks in the Roman city (see discussion in chapter 7). ריאטות, *ri'atot,* appears in Ms. Leiden as ריטאות, *rita'ot,* and should probably be emended to רימאות, *rima'ot,* with the same *tet-mem* interchange. This would correspond to the Greek ῥεῦμα, stream (with a Hebrew feminine plural termination).[55]

Although the passage in Midrash Psalms is anonymous, in B. Baba Batra 75b it appears in a closely parallel form[56] in the name of Resh (= Rabbi Simon b.) Lakish. The continuation of the text in Midrash Psalms is attributed to Rav Naḥman [b. Yaakov] (Babylonia, d. ca. 320 C.E.),[57] again pointing to a third-century dating of our text. In all probability our text is by Rabbi Simon b. Lakish,[58] and should be dated mid-third century, C.E. In this chronological context it would correspond to the Palestinian Messianic trends of the 250s, already noted by scholars.[59] It may possibly have been affected by the millenial speculation of the Romans around the mid-third century. For the year 248 C.E., the thousandth year of Rome, ushered in the *saeculum novum,* and the notions of victory, concord, and, above all, renewal were stressed.[60]

We have already noted in passing Pliny's description of Agrippa, the aedile's work, completed in 190 B.C.E. He writes (36.121): "Agrippa, moreover, as aedile added to these the Aqua Virgo, repaired the channel of the others and put them in order, and constructed 700 basins (*lacus*), not to speak of 500 fountains (*salientes*), and 130 distribution reservoirs (*castella*), many of the latter being richly decorated. He erected on these works 300 bronze or marble statues and 400 marble pillars; and all these he carried out in a year . . . ." What Rabbi Simon b. Lakish seems to be saying in our Midrash is that the renovated Jerusalem will be even more wonderous than mighty Rome and will have more towers, arches, *nymphaea,* and water channels than the world's greatest city.

Cataracta—Sluice Gates

Water coming from any major source, whether an aqueduct, an open channel, or a water tower, often had to have its flow regulated. One of the easiest methods, increasing or decreasing flow as necessary, was to collect the water in a large pool and construct a sluice gate at the exit.[61] Sometimes one was even created at the exit of the *castellum.*[62] Such a sluice has been found at Ḥamat Gader.[63] It consists of a metal or wooden plate that slides down vertical grooves, closing off the exit canal and thus forcing the water level to rise in the collecting pool that was next to the fountain head. An additional and larger example of such a sluice was found in the Roman dam on Nahal Taninim, north of Caesarea.[64]

This system is mentioned once in the Yerushalmi, in Moed Katan 1.1, 80b, which talks of an *agtrgtiia,* representing the Greek κατα῾ρ῾ράκτης, Latin *cataracta,* here meaning a sluice gate.[65] In this particular text, however, we are speaking of an agricultural technique, and indeed this method was most frequently used in irrigation.[66]

Piping

We have already noted that the water was distributed from the water tower to the bathhouse and the public fountains. In addition, private users were supplied through a network of pipes that spread across the city. This system transported fresh water that was cold and relatively clean. Such pipes were sometimes called ψυχρόφορον, a term found in a fourth-century (?) Hebrew Palestinian magical text, meaning a pipe that transfers cold water.[67] The Mishnah in Shabbat 3.4 relates how the people of Tiberias connected a pipe (סילון—σωλήν)[68] of cold water (צונין, *ẓonin* = *ẓonenin*) to a water [channel] of hot water. This was either to heat the cold water or to cool the hot water.[69] Even if the *silonim* were closed pipes, they received their waters from open canals, carrying water from a major source. These waters often became infected and infested with organisms (such as leeches), and it was for this reason that the rabbis counseled against drinking directly from the *silonim,* despite the fact that they were closed.[70]

These pipes consisted of closed earthenware interlocking sections, some of which were bent with elbow joints[71] and some of which had a belly to collect silt deposits.[72] They could be made of a variety of materials but most commonly were of earthenware or lead but sometimes were of wood, glass, or even bone.[73] Perhaps only the wealthy citizens had water piped into their houses.[74] Others relied on the public fountains[75] and on their private cisterns.[76]

Channels

I have referred several times to open channels (*amot ha-mayyim*)[77] through which water flowed from the *castellum* or some other source, at times close to the main street,[78] and sometimes terminating at the *nymphaeum.* These were well built, at least 65 cm deep and about 25 cm wide.[79] At certain points they had a junction[80] from which a pipe system led off in different directions, and on occasion they passed through the streets and into individual courtyards.[81] Some of these channels were interurban and brought water from great distances, such as from the aqueducts. (The one from Abella to Sepphoris is mentioned in the Tosefta,[82] and there is also one in Tripoli, Lebanon.[83])

Drainage and Sewage

Literary evidence has helped us understand how water was conveyed from its source by aqueducts, pipes, or canals to the city, where it was collected in a water tower and distributed domestically. Now we must pose the question of how surplus water was disposed of: In other words, what sort of *drainage* system existed? In addition, we must seek out what our sources disclose about the conveyance of domestic human waste: In other words, what sort of *sewage* system existed? Were these two systems identical or separate? Was there one system of canals for draining water and a separate one for carrying sewage, or was the same facility used for both functions? Trevor Hodge writes that "in cities it was often convenient to use one conduit for both."[84] Rabbinic sources are not explicit on this point, and their terminology is not precise. It is, therefore, often difficult to distinguish between these two different functions. Nonetheless, there is enough information to give us something of a picture of how these systems functioned in Rabbinic Palestine.

Sewers

There were certain restrictions placed on the disposal of sewage in public places,[85] but obviously much domestic waste had to find its way into the sewage system. Both public and private toilets would require a method of disposing of the accumulated waste, other than carting it off as manure to nearby farms.[86] There were public toilets in many Palestinian cities[87]—the one in Tiberias was especially well known (see B. Berachot 62a)—and no doubt they were regularly flushed by running water[88] (fig. 9.1). However, Carcopino's remarks should not be taken lightly when he writes that only the sewage of the ground floor and the public latrines that stood directly along the route of the *cloaca* (sewer) was collected.[89] No effort was made to connect the systems with the private latrines of the separate *cenacula*. Very few houses were designed so that

Figure 9.1 Public latrine, Ephesus. (From W. H. Stephens, *The New Testament World in Pictures* [Cambridge: Lutterworth Press, 1988], p. 101, no. 135. Used with permission.)

the upstairs latrines could empty into the sewer below. He further writes: "Of all the hardships endured by the inhabitants of ancient Rome, the lack of domestic drainage is the one which would be the most resented by Romans of today."[90] This is probably no less true of other ancient cities of the Roman world.

Despite the structural limitations of city sewers, a great deal of waste and refuse did obviously find its way into the sewage system and thus out of the city confines. Indeed, there are some specific references to sewers in our sources. In M. Moed Katan 1.2 are we told that:

> The Rabbis say: One may build a water-conduit during the Sabbatical Year, and during the mid-festival (*Ḥol ha-Moed*) one may repair what has broken down, and one may repair the damaged waterways (*kilkulei ha-mayyim*) in the public domain, and clean them out.

The famous thirteenth- to fourteenth-century Spanish commentator Rabbi Yom-Tov Alshvili (usually called by his acronym Ritva) explains *kilkulei ha-mayyim* as follows:

> They are the sewers (*bivin*) which take out all the usage, and if they are damaged, the city will be harmed with slime and excrement, and it is they that are called *kilkulei ha-mayyim,* because the filthy waters go through them. . . .

Likewise, the thirteenth-century Provençal commentator Rabbi Menahem Meiri writes:

> This is referring to the large sewers they had on all [major] roads going from one end of the city to the other. . . . And every individual house had a small sewer, connecting up with the main sewer, and the city sewage goes out through it. And they have small apertures the size of a handbreadth, to clean them out, because at times they are damaged by blockages of excrement and silt, so that the water cannot pass through properly. And (the rabbis) said one can repair them and clean them out . . . and unblock them. . . .[91]

It would appear that these commentators saw *kilkulei* as a wordplay on *cloacae* or *colliquia,* the Latin for sewer. Clearly, it was a public necessity to keep them clean, clear, and unblocked for the health and good spirits of the city folk.

Furthermore, in Y. Moed Katan 1.2, 80b, we read that:

> The *aira* (איירא) of Sepphoris was damaged on the midfestival and the students [of the academy] were of the opinion that it was permitted [to repair it, deriving their view] from here (i.e., the Mishnah cited above): ". . . and one may repair the *kilkulei ha-mayyim*. . . ."

Elsewhere I have shown[92] that the correct reading in this Yerushalmi text should be *amara* (אמרא, instead of איירא, with the two *yods* corrected to *mem*). *Amara* equals ἀμάρα—*cloaca,* sewer, as we learn from a medieval Greco-Latin glossary[93] and from Syriac.[94] This was probably a main "collector drain" that might well be served by a number of smaller branches running down side streets,[95] the most famous of which was the great *Cloaca Maxima* at Rome.[96]

We know a good deal about the water intake system of Sepphoris. The city had wells, canals, water cisterns, and reservoirs from which water was drawn by large wheels.[97] It also had many markets and local industries (see chapter 1). No doubt a great deal of waste was generated, much of which flowed through the main *amara* sewer. A blockage of such a sewer would cause the local inhabitants considerable discomfort and might as well constitute a health hazard. Hence the rabbis permitted its repair on the midfestival. Indeed, there were people whose job it was to keep these sewers constantly clear and unblocked. In Rabbinic sources such a person is called a *goref bivin,* a "scraper clean of sewers."[98] Diocletian's *Edict of Maximum Prices* (301 C.E.) fixes the daily wage of such a *cloacarius,* with maintenance at 24 denarii per day.[99]

Drains

There appear to be a number of terms referring to drains or parts of the drainage system. The term *ẓinor,* literally meaning "a pipe," usually is related to the problem of water drainage. At times it seems to be used to indicate a gutter and is thus synonymous with *marzev.*[100] But more frequently it refers to the pipe connected to the gutter along the edge of the roof, which, fixed with brackets to the wall, leads the rainwater down to the ground.[101] These drainage pipes ran downward close to the ground, and people at times drank rainwater from them.[102] Sometimes this pipe communicated with a large public drain, which ran along the street and was covered with a vaulted roof. In Y. Kilaim 9.1, 31d we read that one does not pour water on the Sabbath into a drain, 4 cubits [wide], covered with a vaulted cover, in the public domain[103]. . . . Pipes may not pour into it. The reason given is that people should not say: This man's [private] drainpipe pours water [into the public domain] on the Sabbath.[104]

Furthermore, in Y. Avodah Zarah 33,42a we are told that when Rabbi Yasa b. Ḥalfuta (Rabbi Yose [b. Ḥalafta] fl. late second century) died, the drains of Laodicea ran with blood, while in B. Sanhedrin 109a[105] it is related that when Rabbi Yose died, the gutters (*marzeivei*) of Sepphoris ran with blood.[106] That these unique phenomena were seen and noted indicates that they took place in a public area; hence, these drains were most likely in the main streets.

On occasion these drainage canals ran straight under a building blocking their path. This may well explain the passage in M. Oholot 3.7, in which we read of a vaulted drain running under a house.[107] They also sometimes ran under streets (as is shown by Schwartz in chapter 10). In Derech Ereẓ Rabba 3.3 (Masechtot Derech Ereẓ, ed. M. Higger, Brooklyn, 1935, pp. 159–60) we read in the name of Rabbi Eliezer

b. Jacob (second century C.E.) of a great palace (טרקלין, *triclinium*) with a tanner's canal going through it (ביב של בורסקי). The parallel in Kallah Rabbati 3.2, ed. Higger p. 302, has: It is like unto a king who built a beautiful palace (פלטורין, *palatium* or *praetorium*) and caused a river (i.e., canal: נהר) of tanners to pass through it. The stenchful water of the tannery passing through a beautiful palace is likened to fowl language in the mouth of a wise man. Since many wealthy Roman establishments had in the middle of the house an impluvium, with a marble fountain and jets of water frequently decorated with reliefs, several specimens of which have been found at Pompeii,[108] the point of this parable is even more cutting: instead of a beautiful pool with a gushing fountain, he placed a leather tanner's evil-smelling gutter channel in the center of his palace.

Many houses had storage (and drainage) cisterns under their ground floors built to catch the winter rains and store them through the summer seasons.[109] Some cisterns discharged their overflow into a public drain[110] through a drainpipe narrowing at its exit point.[111] Several courtyards with individual drains subsequently joined with one main drainage canal, probably at a junction on the street.[112] There was always a danger of flooding, which would damage the house and its contents,[113] and sometimes dogs, and certainly rats, crept into the house through these drains.[114]

The main drain of the city was called the *bubia de-medinta,* the city drain.[115] Often it was open and of considerable size, so much so that a citizen might fall in and hurt himself.[116] They required constant attention, and there were people whose entire job consisted of keeping the drains clear and unblocked. This task fell to a person called the *goref bivin,* the already noted "scraper clean of drains."[117]

Summary of the Sewage System

We have seen most elements of both sewage and drainage systems either mentioned directly or alluded to in Rabbinic sources. The resultant picture is very close to the one Trevor Hodge presents in his definitive summary:

> Rainwater was disposed of depending on where it fell. If it fell on a house, the roof . . . funnelled it into a cistern somewhere in the interior. In other words, the function of the roof on an ancient house (other than keeping the interior dry) was not so much to shed water as to collect it. A great deal of the rain falling on a town, therefore, never did get drained away. Indeed, it was kept. Rain falling on the streets and open places, on the other hand, found its own way down hill, following the lie of the land. It was joined by waste water thrown out of the houses and from any other source. . . . Where convenient or necessary through the city surface gutters on runnels would be provided to send the water in the right direction. . . . Buildings lying across its natural course, which could otherwise have acted as dams with water building

up behind them, in this way had it led round the sides [or in some cases according to Talmudic sources, it wound underneath them, D.S.]. Any kind of subterranean accommodation . . . required special treatment to stop them simply filling up. . . . In the streets, it was largely this surface water problem that led to the raised sidewalks so familiar from Pompeii and Herculaneum, with stepping stones (*pondera*) at the street corners to enable pedestrians to come from one side to the other without stepping down [see discussion in chapter 6, D.S.].

Where sewers were provided, the simplest form was an open ditch. . . . Even at Rome itself . . . at the height of the empire . . . a lot of the city still relied on open sewers down the middle of the streets; passers-by were often knocked into them for the fun of it by Nero, sallying forth incognito on one of his nocturnal escapades (Seutonius, Nero 2.6). . . . Pliny (Ep. 10.98) tells us that in Amastris in Bythnia, a city that he otherwise describes as elegant and beautiful, there was an open sewer running down the main street, which he is proposing to cover over. . . . The street drains would possibly discharge into a large central collector sewer. . . . In shape . . . the one in Cologne had a vaulted roof and is more or less the same proportions as an ordinary aqueduct conduit, though a lot larger. . . .

The last stage of drainage came when the drain with its cargo of rainwater, overflow, and assorted detritus reached the edge of the city. If the city was built on a river, as so many cities were, there was no further problem. The drain simply emptied into it, and its contents were washed away downstream, to find their way wither they would. . . . Cities with no convenient river fell back on other expedients for disposal . . . a method nowadays called "the soakage system." The main drain . . . divides, when it has left town, into a number of smaller channels, so that the waters which had first been collected together, again separate into little rivulets. They run along the little drains underground from some distance and then flow out into the lower-lying plains where they soak away. . . .[118]

The "soakage system" may possibly have been used by many Palestinian cities that had neither rivers, lakes, nor seas into which to drain their sewage. There may even be an oblique reference to this system in a parable cited in Y. Ḥagiga 2.1,77c and attributed to Rabbi Eleazar (d. ca. 280 C.E.):

It is like unto a king who built his palace on a site of sewers (*bivim* ביבים), on a site of dung deposits, on a place of putrid stenches. Someone who comes along and says, "This palace is [built] on a site of sewers, on a site of dung deposits, on a place of putrid stenches," is he not offensive?

Apparently, the king had not been able to find a free and unbuilt area within the city confines (walls?) and therefore had to locate his palace just outside the city. As is well-known, the municipal rubbish dumps were generally just outside the city,[119] and the stench and the putrifaction were great. It would seem that he chose a spot that was also on the confluence of several sewers that he hoped were meant to seep into the earth. However, in this particular case, the "soakage system" was singularly unsuccessful.

Notes

1. See the magnificent volume edited by D. Amit, Y. Hirschfeld, and J. Patrich, *The Aqueducts of Ancient Palestine: Collected Essays* (Jerusalem, 1989) [in Hebrew], pass. See also M. Hecker, "Water Supply of Jerusalem in Ancient Times," in *Sefer Yerushalayim,* ed. M. Avi-Yonah (Jerusalem, 1950), p. 219 et seq.; R. Amiran, "The Water Supply of Jerusalem," *Qadmoniot* 1 (1968): 13–18; and A. Mazar, "The Ancient Aqueducts of Jerusalem," *Qadmoniot,* vol. 19, no. 120 (1972): 120–25 All of these publications are in Hebrew.

2. See L. I. Levine, *Roman Caesarea: An Archeological-Topographical Study, Qedem* 1 (Jerusalem, 1971), pp. 30–36, for a fine summary with the relevant bibliography. In the later fourth century C.E. under the proconsulship of Fl[avius] Florentinus the two aqueducts—the high and the low one—were completely renovated. See Levine, *Roman Caesarea,* p. 31, and H. Hamburger, "A New Inscription from the Caesarea Aqueduct," *IEJ* 9 (1959): 189 et seq. Florentinus functioned 385 C.E. See S. Krauss, "Les Divisions Administratives de la Palestine à l'Epoque Romaine," *REJ* 46 (1903): 124, citing P. Von Rohden, *De Palaestina et Arabia provinciis Romanis quaestiones selectae* (Berlin, 1885), p. 47.

3. See the excellent and exhaustive work of A. Trevor Hodge, *Roman Aqueducts and Water Supply* (London, 1992), pass. and pp. 25, 100–102 for inspection shafts and manholes.

4. See Amit, Hirschfeld, and Patrich, *Aqueducts,* pp. 169–95.

5. On planning and surveying see Trevor Hodge, *Roman Aqueducts,* p. 172 et seq. The standard work on surveying is O. A. W. Dilkes, *The Roman Land Surveyors* (Newton Abbot, 1971).

6. Loeb translation by F. Granger, vol. 2, pp. 181–89.

7. Note that Pausanias 10.4 dismisses the claim of a town to be a *polis* because it had "no public buildings, no gymnasium, no theatres, no market place, *no water conducted to a fountain.*"

8. See Y. Hirschfeld, "Water Supply Networks in the Roman Baths at Hammat-Gader" [in Hebrew] in *Aqueducts,* pp. 141–55, and note in Z. S. Winogradov's article "The Ancient Aqueduct of Tiberias" [in Hebrew], pp. 123–32, the canal supplying the baths at Tiberias.

9. See Amit, Hirschfeld, and Patrich, *Aqueducts,* pp. 120–21, fig. 9, Caesarea; ibid., p. 139, Susita.

10. On the problem of air pressure, see Trevor Hodge, *Roman Aqueducts,* pp. 155, 241–45.

11. See Amit, Hirschfeld, and Patrich, *Aqueducts,* p. 128, on Tiberias; ibid., p. 139, on Susita. On pressure pipelines see Trevor Hodge, *Roman Aqueducts,* p. 108.

12. Trevor Hodge, *Roman Aqueducts,* pass., H. Plomner, *Vitruvius and Later Roman Building Manuals* (Cambridge, 1979). See also H. Fahlbusch, *Wasserversorgung in antiken Rom* (Wien and Munchen, 1983), based on Frontinus. In Amit, Hirschfeld, and Patrich, *Aqueducts,* pp. 29–45, passages from Vitruvius and Frontinus are given in Hebrew translations by Lea Di Segni.

13. See my articles "Meḥkarim be-Realia Talmudit 2, Kastelin," in *Sinai* 94

(1984): 233–36; "Meḥkarim be-Realia Talmudit 3, Talmi," ibid. 95 (1984): 174–78; and most recently my book *Material Culture in Ereẓ-Yisrael During the Talmudic Period* (Jerusalem 1993) [in Hebrew], pp. 29–37.

14. I have not rendered this passage literally, since the halachic details are too complex to be discussed here in full. I have, however, given, in an abbreviated manner, an accurate sense of the text. See below.

15. See Trevor Hodge, *Roman Aqueducts*, pp. 154–55.

16. See M. Mikvaot 4.3.

17. See Trevor Hodge, *Roman Aqueducts*, pp. 117, 420, n. 51, with examples from Samothrace and Pella and the relevant bibliography.

18. For a detailed analysis of this issue, see my article "Meḥkarim be-Realia Talmudit 3, Talmi," pp. 174–78, and in my *Material Culture*, pp. 33–37.

19. See T. Krauss and T. von Matt, *Pompeii and Herculaneum, The Living Cities of the Dead* (New York, 1973), p. 57, figures 63 and 64, and my *Material Culture*, p. 31–32.

20. בברכין and not בכרכין. See my discussions in "Meḥkarim be-Realia Talmudit 2, Kastelin; pp. 233–36, and in *Material Culture* pp. 29–32, contra S. Liebermann, *Tosefeth Rishonim*, vol. 4 (Jerusalem, 1939), pp. 16–17.

21. On the identification of Asia, see S. Klein, *Sefer ha-Yishuv*, vol. 1 (Jerusalem, 1939), pp. 122–23 s.v. עסיא = אסיא , that this place is Eẓion-Gever, present-day Eilath. Cf. ibid., p. 76, n. 8, and Klein, apud *Jacob Freimann Festschrift* (Berlin, 1937) [Hebrew section], pp. 116–27.

22. See W. Smith, W. Wayte, and G. E. Marindin, *A Dictionary of Greek and Roman Antiquities*, vol. 1 (London, 1891), pp. 154–56; Kubitschek, apud *PWRE* 3, no. 2 (1899): 58; C. Thierry, *Dictionnaire des antiquités Grècques et Romaines*, vol. 1, ed. Ch. Darenberg and E. Saglio (Paris, 1877–1919; reprint, Graz, 1969), pp. 936b–40a S.V. Castellum. See further J. C. Landels, *Engineering in the Ancient World* (Berkeley and Los Angeles, 1978), pp. 47–48.

23. Pliny 36.121, ed. Loeb, vol. 10, pp. 96–97, and see ibid., note 6.

24. Leviticus Rabba 19.2, ed Margulies, p. 418; parallels in Deuteronomy Rabba 8.3, Canticles Rabba 4.11, Midrash Proverbs 5.3.

25. See A. Reifenberg, *The Desert and the Sown: Rise and Fall of Agriculture in the Levant* (Jerusalem, 1955), p. 72.

26. Y. Avodah Zarah 3.2, 42c. See further the place name *Castella* (קסטלה), near Tyre, in the famous Reḥov inscription; Y. Sussmann, "Ketovet Hilchatit mi-Beit Shean," *Tarbiẓ*, 43 (1974): 88, 126–27, n. 263. Lieberman, "He'arah be-Tarbiẓ mem-heh," *Tarbiẓ* 45 (1976): 62–63, believes that this was a place named after its water tower (and has nothing to do with *castra*).

27. However, Z. S. Winogradov "The Ancient Aqueduct of Tiberias" [in Hebrew] in *Aqueducts*, p. 131, suggests identifying this *castellum* with the remains of a city water catchment in Tiberias.

28. A. Frova, *Caesarea Maritima* (Milan, 1959), p. 14 ff; Hirschfeld, *Aqueducts*, pp. 20, 27, n. 126.

29. See bibliography cited in note 1 and Trevor Hodge, "Aqueducts," in *Roman Public Buildings*, Exeter Studies in History No. 20, ed. I. M. Barton (Exeter, 1989), pp. 128–49; Trevor Hodge, *Roman Aqueducts*, and Amit, Hirschfeld, and Patrich, pass; *Aqueducts*, pp. 20–21.

30. ἀγωγός alone, without ὕδατος (water), in Just. Nov. 128.16 (pl.)

31. ἀγωγός ὕδατος. See Monumenti Ancyrani versio Graeca (Res Gestae Divi Augusti), ed. E. Diehl[3] (Bonn, 1918), 19.5 (pl.) (p1.).

32. Cf. Yalkut Shimoni sec. 742.

33. See editor's note 403, ibid.

34. P. 130.

35. Levine, *Roman Caesarea,* p. 30, n. 218.

36. Trevor Hodge, *Roman Aqueducts,* p. 133.

37. See M. Schwabe, "A Greek Inscription on a Water-Supply Installation in Southern Palestine [in Hebrew], *BJPES* 9 (1942): 89; B. Lifshitz, "Notes d'épigraphie grècque," *RB* 70 (1963): 255–59; and Levine, *Roman Caesarea,* pp. 30–31.

38. See H. Hamburger, "A New Inscription from the Caeserea Aqueduct," *EIJ* 9 (1959) 189; Levine, *Roman Caesarea,* pp. 30–31.

39. Choricius Gazaeus, *Bibliothecae Scriptorum,* p. 61 sec. 45, apud Levine, *Roman Caesarea,* pp. 30–31 (Levine's translation). Cf. Reifenberg, *The Desert,* p. 72.

40. See for example M. Moed Katan 1.2; cf. Y. Moed Katan 1.2, 80b, and see the discussion in this chapter on Sewers.

41. Parallel in Exodus Rabba 31.3.

42. See my *Greek and Latin in the Mishna, Talmud, and Midrashic Literature* (Jerusalem, 1982), p. 72, on the dialectic form of the word; and Ir Shai, "The Discussion of Water Installations and Aqueducts in Rabbinical Literature—Characteristics and Terminology." in *Aqueducts,* pp. 49, 54, n. 81–82. (Throughout I have used the Latin form *nymphaeum,* plural *nymphaea,* while the Rabbinic term is based on the Greek *nymphaion,* plural *numphaia.*)

43. See Ir Shai, "The Discussion of Water Installations and Aqueducts in Rabbinical Literature—Characteristics and Terminology." p. 139, Susita, pipe to *nymphaeum,* and his note on p. 139. See also G. J. Blidstein, "R. Yoḥanan, Idolatry and Public Privilege," *JSJ* (1975): 155–58.

44. Pliny, *Hist.* 36.121.

45. Trevor Hodge, *Roman Aqueducts,* pp. 8–9.

46. לכרכים = בכרכים. See S. Liebermann, *Ginze Kedem,* vol. 5 (Jerusalem, 1934), pp. 180–85; *Tosefeth Rishonim,* vol. 1 (Jerusalem, 1937), p. 204 (to line 4) on ל = ב. We are talking of *personae,* terra-cotta marble masks, as ornamental escapement for discharging water. See A. Rich, *A Dictionary of Roman and Greek Antiquities* (London, 1874), p. 495 s.v. persona 5. The Gaon, Rabbi Eliyahu of Wilna, emended ופרצוף הדקה in T. Kelim Baba Meẓia 1.10, p. 578, to read ופרצופין הכרכין, but this emendation has no basis in manuscripts or early testimonia.

47. Since the water, being publicly owned, is unaffected (see above).

48. See Y. Tsafrir, *Ereẓ-Yisrael from the Destruction of the Second Temple to the Muslim Conquest,* vol. 2 (Jerusalem, 1984), p. 78; ibid., pp. 76–80 on the *nymphaea* of Gerasa and Bostra.

49. See W. H. Stephens, *The New Testament in Pictures* (Cambridge, 1988), p. 96, n. 127.

50. Hirschfeld, *Aqueducts* "Water Supply Networks in the Roman Baths at Ḥammat Gader" [in Hebrew], pp. 144–45.

51. See A. Kohut, *Aruch Completum,* vol. 4 (Vienna, 1878) pp. 67b–68a s.v. טפף.

52. See S. Krauss, *Griechische und Lateinische Lehnwörter im Talmud, Midrasch und Targum,* vol. 2 [*LW*²] (Berlin, 1899; reprint Hildesheim, 1964), p. 358 s.v. ניטפאות, in Löw's correction, accepting Buber's note ad loc.; Kohut, *Aruch Completum,* vol. 4, p. 68, n. 15.

53. Cf. H. Jacobson's comments in his article, "Greco-Roman Light on Rabbinic Texts," in *Illinois Classical Studies* 5 (1980); 61, and see H. B. Rosén, *JSS* 8 (1963): 63.

54. See Buber, followed by Kohut, *Aruch Completum,* vol. 4, p. 24 s.v. טטפראות, suggesting τετράπυρος = τετράπυλος But Krauss, *LW*², p. 262b. s.v. טיטרפלין, does not accept this suggestion. Perhaps *tt[r]pra'ot,* with the common L>R interchange. See F. T. Gignac, *A Grammar of the Greek Papyri of the Roman and Byzantine Periods,* vol. 1, *Phonology* (Milano, 1975), pp. 103–106. The loss of an interconsonental *rho* is also frequently found in *koine* Greek. See ibid., pp. 107–8.

55. Reject Krauss, *LW*², p. 578b s.v. ריאטות, who suggests emending to דוכטאות *ductus* (?), and follow Kohut, *Aruch Completum,* vol. 8, addenda 18a. See also ibid., vol. 4, p. 68b s.v. טפף, citing a reading דיכטאות, and explaining it as δοχή [= δοχεῖον – receptacle]? It was this reading on which Krauss based his suggestion. At first I thought to emend ריאטות to ריאינות, from ῥιαινα = πηγή, λιβάς, cited in Hesychius, and meaning: spring, fount, stream source. For *tet* broken into *yod nun,* see Sperber, *A Dictionary of Greek and Latin Legal Terms in Rabbinic Literature* (Jerusalem, 1984), pp. 95, 146 (*nun vav = tet*). *Yod nun* = *tet* is much the same phenomenon. This would make good sense in terms of the question: *From* where would the water come? However, היכן עולים here must mean: *to* where will the water flow? Since the answer is: על תשע מאות, *on* nine hundred . . . , not *from* nine hundred, we cannot be speaking of streams. See also S. S. Miller, *JJS* 49/1 (1998): 51–66.

56. See R. Rabbinowicz, *Dikdukei Soferim* ad. loc., p. 238 for variant readings.

57. He had strong connections with Ereẓ Yisrael and learned Aggadic traditions in the name of Rabbi Yoḥanan from Rabbi Isaac (B. Taanit 5a, B. Sanhedrin 80b). He himself was a well-known aggadist (B. Berachot 23b).

58. He knew the word νύμφη; see B. Rosh Ha-Shanah 26a and my discussion in my *Greek and Latin,* pp. 69–70.

59. See A. Marmorstein, "Doro shel Rabbi Yoḥanan ve-'Otot ha-Mashiaḥ'," *Tarbiẓ* 3, no. 2 (1932): 161–80.

60. See R. MacMullen, *Enemies of the Roman Order* (Cambridge and London, 1966), pp. 117, 156–61, 333–35, n. 30–32, and my comment in *Yehudim ve-Yahadut bi-Yemei Bayyit Sheni, ha-Mishnah ve-ha-Talmud* (Jerusalem, 1993), pp. 245–246, and also in my "*Aluf Magdaliel:* Diocletian," chap. 19 in *Magic and Folklore in Rabbinic Literature* (Ramat-Gan, 1994), p. 130.

61. Trevor Hodge, *Roman Aqueducts,* pp. 165, 169.

62. Ibid., pp. 285–87. There is one such at Nîmes.

63. Y. Hirschfeld, "Water Supply Networks in the Roman Baths at Hammat-Gader" [in Hebrew] in *Aqueducts,* p. 150.

64. Ibid.

65. I have discussed this text in detail in my *Material Culture,* pp. 42–45, where I beg to differ slightly with Feliks' interpretation in his *Ha-Ḥaklaut be-Ereẓ-Yisrael bi-Tekufat ha-Mishnah ve-ha-Talmud* (Jerusalem and Tel Aviv, 1963), p. 344.

66. Trevor Hodge, *Roman Aqueducts,* pp. 249–50.

67. See Sperber, *Sefer ha-Razim,* ed. M. Margalioth (Jerusalem, 1966), p. 84.

68. See Y. Brand, *Klei Haḥeres be-Sifrut Hatalmud* (Jerusalem, 1953), pp. 378–80.

69. See commentators ad loc., and Ir Shai, "The Discussion of Water Installations," in *Aqueducts,* p. 53, n. 65.

70. T. Avodah Zarah 5.6, ed. Zuckermandel p. 469; B. Avodah Zarah 12ab; Ir Shai, *Aqueducts,* p. 53, n. 65. It is not altogether clear if these texts are talking of open gutters or closed pipes. The Greek word σωλήν bears both of these meanings. Since the *silon* apparently received its waters from an *amah,* an open channel (M. Shabbat 6.3, 4), it would seem we are dealing with a closed pipe. See also Y. Eruvin 10, 26b, which speaks of square-shaped *silons.* On open piping, see Trevor Hodge, *Roman Aqueducts,* pp. 315–16 and below.

71. T. Mikvaot 5.5 and cf. above. See Trevor Hodge, *Roman Aqueducts,* pp. 44, 117, 307–15, and Hirschfeld, *Aqueducts,* pp. 144–45, 152–53 on Ḥamat-Gader.

72. M. Kelim 2.3, T. Kelim Baba Kama 2.31.

73. On earthenware–terra-cotta pipes, see Trevor Hodge, *Roman Aqueducts,* pp. 111–13. On lead pipes, see above the passage cited from Vitruvius. He also discusses the medical danger of such a pipe system. See also Trevor Hodge, *Roman Aqueducts,* pp. 15, 307–15. On wood pipes see Trevor Hodge, *Roman Aqueducts,* pp. 109, 307–8. On bone pipes see M. Mikvaot 6.8, T. Mikvaot 5.5.

74. See Y. Brand, *Klei Haḥeres be-Sifrut ha-Talmud* (Jerusalem, 1953), p. 378.

75. See above our citation from Choricius of Gaza, and see J. Carcopino, *Daily Life in Ancient Rome* (Harmondsworth, 1956), p. 51.

76. This was true up to the twentieth century in Jerusalem and other cities (Safed).

77. See Trevor Hodge, *Roman Aqueducts,* pp. 315–16.

78. See T. Eruvin 10.3.

79. Ibid. These are not necessarily the optimal measurements. See Trevor Hodge, *Roman Aqueducts,* p. 225. These measurements are determined by the laws of Shabbat (*shiurim*). Cf. chapter 6 on street measurements in Rabbinic sources.

80. See Trevor Hodge, *Roman Aqueducts,* pp. 317–20 on junctions.

81. See M. Eruvin 8.7, T. Eruvin 6(8), 26, ed. Lieberman, p. 125; see Lieberman, *Tosefta ki-fshuṭah,* vol. 3 (New York, 1962), pp. 436–37 to lines 85–87. Cf. ibid., 6(8), 25, p. 125 on "the channel of water below the window," and ibid., p. 436 to lines 81–82. Lieberman believes that this refers to a smaller drain or ditch to carry off rainwater. Ostia possessed an aqueduct, municipal channels, and private conduits. See Carcopino, *Daily Life,* p. 50.

82. T. Eruvin 6(8), 26, ed. Lieberman, p. 126; cf. Lieberman, *Tosefta,* vol. 3, p. 437 to lines 92–93. See further S. Klein, *Ereẓ ha-Galil* (Jerusalem, 1967), p. 93 and p. 30 for an identification of this channel or aqueduct. See further, Zvika 20. Tsuk, "The Aqueducts to Sepphoris" [in Hebrew], in *Aqueducts,* pp. 101–108.

83. T. Eruvin 6(8), 25; see Ir Shai, *Aqueducts* p. 52, n. 42.

84. Amit, Hirschfeld, and Patrich, *Aqueducts,* p. 332.

85. See B. Baba Kama 6a; T. Baba Kama 2.6, ed. Zuckermandel, p. 348.

86. On agricultural manure, see Feliks, *Ha-Ḥaklaut,* pp. 91–115. There he discusses trade in manure (pp. 100–102) and different kinds of manure and their manufacture (pp. 102–6).

87. See Canticles Rabba 1.2; Exodus Rabba 31.11; Ecclesiastes Rabba 1.8.3: כורסוון לרבים—toilets for the people; and see S. Krauss, *Kadmoniyyot*

ha-Talmud, vol. 1, part 2, pp. 406–10. The public latrine appears frequently with the bathhouse בתי כסאות ובתי מרחצאות. However, on occasions the full term was abbreviated thus: בה"כ, or ב"כ (= בית הכסא, בית כסא, or in the plural), and the abbreviation was later mistakenly understood as בית הכנסת, בתי הכנסת, synagogue(s). For several amusing examples of this error, see R. Margaliot, *Meḥkarim be-Darkei ha-Talmud ve-Ḥidotav* (Jerusalem, 1967), pp. 27–28.

88. See Stephens, *New Testament World,* p. 101, including a picture of a limestone toilet seat at Tel al-Ajjul, now in the Rockefeller Museum, Jerusalem. See also Carcopino, *Daily Life,* p. 53, who describes the social aspects of the Roman *forica,* how people met, conversed, and exchanged invitations to dinner without embarrassment (Martial II, 77, 1–3) and how they were decorated with a lavishness that we would not expect. "All around the semi-circle or rectangle which it formed, water flowed continuously in little channels, in front of which a score or so seats were fixed. The seats were of marble, and the openings were framed by sculptured brackets in the form of dolphins, which served both as a support and a line of demarcation. Above the seats it was not unusual to see niches containing statues of gods or heroes, as on the Palatine, or an altar to Fortune, the goddess of health and happiness, as in Ostia; and not infrequently the room was cheered by the gay sound of a playing fountain as at Tingad. . . ."

89. Carcopino, *Daily Life,* p. 52.

90. Ibid.

91. Of course, these descriptions probably reflect their own contemporary scene.

92. D. Sperber, "The איירא > אמרא of Sepphoris" [in Hebrew], *Sidra* 8 (1992): 163–66, idem, *Material Culture,* pp. 14, 20.

93. Hermeneumata Monacenis, mid-twelfth century, apud *Corpus Glossariorum Latinarum,* vol. 3, ed. G. Goetz (Leipzig, 1892; reprint, Amsterdam, 1965), p. 196, line 56: *Amara clauaca.*

94. See C. Brockelmann, *Lexicon Syriacum,*[2] (Halis Saxonum, 1928), p. 27a s.v. אמארא.

95. See Trevor Hodge, *Roman Aqueducts,* p. 333.

96. Ibid.

97. See Klein, *Ereẓ ha-Galil,* p. 93; Tsuk, *Aqueducts,* pp. 101–8; and Ir Shai, *Aqueducts,* p. 47.

98. See Exodus Rabba 6.1. See also Aggadat Bereshit chapter 2, ed. Buber p. 4 (where Buber's interpretation of the problematic text is not convincing).

99. Edict of Diocletian 7.32, ed. E. S. Graser in *An Economic Survey of Ancient Rome,* vol. 5 of *Rome and Italy of the Empire,* ed. T. Frank (Baltimore, 1940), pp. 342–43.

100. Brand, *Klei Haḥeres,* p. 463.

101. Ibid.

102. T. Eruvin 9(6).23; M. Eruvin 10.6.

103. See T. Eruvin 9(6).18: ביב שהוא קמור ד' אמות ברשות הרבים. On the vaulted covers of some sewers, see Strabo (fl. ca. 60 B.C.E. to ca. 24 C.E.), *Geography* 5.3.8.

104. T. Eruvin 9(6).22.

105. = B. Moed Katan 1b.

106. On these two different traditions of the same event, or complementary ones, see A. Hyman, *Toldoth Tannaim Ve'Amoraim*[2], vol. 2, (Jerusalem, 1964), p. 713b (whose interpretation is questionable).

107. Cf. T. Ahilot 5.3. See also N. Avigad, "Excavations in the Jewish Quarter of the Old City" [in Hebrew], *Qadmoniot* 5, no. 3–4 (1972): 96, for a Roman underground drainage tunnel in Jerusalem.

108. See T. Shabbat 16.18, ed. Lieberman, p. 79 = T. Beẓa 2.10, ed. Lieberman p. 289, that sometimes the "triclinium" was heated, that is, the water in the impluvium was heated, and people bathed in it. See Lieberman, *Tosefta,* vol. 3, p. 277, to Shabbat 16.18 and vol. 5, p. 953, to Beẓa 2.10, and Krauss, *Kadmoniyyot ha-Talmud,* vol. 1, part 2, p. 438. The impluvium consists of a basin with water and is usually found in the atrium. See Varro, Res. rust. 1.13; Sen. Ep. 86; Salientes constanus in impluvium. See Darenberg at Saglio 1/1, s.v. atrium p. 132a.

109. See T. Eruvin 9.(6).26 . . . ביבין המקשטין תחת הבית vaulted drains under the houses and under the courtyards.

110. M. Ohalot 3.7; T. Ahilot 5.3: a vaulted drain under the house four handbreadths [deep] and at its exit it is four handbreadths. . . .

111. T. Ahilot 5.3.

112. See T. Baba Meẓia 11.20: Five courtyards use one *biv.*

113. T. Eruvin 11.10.

114. See Mechilta de-Rashbi to Exodus 12:30, ed. Epstein—Melamed, p. 29.

115. See Y. Taanit 4.5, 68d; Lamentations Rabba 2.2, ed. Buber p. 102; Y. Eruvin 5, 23c, where *ḥaviẓ,* ditch, also bears this meaning. On *bubia de-medinta* see my comment in *Greek and Latin,* p. 159. See further T. Ahilot 18.6 and Krauss, *Kadmoniyyot ha-Talmud,* vol. 1, part 2, p. 403, which speaks of drains connecting one area with another.

116. See Exodus Rabba 18.8.

117. See Krauss, *Kadmoniyyot ha-Talmud,* vol. 1, part 2, pp. 402–6.

118. Trevor Hodge, *Roman Aqueducts,* pp. 335–43. On open sewers and sewage disposal in general in antiquity, see L. Mumford, *The City in History* (Harmondsworth, 1966), pp. 249–53.

119. Mumford, *City,* pp. 249–353. See also B. Baba Kama 82b, Avot de-Rabbi Nathan 1, chapter 35, 526, ibid., 2, 39, 54a; S. Krauss, *Kadmoniyyot ha-Talmud,* vol. 1, part 1, pp. 94–95, 100–101.

10

Archeology and the City

Joshua J. Schwartz

The complexities of city life in the Roman period and the rich varieties of urban existence during that time have not always been revealed by the spade of the archeologist. Much mentioned in the literary sources of the time has not been uncovered in archeological excavations and even when perchance it has been, it has not always been correctly identified. In any case, the limitations of present-day research often make such identification all but impossible. For example, literary sources, both Jewish and non-Jewish, mention buildings or monuments in Late Roman period Caesarea. We know, however, very little about what this city or the buildings in it looked like.[1] Moreover, there are dozens of unidentified "public buildings" that have been uncovered in the course of archeological excavations that await some shred of additional information or keen analysis to determine or to corroborate their purpose or function. Thus, it would be the lucky archeologist who would discover and excavate a tavern (*kapelia*) or a prison, for instance, in one of the Roman-period cities of the Land of Israel. And even if by chance he did discover a structure that fulfilled one of these functions, it is doubtful that he would ever really be able to prove it.[2]

Moreover, Roman-period cities were built to accentuate the public aspects of city life, and this type of building did not always tell the full story of urban life. Interurban competition and the occasional economic windfall often resulted in spurts of public building activity of a monumental and elaborate nature. There was often more form than substance behind this type of building, and occasionally this form was more vain, sterile, and ostentatious than the actual life of the city.[3] The archeologist by nature, however, gravitates toward excavation of the grand. It is the public life of cities that archeologists try to reveal, and even this might be more fleeting than they are willing to admit. The more private aspects of urban existence often remain hidden or within the realm of the historian, not the archeologist.[4]

In spite of all this, however, it is impossible to fully understand city life without recourse to the physical remains of the city uncovered and studied by the archeologist. This chapter summarizes the major relevant archeological remains of the cities of the Land of Israel during the Roman period and provides a backdrop to the rich corpus of Rabbinic and Classical material on urban life presented earlier in this book.[5]

Urban Planning

Roman cities, including those in the Land of Israel, were supposed to be built in accordance with the principles of urban planning of the time. This was often easier said than done, and not every Roman city ended up looking like Thamugadi in North Africa, built by Trajan around 100 C.E., an almost perfect square, divided into insulae by crisscrossing streets, with some, like the *cardo, decumanus,* and a few others, colonnaded and with a civic center located at the intersection of the two main thoroughfares.[6] Many of the Roman-period cities of the Land of Israel were "built" in or on existing Hellenistic-period cities. Sometimes not too much changed. Thus, for instance, Roman-period Ashdod (Area A), at least up until the War of Destruction (66–70 C.E.), maintained the existing plan of the Hellenistic city, with an *agora* and with a number of streets dividing various residential areas into insulae.[7] Roman-period Gerasa, however, was apparently constructed on the western bank of Wadi Jerash, while the "old city" was on the eastern bank. Thus, the majority of the city may have been constructed anew, but the Temple of Zeus, for instance, constructed between 161 and 166 C.E. on an earlier structure of which nothing remains, still faces the older city on the other bank of this river.[8]

Roman planning in the East relied heavily upon visual impact: buildings and groups of buildings were arranged axially, and vistas were created by careful locations of buildings to embellish cities as well as to hide the unsightly.[9] Topographical considerations were also of great importance in planning a city. Thus, for instance, Wadi Jerash, mentioned above, effectively divided the valley in which the city is located into two parts, allowing for the construction of a new city, connected to the old one by a number of bridges.

Local topography, however, was not always so kind to orthogonal town planning considerations. Thus, for example, Naḥal Ḥarod and Naḥal Amal cut through Beit Shean. The city was also surrounded by hills and to the north Tel Iṣṭaba. There may have been massive Roman-period building in Beit Shean, as we will see later on, but topography severely limited opportunities for symmetry in Beit Shean town planning (see fig. 10.5).[10]

The same is true for Philadelphia. The hilly topography, as well as Wadi Amman, which divides the city in half, determined the nature of this Roman city. To the north was the acropolis with a temple, while in the valley to the south was the civic center. The wadi, and not the principles of town planning, determined to a great extent the orientation of the streets.[11] Similarly, the main street in the Roman city of Sebaste in Samaria did not even pass through the center of town located at the top of the acropolis but skirted the city to the south of the acropolis. Nor was there another main street that intersected this thoroughfare but rather a narrow alleyway ascending with stairs to the acropolis.[12]

This does not mean that there was no city planning in Roman-period Land of Israel. In spite of the problems regarding the street system of Sebaste, the city planners made sure that at least the acropolis, with forum, basilica, theater, and temple, should be built in accordance with accepted theory.[13] Likewise, the builders of Aelia Capitolina (= Jerusalem) constructed a large circular courtyard in front of Porta Neapolis (= the Damascus Gate) because the *cardo maximus* would have intersected the gate at too sharp an angle (see fig. 10.1).[14]

Sometimes an apparent lack of symmetry actually reflected a very high level of planning. For instance, the eastern and western parts of the northern gate complex of Gerasa were not symmetrical; the eastern section was much larger. This was because the road outside the gate intersected with the gate and the *cardo* that began there at a very sharp angle, a problem similar to the one that existed at Jerusalem. The asymmetrical gate complex actually solved the problem of perspective, and the traveler never realized that there even was a problem.[15]

Caesarea had a complex street system reflecting thoughtful planning in city construction[16] (see fig. 10.2). Major streets indicating a high level of planning have been uncovered in a number of other cities, such as Gerasa, which had two *decumani* as well as a *cardo maximus*.[17] Ashkelon had both a *cardo* and a *decumanus,* although they apparently intersected in a somewhat diagonal manner and not at a right angle.[18] Antipatris[19] and Tiberias[20] each had a *cardo,*[21] and archeological excavations have uncovered *decumani* in Gadara,[22] Abila,[23] and Hippus (Susita)[24] in the Decapolis. Neapolis had a major east-west thoroughfare that can be defined as a *decumanus.*[25] We shall, of course, have more to say on urban streets and their construction later on. For the moment, it is sufficient to cite these examples as proof of city planning in the Roman period.

Urban Security

If a city did not have the means to defend itself or to provide adequate security for its residents, then all planning could well turn out to be for nought. Greek cities always had walls, although they were not always constructed along the shortest perimeter. Roman cities also usually had walls, and this was particularly true in the provinces, where cities often had to face hostile forces. These walls, unlike their Greek counterparts, often reflected a much higher degree of planning and coordination with street grids, reflecting the Roman military spirit.[26]

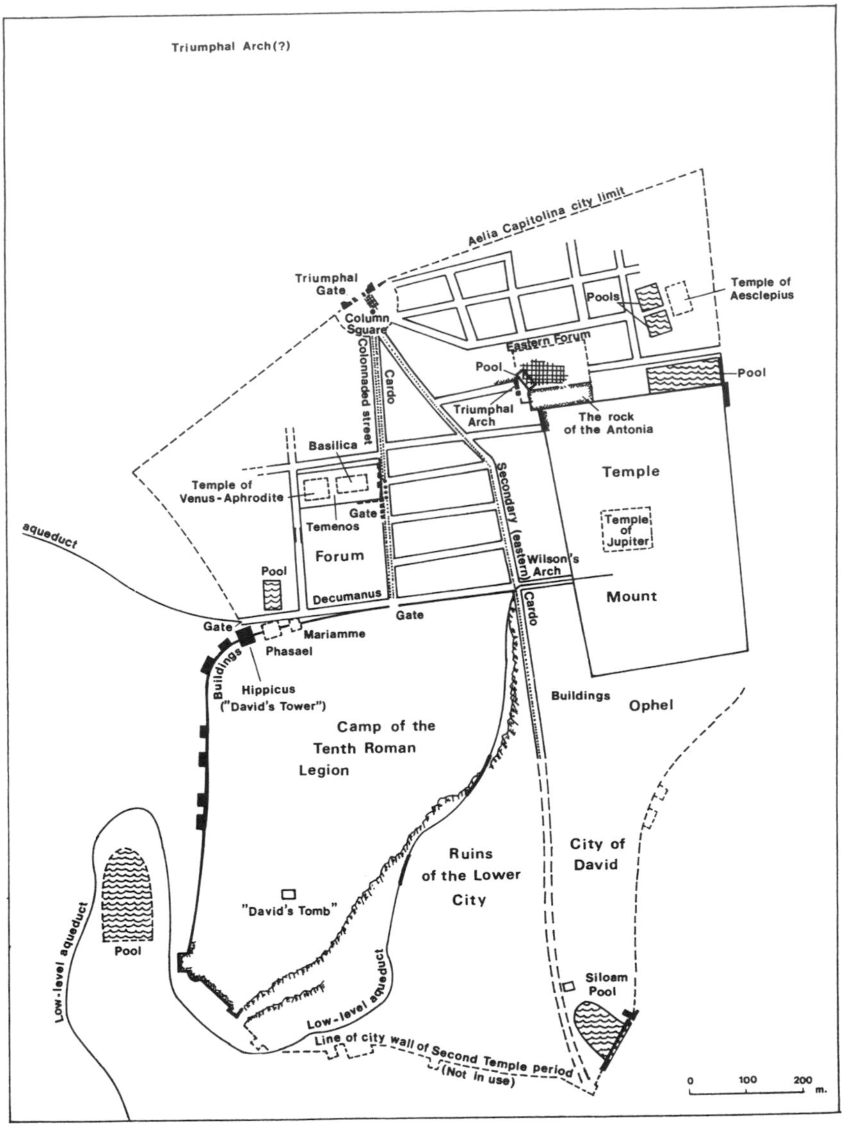

Figure 10.1 Jerusalem in the Roman period.

Walls were important, a sign of independence, and were usually expensive to build and maintain. They also reflected status and privilege, and therefore walls as well as gates could also be important public monuments. They also had economic significance, with markets and shops located in gate complexes or even in other sections of the wall.[27] Walls also served as the boundaries between the intra- and extramural parts of a city. Certain institutions or buildings that were clearly part of the city, such as cemeteries, ampitheaters, and types of industries, were

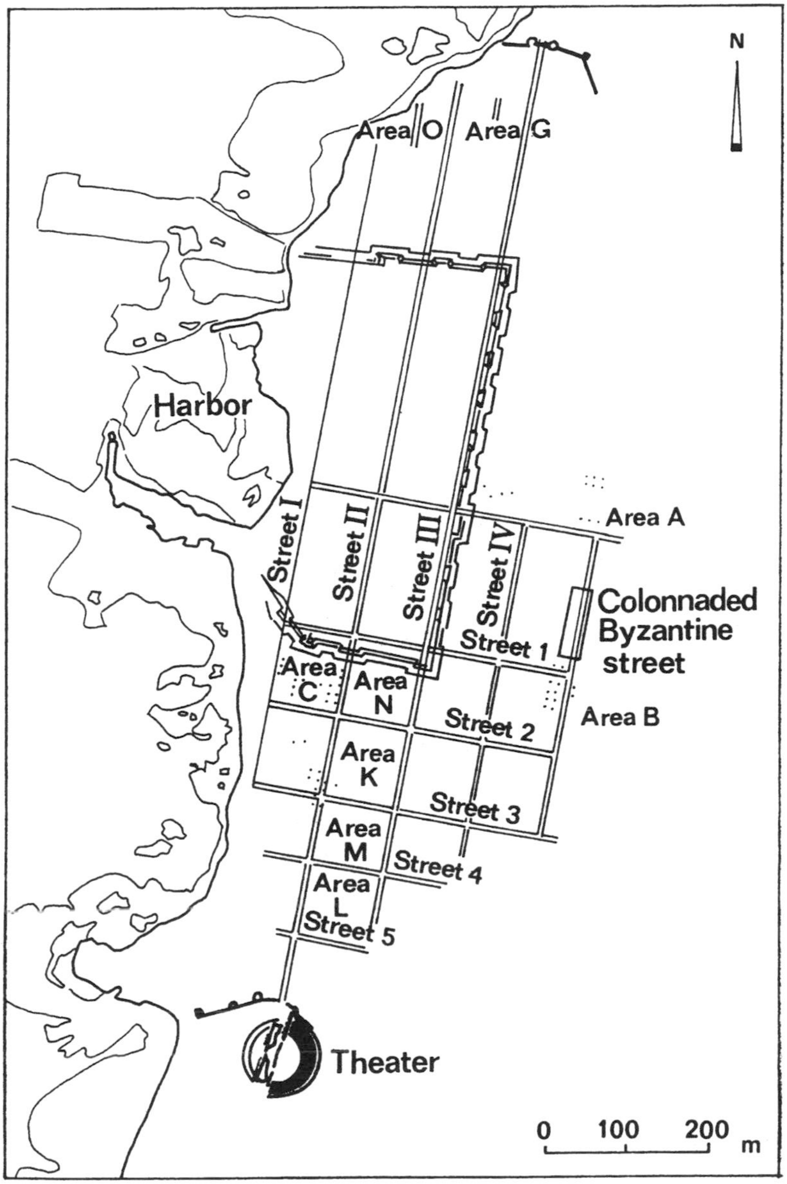

Figure 10.2 Streets of Caesarea in the Roman Byzantine period.

located outside the walls, even though they still belonged to the city. Suburbs of a successful city began to develop outside the city walls and eventually may have been incorporated into the city itself. This expansion sometimes resulted in new wall construction to include the suburbs, while the old wall surrounded the "ancient" city.[28]

In spite of the important functions of the walls and the status they imparted, not every Roman-period city had walls; this was especially true in periods of peace, such as the Pax Romana, or in other times of relative quiet.[29] Walls were expensive. If there were no security threats, the central government was not always willing to subsidize the costs involved, and many cities could not afford to build them. Thus, for example, archeologists have not discovered any signs of walls surrounding Roman-period Lod (Diospolis) or Beit Guvrin (Eleutheropolis), and the Madaba Map depicts Jamnia (Jabneh) and Azotus Paralius (Ashdod-Yam) without walls. Topographic considerations apparently made it impossible to construct a wall around Philadelphia.[30] In fact, even Aelia Capitolina did not have a wall from the time it was built after the Bar-Kochba War until some time in the early third century C.E.[31]

In spite of all these problems, if the city could afford to build the wall or find some other way to support its construction, then it certainly preferred to have this added aspect of security. Unfortunately for our purposes, though, walls do not always make very interesting archeology, and not many Roman-period walls of the Land of Israel have been excavated. Gates, however, are considered somewhat more interesting, and in addition to providing important information regarding urban planning, they are also helpful in understanding the history of the walls themselves.

One of the best examples of an urban wall is found in Gerasa. The city wall, about 3.5 km, was constructed from uniformly cut hewn stones and had 101 towers separated by distances ranging from 17 to 22 m. It was 3 m wide, and there were six gates, two of which, however, were "water gates." The course of the wall conformed closely to the contours of the surrounding topography and thus was not regular or orthogonal in plan.[32]

Other big Roman-period cities also had large or expansive walls; unfortunately, often not much of them remains. For example, the walls of Sebaste enclosed an area of 640 dunam. Little of these walls has survived. The city gate was in the west and was protected by two circular towers. The towers are dated to the Herodian period, their square bases to the Hellenistic period, and the walls between them to the third century C.E.[33]

The Madaba Map occasionally gives a good indication of the course of an ancient wall, but the remains have often been disappointing. This is the case, for example, regarding the walls of Neapolis, where only little has been discovered.[34] The same is true regarding Ascalon, although analysis of mortar taken from the Crusader Wall has shown that the walls of Roman-period Ascalon were rebuilt some time between 270 and 400 C.E.[35]

Three walls of Tiberias are mentioned in literary sources. One was built by Herod Antipas, the founder of the city, and this wall was later reenforced by Josephus. Another was built in the third century C.E. by Rabbi Judah Nesiah. The last one was built in the middle of the sixth century C.E. during the reign of Justinian.[36] The most prominent remains are from the latest wall and are beyond the purview of our discussion. Remains of an earlier wall can be seen along the eastern slope of Mt. Berenike. This wall may have been part of the one built by Rabbi Judah Nesiah, although it is possible that it was part of the original city wall of Tiberias.[37]

All of these walls undoubtedly had a large number of gates. At present, only one gate of Tiberias, the southern one, has been uncovered. Originally, when the city was founded, this gate with its circular towers was free-standing and not connected to the walls of the city. It served, perhaps, as a sign of the municipal boundary of Tiberias. Only later, during the Roman or Byzantine period, was the gate connected to the city walls and then became similar in structure to the gate at Sebaste[38] (see fig. 10.3).

A similar type of city wall gate apparently existed at Hippus. Remains of a round tower have been found at the eastern gate of that city. Although not much is known about this wall, perhaps it was already built during the Early Roman period and continued to exist throughout the rest of the Roman and Byzantine period.[39]

Round towers and a city wall gate have also been found at the northern section of Caesarea, which has traditionally been identified as Straton's Tower, and this entire complex was identified as Hellenistic. The walls, though, probably continued to exist during Roman times.[40] Somewhat to the south of these towers, in Section G, archeologists have uncovered approximately 9 m of an Early Roman wall built in a header-and-stretcher pattern.[41] A somewhat similar situation existed in Dor to the north. The Hellenistic-period wall continued to exist into the Early Roman period. By the Late Roman period, however, that city was unfortified[42] (see fig. 10.4).

Sections of the eastern and western towers of the northern gate to Roman-period Aelia Capitolina have also been uncovered. At first, the gate-and-tower complex served as a free-standing triumphalistic monument, and indeed there were no walls around Jerusalem when Aelia Capitolina was originally constructed. Later on toward the end of the third century C.E. when the city walls were rebuilt, the tower-and-gate complex was incorporated into the walls. Remains of the walls of that time have been found nearby in the area of the modern-day Damascus Gate and at a number of other spots in Jerusalem, such as at the Citadel[43] (see fig. 10.1).

City walls were not the only means of urban defense or security. Many cities also had an acropolis, a fortified strategic area within the city. The acropolis could, of course, contain many types of buildings, but it usually had a wall, fortifications, and a fortress. There were cities with both city walls and a fortified acropolis as well as cities lacking walls, for whatever reasons, but having an acropolis. Abila had walls and also a fortified acropolis.[44] The same was true of Sebaste, which as

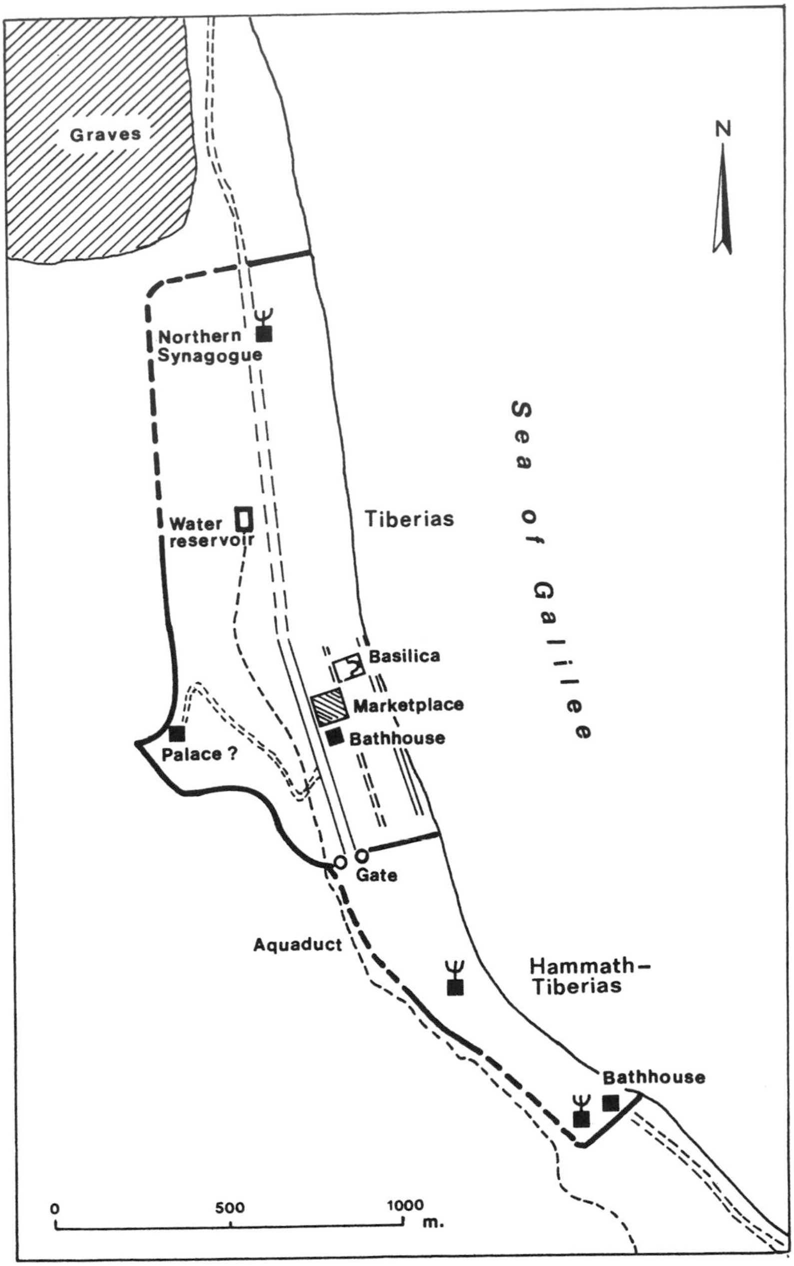

Figure 10.3 Tiberias: City plan.

a Roman city was unique in that it had a new acropolis, not the Hellenistic one with the round towers but rather the area of the temple of Agustus.[45] Philadelphia, however, had no city walls because of topographic difficulties; it did have a strong acropolis serving not only as a

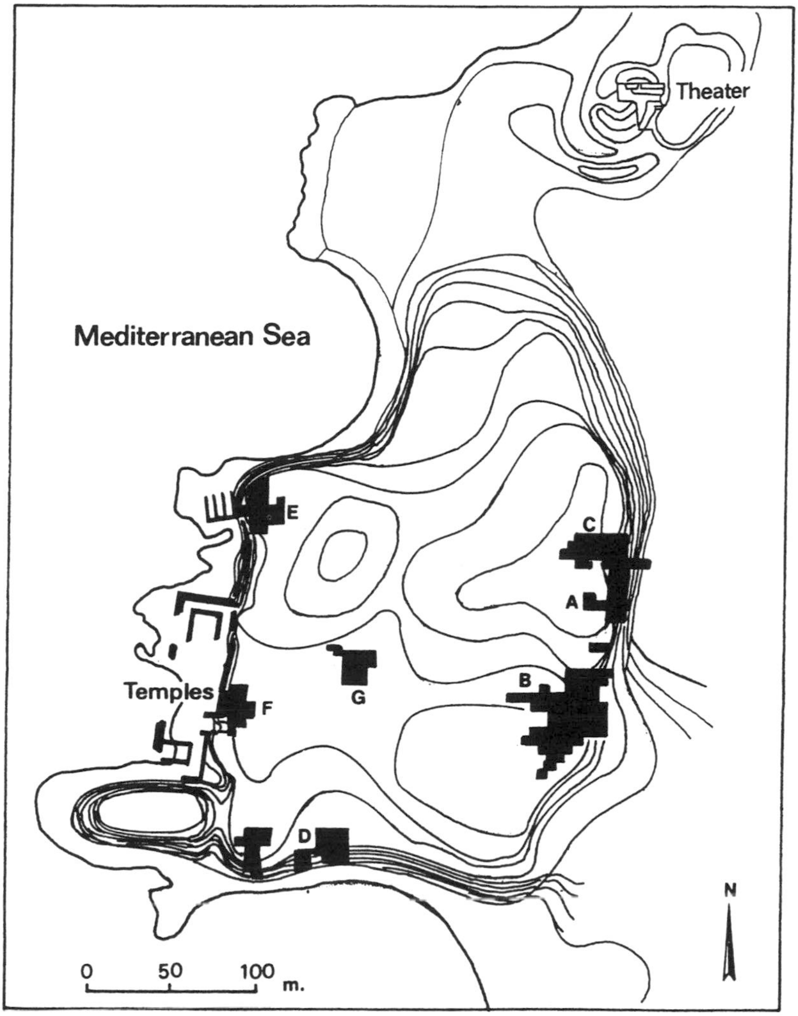

Figure 10.4 Tel Dor.

fortress but also as a religious center.[46] The Crusader-period fortress at the top of the hill on which Sepphoris is located was constructed on earlier remains, possibly a Roman-period fortress that may have also included some of the nearby buildings.[47]

City Center: Politics, Administration, and Economy

Having solved its problems of security, the city was able to grow and flourish, at least in theory. "Official" city life was tied to the city "center," often located in the geographic center of the city, but not necessarily so, particularly in those cities still drawing upon Greek or Hellenistic models of town planning. Also, it was not always easy in the ancient world to differentiate between matters of politics and economics and the market place, which, at least the main one, was usually located near the buildings connected with municipal administration.

The original model for the "city center," once again remembering that this need not be the geographic center, was the Greek agora, originally a large open space for political or economic assembly. As time went on, various public buildings would be built around the agora. The Roman version of all this, the forum, was a much more planned design and was often located at the intersection of the *cardo* and *decumanus*. There could, of course, be a number of fora in large cities. The forum usually contained an open square or plaza surrounded by porticoes and buildings such as the basilica, where the court usually met or where activities undertaken in the forum in good weather or during the day could take place at night or in bad weather. One could also find in the area of the forum the *bouleterion* (*curia*, or town hall), municipal archives, and a major temple. Around the forum were shops, markets, and offices; all of this eventually evolved into an enclosed area, linked to but independent of the street system.[48] We shall present the archeological material relevant to this section of the city and particularly that regarding matters of municipal administration and economy. We shall discuss religion and temples in a later section of this chapter, since temples can be found in many parts of the city and not just in the forum.

In spite of the importance of the buildings and institutions connected to the city center, few fora and basilicae have been discovered and excavated. However, increased archeological activity has been rapidly adding new remains to the old catalogue of such buildings.[49] It is important to point out that although the forum technically may have replaced the agora, in the Land of Israel the difference between these two institutions was not always pronounced. We shall first present, therefore, those remains that have been identified by scholars as associated with agorae followed by those connected or identified with fora.

We have already pointed out that Early Roman–period Ashdod continued to maintain the plan of the Hellenistic city, including an agora.[50] Roman-period Philadelphia had a large agora located in the lower city and to the north of the theater. To the south, west, and east it was surrounded by porticoes, while to the north there was the colonnaded street serving as the main thoroughfare of the city.

As previously mentioned, in spite of the importance of the forum and the buildings dependent on it or connected to it, not many fora have been discovered, and those that have been excavated have not been completely uncovered or understood. The classic examples of forum and basilica are those excavated at Sebaste. Between the acropolis of that city and the modern-day Arab village of Sebastiya was a Roman-period forum measuring 72.50 × 128 m. The forum was surrounded by roofed stoa. About a third of the columns have survived in situ. The final form of the forum dates to the third century C.E., but it undoubtedly existed in some form or fashion as early as the Hellenistic period. In the middle of the western wall was a passageway from the forum to the basilica. The basilica measured 68 m long and 32.60 m wide. At the eastern end of the basilica was a platform with a semicircular niche and four seats. Most of the visible remains date to the second century C.E., but the basilica itself undoubtedly dates to an earlier period, perhaps even to the times of Gabinius.[51]

A reevaluation of existing remains has added a new forum-basilica complex to our list. Some seventy years ago, J. Garstang and W. Phythian Adams discovered and excavated the remains of an impressive building in Ascalon, measuring some 110 m in length and 35 m in width. The excavators identified the building as a *bouleterion* constructed during Herodian times. The building consisted of a semicircular hall with tiers of seats, square rooms on the sides, a forecourt, and a large courtyard. A portico ringed the courtyard. The entrance to the apsidal hall was through columns carved in the form of Nike, goddess of victory, on one side and Isis and the infant Horus on the other. Unfortunately for Garstang's analysis, the statues have been dated to the third century C.E., disproving any Herodian attribution. Moreover, the building is today commonly identified as a small forum with a basilica. Surprisingly, this was also not the only basilica in Ascalon. Another basilica was found in the early nineteenth century somewhat to the north of the remains just described. Unfortunately, there is nothing to be seen of this basilica today.[52]

Apart from Sebaste and Ascalon, there are no other cities in which the entire forum-basilica complex has been discovered. There are a number of cities such as Dor[53] and Banias[54] in which both forum and basilica have been found, but they were located in different sections of their respective cities and not as part of one complex.

As we have already stated, major cities may have had more than one forum. This was certainly the case in Late Roman–period Aelia Capitolina. The eastern forum was located in the area of the present-day Monastery of the Sisters of Zion, and the western and major forum was located in the area of what would become the Church of the Holy Sepulcher[55] (see fig. 10.1). The Roman-period city of Gerasa had two and maybe even three fora.[56] Cities like Antipatris[57] and Pella[58] apparently had to make do with just one forum.

There are also a number of cities in which basilicae have been discovered. The basilica of Beit Shean was one of the first buildings constructed in the civic center of that city, apparently in the first century C.E. Located to the south of the tel and on the northeastern bank of Nahal Amal, the basilica was a large building with a northeastern-southwestern orientation. During the second century C.E. when the civic center was redesigned in light of new developments in the street system, the area of the basilica was somewhat curtailed, and the "major monument" was built there. By the fourth century C.E., the basilica no longer functioned[59] (see fig. 10.5).

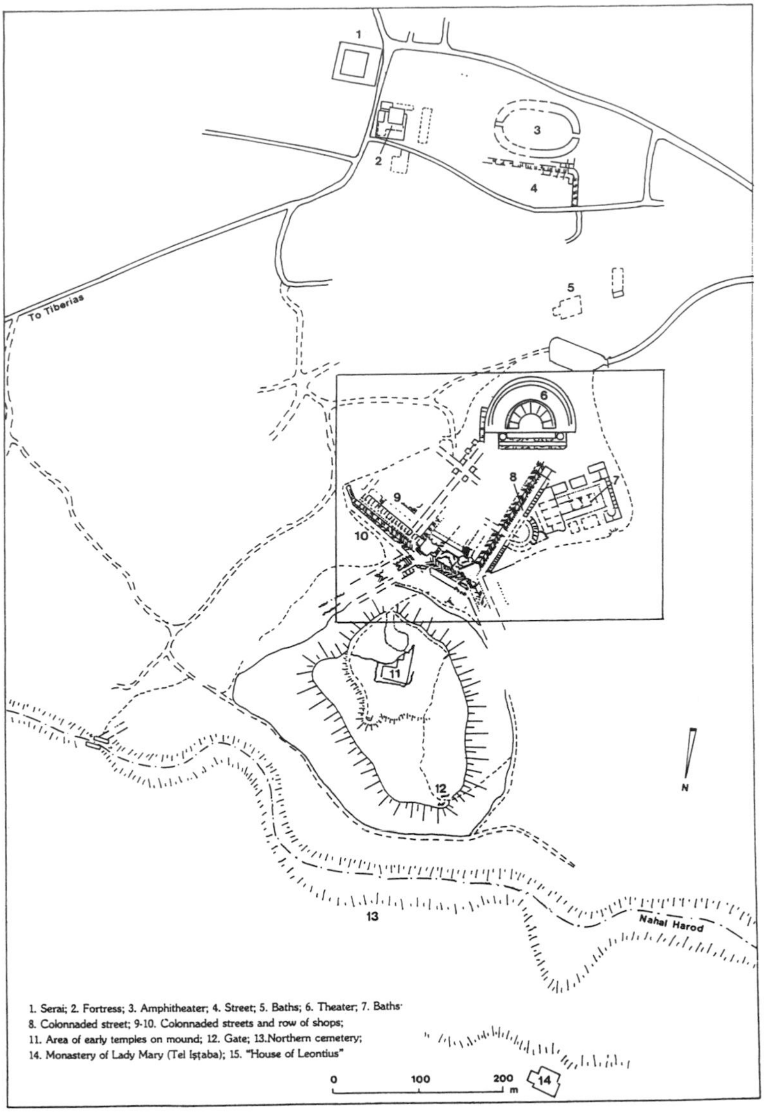

Figure 10.5 Beit-Shean. Key: 1. serai; 2. fortress; 3. amphitheater; 4. street; 5. baths; 6. theater; 7. baths; 8. colonnaded street; 9–10. colonnaded streets and row of shops; 11. area of early temples on mound; 12. Gate; 13. northern cemetery; 14. monastery of Lady Mary (Tel Istaba); 15. "House of Leontius."

A basilica was also found at Tiberias to the west of the highway leading into the modern-day city. This secular or civic basilica was apparently built in the second century C.E. and was part of a large complex surrounded by a wall and containing rooms, courtyards, and underground drainage systems in addition to the basilica building itself[60] (see fig. 10.3). Remains of a basilica have also been found in Beit Shearim, showing that Roman-period civic structures apparently also existed in smaller Jewish "cities."[61]

Another building often found in the forum-basilica complex was the *bouleterion,* or town hall. As was the case in the other civic structures already mentioned, not many Roman-period town halls have been discovered. In Beit Shean near the northeast corner of the bathhouse there are remains of a building that has been identified as either an *odeion* or *bouleterion,* although the tendency in scholarship today veers more toward classifying it as the former. In any event, there certainly was a *bouleterion* in Beit Shean because a recently discovered inscription there mentions a number of members of the *boule,* or town council.[62] It is also possible that a small unroofed building uncovered in Field C in Caesarea may have been a *bouleterion.*[63]

Shops and markets were also an integral part of the civic center,[64] although, of course, they could be located elsewhere. Sometimes they were planned in accordance with Hellenistic-Roman concepts of markets, and sometimes they were the result of "organic" growth and resembled latter-day oriental bazaars. Although it is not always easy to identify individual shops, markets and stores in the city center or in other important urban areas are usually easier to identify.

Part of the commercial center of Herodian Antipatris, along approximately 100 m of the *cardo,* was excavated by Moshe Kochavi, who uncovered stores lining both sides of the street. This area was apparently destroyed during the War of Destruction[65] and rebuilt during the Late Roman period but on a smaller scale: The *cardo* was expanded, and shops were built only on the western side of the street, since a large villa had been constructed on the eastern side of the *cardo.*[66]

There were also shops along some of the streets of Beit Shean (see fig. 10.5). For instance, the shops built along the western portico of Palladius Street were constructed as part of separate shopping complexes with individual stores. Two such complexes have been excavated. One of these, built in the fourth century, contained nine identical stores. These complexes also had a wooden gallery, or second story, supported by wooden pillars in the center of the store. The shops continued to exist into the Byzantine period, although some were damaged in that time by earthquakes.[67]

In Sebaste, as we have already noted, the main street did not pass through the civic center of forum and basilica but skirted the area to the south. This colonnaded street, dated to the third century C.E., has been described as an oriental-type bazaar street. It had shops on both sides and according to the excavators of the site, the shops on the southern side of the street had two stories, with perhaps the second story serving also as a residence.[68]

Sometimes it is quite clear that stores and markets were constructed within the framework of town planning. Thus, for instance, at the beginning of the fourth century, stores were constructed around the complex of the southern tetrapylon of Gerasa, "rounding out" the structure of that complex.[69] Perhaps this was also true for similar monuments, such as the tetrapylon in Antipatris that led into the forum.[70] In spite of attempts at planning, though, shopkeepers often displayed goods in the street and restricted passage of pedestrians.[71]

Religion

Temples were the center of religious life in the Roman city and were often built in the city center or in the acropolis. They could, however, also be located in different parts of the city. Whenever possible, the temple conformed to the general street orientation, but religious scrupples and peculiarities were often more important than town planning.[72] Generally, wherever it was located, the temple was constructed in such a manner to maintain a prominent place among the buildings of the city.

To create this air of prominence, height was of the essence. The temple was therefore usually built on a raised platform with steps leading to it. The courtyard and area of the altar were associated with most of the public cultic activities. The temple itself, home of the deity, was usually off-limits to the public.

There were, of course, many temples in the Roman-period cities of the Land of Israel. Unfortunately, once again, archeological remains, particularly in the Land of Israel west of the Jordan River, are not very numerous. Much of our information on urban Roman-period temples is dependent on literary sources or depictions on coins, two areas outside the purview of this survey. Thus, there were many pagan temples in Caesarea. The field of archeology, however, has not yet provided the physical evidence for this well-known fact.[73] Recent excavations, though, such as those in Beit Shean or in Banias, have uncovered new remains.

Not all in Beit Shean is "new." The square podium, columns, and capitals found on the tel, belonging to an Early Roman–period temple, were long evident and there was apparently a "holy way," a path that led from a gate at the foot of the tel to the temple on the top. Recent excavations have uncovered a new temple at the intersection of Palladius and Valley (הג'יא) Streets near the southern slopes of the tel. In front of the temple was a large courtyard paved with well-hewn stones. There were depressions in some of the stones in which to place small altars. An inscription on a base of a column mentions the Emperor Marcus Aurelius, during whose reign the temple was built. A series of monumental steps led to a peristyle with four large columns. From here there were additional steps to the temple itself. Only the foundations of the temple have survived. These were built on a podium supported by arches, some of which have also been discovered.[74] A number of altars with dedicatory inscriptions have also been found. These sometimes provide a clear indication of the existence of temples, even if their remains have not yet been found. Thus, altars dedicated to Dionysius and Serapis most likely were connected to temples of these gods.[75]

Recent excavations have also shed light on the cultic history of Banias or Paneas. The sacred cave-temple dedicated to Pan has long been known. Most recently, Z. Maoz claims to have found remains of the Temple of Augustus (Augusteum) mentioned in Josephus (Ant. 15.363) next to the Cave of Pan, making the two cultic sites really part of one religious center. There may also have been a Temple of Hadrian at that site.[76]

One of the most well-known temples was the Augusteum in Sebaste. Although there have been no new excavations there, the existing remains have been reexamined by scholars.[77] The temple was, as the name implies, built by Herod, although the remains belong to the Severan period of the third century. The temple itself was probably surrounded by columns on three of its four sides and was built at a distance from and higher than the temple forecourt. The forecourt was surrounded by double colonnades, typical of Herodian building projects, and the main entrance was probably in the north of the forecourt in the form of a stairway based on arches and reminiscent of the structure of the Temple Mount and winter palaces at Jericho. According to Dan Barag, the temple was part of a royal castle complex built by Herod.[78]

Sebaste had at least one other Roman-period temple. A temple dedicated to Kore was found on the northern slopes of the acropolis. As was the case regarding the Augusteum, the visible remains are Severan, although the temple was undoubtedly built long before then. Only the foundations remain today, but this is enough to determine that the plan of the temple was rectangular, measuring 15.5 × 36 m and within a colonnaded temenos measuring 45 × 48 m.[79]

As I mentioned earlier, most of the temples were built on a podium in order to accentuate their height vis-à-vis surrounding buildings. The usual practice was to start at courtyard level and to build up to create a podium, whether dirt filled or hollow and vaulted. In the Roman temple complex at Dor construction was different. Here the existing level of the tel was used as a podium floor; builders then cut and excavated around it to create the low courtyard and stairways leading to it. According to E. Stern, this was probably done to keep the temple structure level with the street and yet towering above the courtyard and harbor.[80]

Sometimes the relationship between temple and city was not always clear. We indicated previously that there was a Roman-period temple on Tel Beit Shean. There was, however, an additional one, as we also saw, in the center of the city below. The Roman city of Neapolis was located in the valley between Mt. Gerizim and Mt. Ebal. There was, however, a Roman-period temple on Tel a-Ras, located on a northern ridge of Mt. Gerizim. The temple was built during the period of Antoninus Pius and underwent renovations in the beginning of the third century and later again in the middle of the fourth century during the time of Julian the Apostate. In spite of the distance between this temple and the city of

Neapolis, the temple was apparently considered an integral part of the cult in that city. For instance, a large rock-cut stairway led from the city to the temple of Zeus, and the temple was a prominent motif on the coins of Neapolis.[81]

So far, we have discussed temples in the cities of the Land of Israel west of the Jordan River. Far more temples have survived in the area of the Decapolis. A good example is Gerasa. Three and possibly even four temples have been uncovered there. The first one was located in the southern part of the city and built in the first half of the first century C.E. On this same site some 120 years later a temple dedicated to Zeus was built. An extremely interesting feature of this temple is its orientation to the east, which is not in keeping with the town plan and street system of Gerasa. Some scholars have cited this as proof that the early Nabatean (?) city of Gerasa was on the eastern bank of the river that divides the walled settlement. A small temple, referred to as temple C, was found to the southwest of the church of Theodorus. This was, according to scholars, either a "shrine of a hero" or a Nabatean shrine. The most prominent temple was the one built in honor of Artemis, the patron goddess of the city. It took thirty years (150 to 80 C.E.) to build the magnificent 34,000 m^2 complex of this temple. In addition to the temple itself and its courtyard, a "processional road" led from the eastern part of the city over a bridge crossing the river and through a series of monumental stepped gates flanking both sides of the *cardo* and up again into the courtyard of the temple. This was undoubtedly the urban center of Gerasa.[82]

Leisure, Entertainment, and Culture

Roman-period cities often provided their inhabitants with opportunities for leisure-time activities. Many of these activities took place within the private house or residence and are beyond the purview of this study.[83] Other leisure-time activities, however, whether public entertainment or culture or both, took place in specific buildings or complexes constructed for the explicit purpose of providing a venue for such activities.[84] Bathhouses, theaters, ampitheaters, hippodromes, stadiums, and the like fall in this category. "Recreation" was also available in taverns and brothels.[85] Theoretically, the Romans might have considered all of these activities, or at least the "cultural" ones, to be a continuation of Greco-Hellenistic culture, but practically there was not much to be said for any degree of cultural continuity. The Romans did, however, spend time and money on making some of these structures architecturally impressive. This, though, was more often the case in Rome itself or its environs and not in the provinces.[86]

The location and the size of these buildings or complexes was dependent on the size and structure of the building and its relationship to the existing city as well as on available space. The limitation of available space as well as crowding and noise level may have resulted in some of these structures being built outside the city. Sometimes architectural developments also allowed for greater flexibility in the location of these structures. For instance, the Romans, unlike the Greeks, did not have to build their theaters in hollows. In any case, there was not always a great deal of logic in the choice of location for these structures or institutions, and sometimes they were just grouped together.[87]

Bathhouse

The bathhouse played an important role in the life of Roman-period cities.[88] In addition to obvious functional purposes related to bathing and hygiene, it served as a place of gathering, facilitating social and business intercourse. The Roman-period bathhouses uncovered in the Land of Israel have little in the way of architectural surprises, and they all contain the four standard rooms or units: *apodyterium* (dressing room), *tepidarium* (warm bath), *caldarium* (hot bath), and *frigidarium* (cold bath).[89]

The bathhouse discovered at the Roman-period city of Emmaus-Nicopolis confirms the rich literary evidence of baths and thermae in that city and in the general region.[90] The *caldarium, tepidarium,* and *frigidarium* were built along a straight line. The courtyard and *apodyterium* were apparently destroyed in one of the many earthquakes that wreaked havoc on the area. In fact, the original bathhouse, apparently built in the third century, was damaged during an earthquake and rebuilt along smaller lines with some of the rooms taking on new or different functions. For example, the original *tepidarium* became the *caldarium.* It is possible that there was also an additional room that served as an *unctorium,* or oiling room, or *sudatorium,* or sweating room.[91]

The bathhouse at Tiberias, located next to the *cardo* and market, was most likely the major bathhouse of that city and perhaps also one of those mentioned in Talmudic sources.[92] The bathhouse was constructed in the fourth century C.E. and was divided into two units. The western one had the various baths and the eastern one had the dressing rooms and halls for social gatherings. Mosaic floors were discovered in a number of rooms in the eastern section.[93] One fragmentary mosaic depicts different animals and birds. The mosaic is generally referred to as the "donkey mosaic" on account of the representation of two donkey heads found somewhat below the middle section. Another mosaic, found almost in its entirety, depicts fourteen different types of fish as well as numerous types of birds and fowl within different-shaped medallions. This mosaic undoubtedly reflects conditions around the Sea of Galilee, although it is not easy to identify the species depicted there. Underneath this room was a pool, whose exact purpose has not yet been determined.[94]

Other bathhouses have been found in such sites as Beit Shean,[95] Dor,[96] Acco,[97] Ḥamat Tiberias,[98] Gerasa,[99] and Pella.[100] The large bathhouse near the southwestern corner of the Temple Mount in Jerusalem and dating to the period of Aelia Capitolina and afterwards may have been for the use of Roman legionnaires.[101]

Theater

From the time of Herod and onward during the Roman period many theaters were built in the Land of Israel, both to the west of the Jordan River and in the Transjordan.[102] Theaters were built in Hellenistic-Roman cities, in Jewish cities, in Nabatean cities, and even in the countryside removed from cities. Most *poleis* had theaters, but if necessary, presentations could be put on in the agora or local palace. Theaters were constructed only in cities in which there was an interest in what would be presented; the inhabitants of pagan cities were not always interested. The theater did represent, though, the spirit of the *polis* and often epitomized local city patriotism. The theater served the city, and during most of the Roman period, it was the city and its inhabitants who had to pay for it.[103]

Roman-period theaters drew, of course, upon the traditions and architecture of Greco-Hellenistic theaters, but there were changes and developments. Roman-period theaters could be built on flat terrain and did not need to make use of the natural slopes of hills. Theaters in the Land of Israel, though, sometimes still made use of these slopes. Topographic features often saved time and money. The stage in Roman theaters was smaller than that in Greek ones, since the actors did not move around too much. The "orchestra," the circular area between the stage and the seats and benches, used by the Greek dancing chorus, was cut down to a semicircle and sometimes was used to seat important members of the audience.

The most prominent part of the theater was the *scaenae frons,* the decorated wall behind the stage which the audience looked at when not watching the action on the stage. The theater generally faced north or at least not toward the sun, and sometimes a curtain or velum was hung above the seats to provide additional shade.[104]

The first theaters in the Land of Israel were built during the reign of Herod. Two of the three, those in Jerusalem and Caesarea, were in cities. The theater in Jerusalem has never been found, although two "tickets" were discovered in the course of the excavations of the Upper City of Jerusalem. This theater is never heard from again after the time of Herod.[105]

The theater in Caesarea had a more successful history (see fig. 10.2). This theater was part of Herod's wide-ranging building plans for Caesarea, which included an ampitheater and hippodrome. The theater of Caesarea was located in the southern part of the city and apparently outside the walls of the Roman-period city. This theater did not face the north as was common, but rather it faced the sea to the west. The wall behind the stage must have been low, in keeping with Hellenistic building tradition, so as not to obscure the view of the audience. Only later, in the second century, was the *scaenae frons* built. Later on, apparently during the third century, the orchestra was filled with water and served as the cite for "water games." Such would be the fate of many theaters.[106]

It is not quite clear who built the theater at Sepphoris (see fig. 10.6).

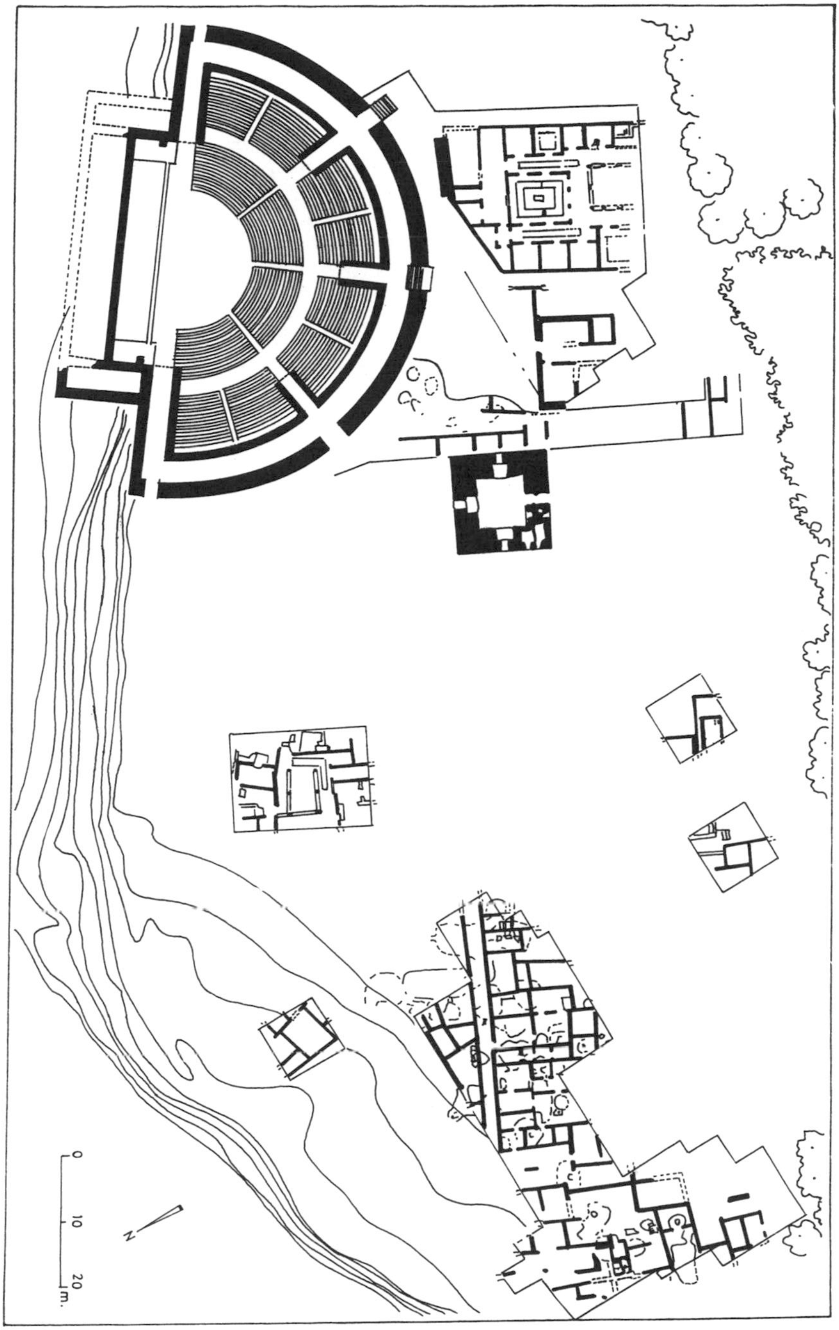

Figure 10.6 Sepphoris: Excavation.

Some scholars claim that it was built by Herod, but others believe that it was his son Herod Antipas who wished to give some Hellenistic flavor to one of his capital cities by building a theater. The theater of Sepphoris is located in the northern slope of the acropolis not far from the rest of the public or municipal buildings located on the acropolis a little bit to the south. The theater had room for about 4,000 spectators, but it is hard to know whether there were 4,000 people interested in what was taking place in the theater. The theater was destroyed either at the end of the Roman period or at the beginning of the Byzantine period.[107]

All of these theaters may have been built in cities, but they had little to do with the city. They were built by rulers to impress or prove their allegiace to Hellenistic culture. The theaters built later on in the Roman-period Land of Israel were, as I have written above, much more oriented to the needs and life of the cities, and they were indeed usually built by the cities and not rulers.

The first theaters built after the War of Destruction were in the Decapolis. The southern theater of Gerasa was built on the slope to the northeast of the temple of Zeus complex (or the earlier temple that was there) at the end of the first century C.E. It was not built with any inherent connection to the developing city plan, and some scholars see its proximity to the temple complex as reflecting perhaps the connection in the Nabatean world between theater and cult. The northern theater of Gerasa, however, built some seventy years later, fits in perfectly with the street network of the city and was located to the south of one of the *decumani* between one of the fora of the city and the Temple of Artemis.[108]

Most of the theaters in the Land of Israel west of the Jordan were built in the late second century or third century and particularly during the reign of the Severans. The city theaters built during this time include those found in Beit Shean, Sebaste, Dor, Shechem (Neapolis), and recently Tiberias.

There does not seem to be any general rule governing location of theaters. The theater in Beit Shean, the largest found so far in the Land of Israel to the west of the Jordan and capable of seating 8,000 spectators, was located in the city center.[109] The theater in Sebaste was located between the acropolis to the east and southeast and the forum to the west. The seats of the theater, or at least some of the rows, were chisled out of the slope of the acropolis.[110] The theater at Shechem (Neapolis) was built at the bottom of the northern slopes of Mt. Gerizim on the periphery of the Roman city. This theater is one of the largest discovered in the Land of Israel and was located along one of the major thoroughfares of Neapolis that passed near the city walls. In the first row of seats there are eleven inscriptions that mention the names of the "tribes" of the city.[111] The theater at Tiberias was located at the foot of Mt. Berenike between the slope of the mountain and the projected route of the major colonnaded street of the city, indicating undoubtedly some degree of planning regarding the site of the building.[112]

Odeion

Some cities had a smaller theater that was known as an *odeion,* although there were cities having both types of structures. Formally, the *odeion* was for musical performances, but in the provinces the size of the potential audience undoubtedly was of importance in determining whether a theater or *odeion* should be built.

One of the best preserved and excavated buildings of this type is found in the southern section of Late Roman period Antipatris. The *odeion,* however, was never completely finished. Thus, for example, it is clear that the *scaenae frons* which was to face the *cardo* was hardly built at all. The same was true for the orchestra and other parts of the building. The earthquake of 363 C.E. probably destroyed the building before it was completed. In any case, the lack of a real theater in this city and the existence of only an *odeion,* and an incomplete one at that, does not say much for the cultural level of Antipatris.[113]

An interesting combination of theater and *odeion* is found at Gerasa, where an *odeion* is located just to the east of the northern theater. Such a combination of the two institutions is unique in the eastern Mediterranean basin.[114] However, a somewhat similar phenomenon has been uncovered in the recent excavations at Beit Shean, in which an *odeion* has been discovered somewhat to the north of the theater.[115]

Stadium

The stadium, used for athletic contests, began to loose its importance during the Roman period. The best example is the stadium built by Herod in the northeastern section of Sebaste and renovated during the third century. The stadium was apparently connected with the local cult of Kore.[116]

Amphitheater

Amphitheaters provided entertainment and "blood" for the masses. Gladiators fought other gladiators, hapless prisoners, or wild beasts. This type of entertainment was incongruous with the mores of the East in general and thus not many amphitheaters have been discovered in the Land of Israel. Moreover, in keeping with the general trend regarding these types of buildings in the East, they were not always used for their original or stated purpose even when they did exist.

In the nineteenth century, members of the Survey of Western Palestine team identified in Beit Shean what they considered to be a hippodrome. The structure, however, disappeared. The modern-day excavations of Beit Shean, however, uncovered the building again, showing it to be an amphitheater, probably dating to the Roman period. The amphitheater was located at the southern border of the city, far from the city center. The amphitheater is somewhat unique. Most amphitheaters are, of course, elliptical. This amphitheater is rectangular with rounded corners in the east, west, and south.[117]

An amphitheater has also been discovered in Neapolis.[118] This ampitheater too is somewhat unique. It was built in the second half of the third century next to a hippodrome that apparently ceased to function a short time before that time. Indeed, many of the stones used in the construction of the building were taken from that now defunct hippodrome. The excavator, Y. Magen, claims that the amphitheater, located in his opinion outside the walls of the city, was built when Neapolis became a *colonia* and Roman soldiers were stationed there. Additional amphitheaters have also been discovered in Beit Guvrin[119] and in Caearea.[120]

Hippodrome

During the Roman period, the hippodrome, or circus, had to compete with the other types of buildings for the hearts and attention of the masses. Later on, during the Byzantine period, as the theater and amphitheater became less popular or were even closed, the chariot races at the hippodrome became the most popular source of public entertainment. Ironically, most archeological evidence relates to the Roman period, while literary sources refer, for the most part, to the Byzantine period.[121]

There was a large hippodrome (450 × 80 m) in Caesarea that was originally thought to have been built during the Herodian period and was clearly outside the walls of Herodian-period Caesarea, although it may have been within the walls of the Late Roman–period city and was within the walls of the Byzantine city. An obelisk, meta cones, and other remains have been discovered there. Unfortunately, the chronology of the structure is not clear. Recently, however, a Herodian period hippodrome has been discovered along the coast next to the amphitheater.[122]

A hippodrome was also discovered in Neapolis, at the foot of Mt. Ebal and along a main road that ran at the base of that mountain. The hippodrome was apparently outside the walls of Roman-period Neapolis. It continued to exist until the beginning of the third century and, as we saw above, was later replaced by an ampitheater.[123] This was not the only hippodrome that was retired or replaced by another type of building. The small hippodrome at Gerasa, located to the south of the walls of the city but near the triumphal arch built in the time of Hadrian and along the main route to Philadelphia, was replaced by a pottery factory (!) some time in the fourth century.[124]

Industrial Areas

Not all the economic activity of the city took place in shops or markets situated near the city center. Much of urban industry, for instance, was relegated to locations outside the walls of the city. Whether this represented incipient sensitivity to matters of urban ecology or just plain common sense is difficult to determine. In any case, not much in terms of urban industry has been discovered by archeologists, although literary sources, beyond the purview of our discussion, do mention various types of industries and factories in cities.

Near the basilica in Beit Shean, archeologists have discovered a pool and the remains of industrial installations that were perhaps related to the dyeing or linen industry, for which Beit Shean was famous.[125] Furnaces for the production of glassware and industrial installations connected with that industry have been found in Acco.[126] Dyeing installations have been found to the west and underneath the synagogue complex at Maiumas Gaza.[127] Other industrial installations have been found in a few other cities, but there is hardly anything unique about them.

Harbors

Location often made the city, and a coastal city had the potential to become part of an international trade network. This, of course, depended on the existence of physical conditions allowing for the construction and development of those structures necessary to fulfill and implement the advantages of a good location. It also often depended on the willingness of the government, at whatever level was required, to make the necessary financial investments. The best example of this was the construction of the Herodian harbor at Caesarea[128] (see fig. 10.7).

The harbor of Herod did not, of course, represent the first attempt to sail the Mediterranean from the Land of Israel. Remains of a wharf have been found north of the "Crusader City" and opposite what was the pre-Herodian Straton's Tower. The water opposite the quay was apparently deep enough only for very small boats to moor alongside it. The small harbor, protected from the waves by the natural contours of the bay, was apparently large enough for a dozen or so ships. This was not what Herod had in mind.

The Herodian harbor is actually three harbors. The internal one may have originally been part of the pre-Herodian harbor of Straton's Tower. The middle harbor was essentially the natural bay and was protected by the protruding cliffs along the north and south. The external harbor enclosed a considerable area of open sea and was created through the construction of two breakwaters, a large one to the south and west and a somewhat smaller one to the north. These protected the harbor from the tempestuous sea, and this was the real contribution of Herod's building effort here (fig. 10.8).

Along the inside of this external harbor there were quays, allowing for the mooring of ships and the loading and unloading of merchandise. Foundation stones of this part of the harbor have been discovered, indicating that the platforms here were 10 to 12 m wide. The middle harbor was smaller, with a series of quays to moor ships being serviced. There was also a system of underwater doors to control and increase the flow of water into the harbor channels. The purpose of

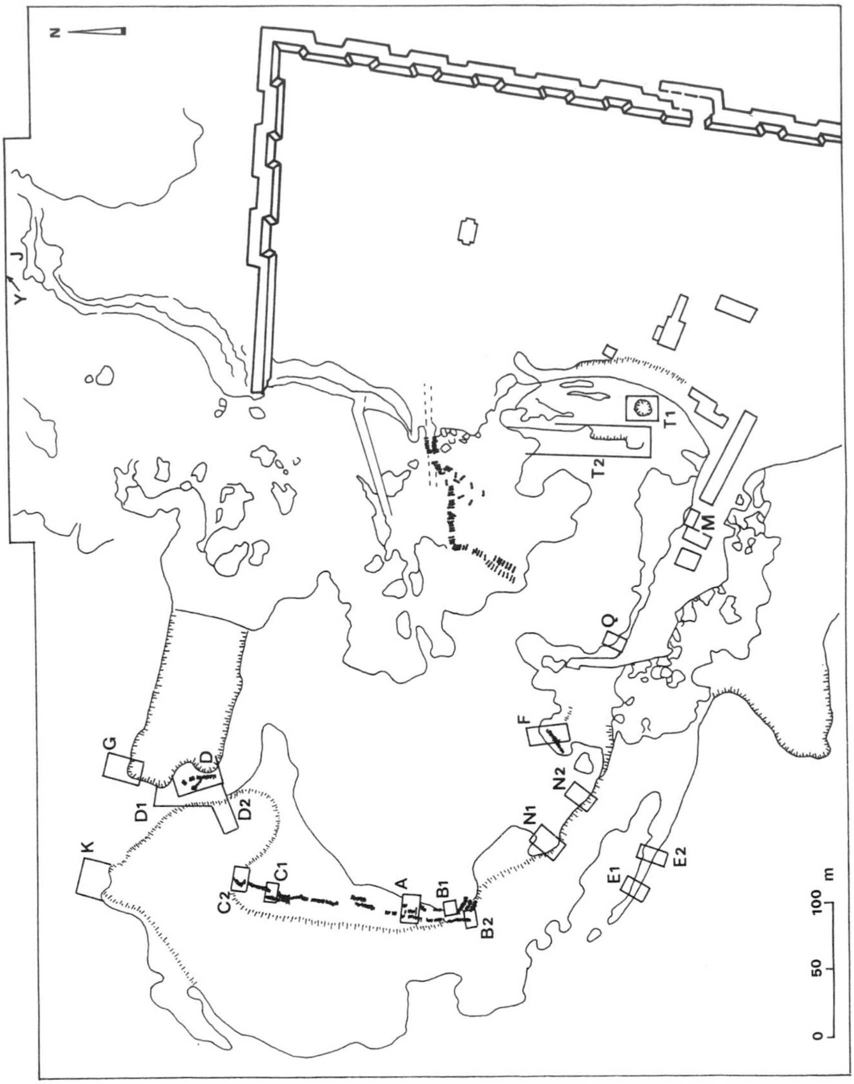

Figure 10.7 Herodian harbor of Caesarea.

this system was to remove silt and sand from the harbor. The internal harbor had a series of warehouses, the remains of which were discovered in excavations during the 1960s and which can be seen today in the Crusader City.

The magnificent Herodian harbor with its breakwaters, however, did not survive that long. By the Late Roman period, the Herodian breakwaters had sunk, making it too dangerous and indeed even impossible to use the harbor areas immediately to the east. It was at this time

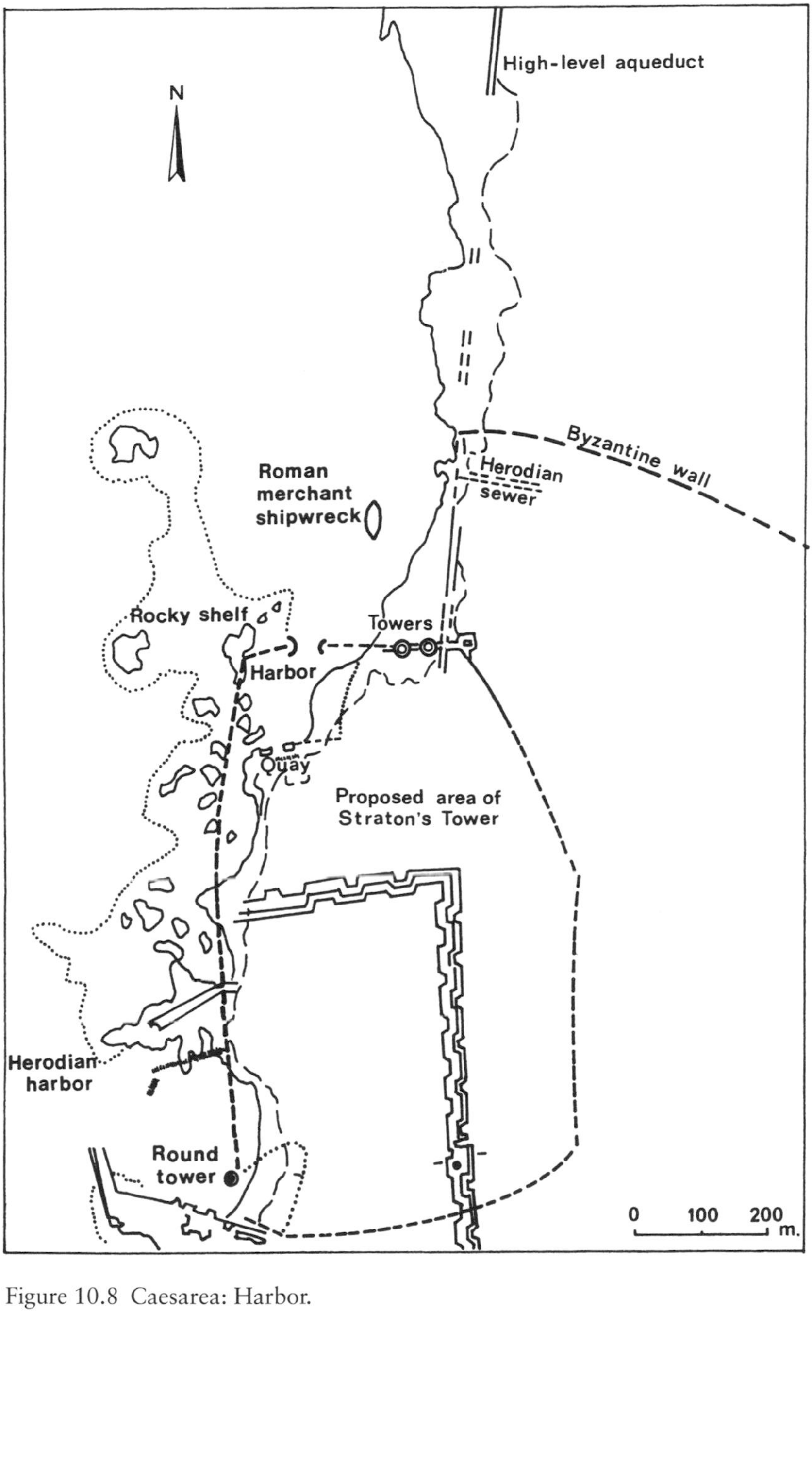

Figure 10.8 Caesarea: Harbor.

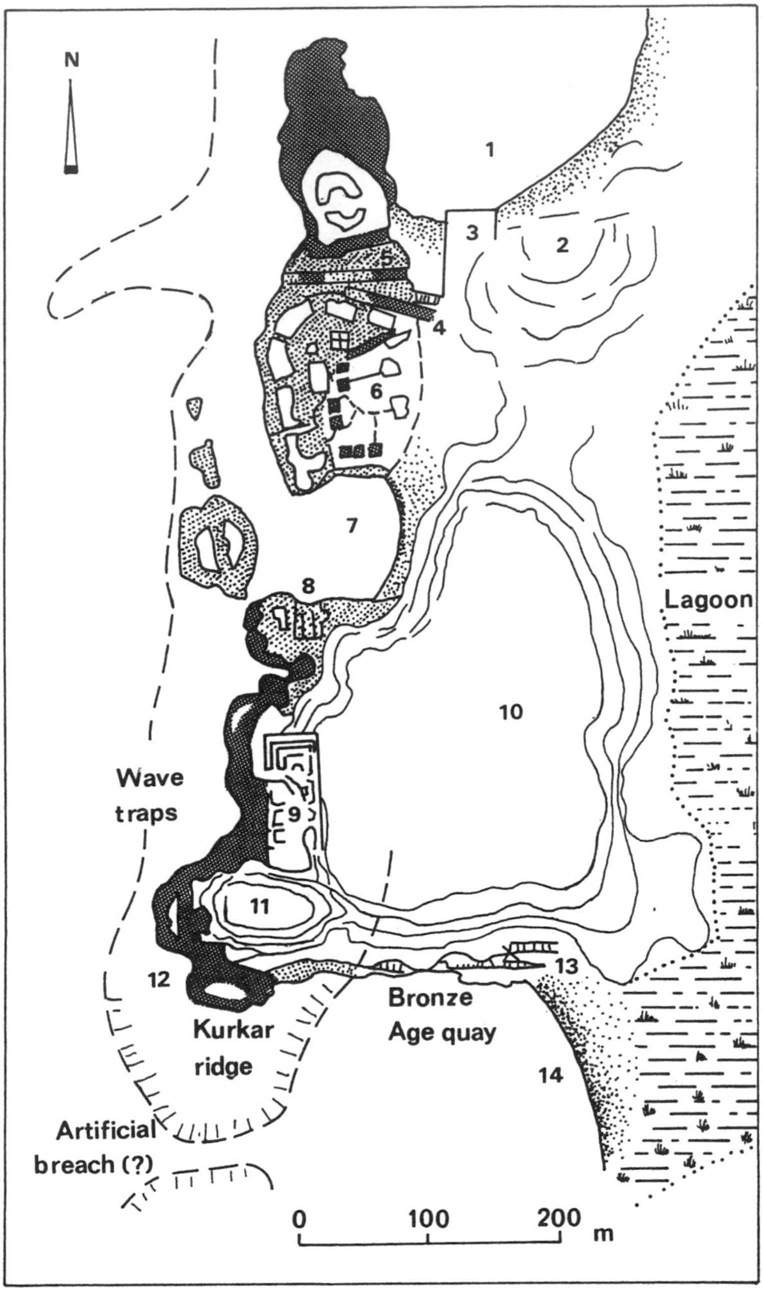

Figure 10.9 Tel Dor: Maritime installation.

that the bay to the south may have been used; the storehouses found along the coast here probably date to this time.

Caesarea was not the only coastal city with a harbor or port.[129] Nearby to the north was the city of Dor, which also had a harbor (fig. 10.9). It is difficult to imagine, though, that the harbor here could have functioned successfully while the Herodian harbor at Caesarea still thrived. The basic assumption among scholars is that these harbors flourished consecutively.[130] There were severe problems of silt accumulation in the northern harbor of Dor during the first centuries of the Roman era, making it difficult if not impossible to use. By the third century, though, a number of factors, some natural, such as the accumulation of large stones serving as a type of breakwater, as well as the construction of a new channel to wash out the silt, rendered the area usable again as a harbor. This, of course, was the time when the harbor in Caesarea suffered a decline.[131]

The harbor in Acco, located from the Persian period and onwards at the place where the present-day harbor is found, was apparently renovated during the first century C.E. The harbor in Caesarea, located after all in a different province, did not cause the decline or closure of the port in Acco. Interestingly enough, as yet, no remains have been found of the harbor in Acco from the Late Roman period (or later on during the Byzantine period), at which time the port of Dor, located like Acco in Phoenicia, was coming back to life.[132]

As mentioned earlier, most other Roman-period coastal cities had some sort of harbor, port, anchorage, quay, or the like, the size and sophistication of which usually depending on local coastal topography. The archeological remains, however, are not always that clear. For example, along the coast of Apollonia it is possible to see remains of walls jutting out from the beach rock. These were remains, according to some scholars, of buildings connected in some manner to the loading and unloading of merchandise from the natural bay of Apollonia. It is, of course, impossible at the moment to prove this, and the dating of these remains to the Roman period is not certain.[133] The situation is similar in Yavneh-Yam (Maḥoza de-Yamniya) in which the possible remains of the Hellenistic harbor have been found, but no remains of the Roman harbor have been discovered, in spite of some "circumstantial evidence" as well as a number of literary references.[134] The same is also true in Ascalon.[135]

Harbors existed not only in the coastal cities along the Mediterranean but also in some of the cities located on the Sea of Galilee. The best example of such a city harbor is found at Tiberias, or to be more exact, at Ḥamat Tiberias.[136] The harbor of Tiberias and the general region was the most important harbor along the Sea of Galilee, although in actuality it was more of a series of anchorages, with a pier and breakwater at which fisherman could moor their boats. The columns on the shore are remains from a building probably dating to the Muslim-period harbor and thus are not relevant to our discussion.

Streets

Ultimately, the individual as well as the combined function of the component parts of the city was determined by location and accessibility, the latter being influenced to a great extent by the local street network. We began our survey with issues of city planning and saw how major streets and street networks often reflected principles of urban development and planning. We also saw how streets and thoroughfares developed "organically," usually to solve immediate urban problems on an ad hoc basis. Building the street was alone not sufficient; making repairs and maintaining it were also required. Without regular maintenance, the best planned street could hardly fulfill its purpose. We shall now examine some of the physical elements connected with Roman-period urban street systems. As we shall see, a great deal of information has been added to our knowledge by recent excavations. Needless to say, we shall not mention every single Roman-period urban street.

Excavations in Beit Shean have uncovered a number of streets, some of which we have already mentioned (see fig. 10.5). One such street, called Palladius Street by the excavators of the site on account of an inscription found there, ran for 180 m.[137] The street was built in the middle of the fourth century and thus can be included in our discussion. It was paved with large basalt stones, as were the rest of the streets uncovered in Beit Shean, which were placed at an angle to the direction of the street, as was common at this time.[138] Underneath the center of the street was a deep drainage channel; other channels fed into this one. The stones over this central part were somewhat gabled, causing a slight incline from the center to the sides.

The width of the street varied from 7.20 to 7.50 m.[139] On the northwest was a raised stylobate upon which were columns that supported a roofed stoa. Pedestrians reached the stoa by climbing stairs placed along the street at regular intervals.[140] Behind the stoa were shops. The respective widths of the stoa and shop complex were almost identical, indicating a high degree of planning.[141]

Another street in Beit Shean was "Valley Street" (הגיא), which ran from the central monument to the northwest part of the city and was apparently constructed in the second century C.E.[142] The basic plan of this street was similar to that of Palladius Street, with stylobate, stoa, and shops. The street was extremely wide. The width of the entire complex without the shops was 23.50 m, while that of the open street, between the stylobates on both sides of the street, was 11.5 m. As on Palladius Street, there was a system of drainage channels leading to and under the street.

Another good example of a Roman-period city street was uncovered in Jerusalem (Aelia Capitolina) on Notsrim Street.[143] The large, elongated stones of the street were striated along their width, apparently to help pedestrians and animals avoid slipping and falling on the stones. Similar types of stones were found in the area of the forum in Aelia Capitolina, located today in the Monastery of the Sisters of Zion.

The physical construction of streets was influenced by local topography and geology. This, for instance, explains the basalt stones in Beit Shean and Tiberias or the limestone in Jerusalem. In Dor, near the sea, one could find a cobbled stone courtyard as well as a seashell-paved walkway as part of the same street complex.[144]

Sometimes, the original plan of a street proved to be unsuccessful. For example, the original Roman-period street in Antipatris had deep depressions in the street in front of the stores, probably so that large jugs or jars could be placed in them. This may have been convenient for shopkeepers, but it probably just caused clutter and accidents. When the street was rebuilt in the Late Roman period, these depressions were eliminated, and the street was thus effectively widened.[145]

Water

Water was not just a matter of drinking but was an essential civic amenity. The general health and happiness of the city population depended on a constant supply of water, whether for private or for public use. The obligation to supply water also often offered the cities another opportunity to engage in elaborate construction projects, supplying water at ornate and sometimes even at magnificent fountains. A constant supply of water was also necessary for less aesthetic purposes such as drainage and the removal of sewage.[146]

The cities of Roman-period Land of Israel, like most cities in the Roman Empire, needed a great deal of water. Unfortunately, there was not always a large natural supply close by and water often had to be brought from a distance through a series of channels, pipes, or aqueducts. But even if there was a good supply of water nearby, it would not have mattered. Having an aqueduct was also a matter of urban pride, and there was not a city in the Land of Israel in the Roman period that did not have some sort of aqueduct. Complex and sophisticated Roman-period aqueducts have been discovered in cities such as Jerusalem, Caesarea, Sebaste, Dor, Tiberias, Hippos, Gerasa, Acco, Sepphoris, Beit Gubrin, and Emmaus.[147]

Once this water was brought to the city, it also had to be distributed. Sometimes this was just as hard and complicated as getting the water to the city in the first place. There were various systems of channels, receptacles, conduits, and reservoirs through which the water was transported to fountains and other points of distribution. There were also drainage and sewage systems through which wastes could be removed from the city.[148] Since the aqueducts that brought the water up to the city walls are not really urban institutions, we refrain here from discussing the many physical remains of these aqueducts. We shall, though, discuss the remains of the internal physical urban water systems.[149]

In one of the distribution systems, the water ran from the aqueduct to a two-tiered receptacle with four cubicles called a *castellum*. The water passed relatively slowly through this system so that refuse could be removed and that the water could be transferred efficiently to its final destination through other reservoirs and channels. The *castellum* was usually located at a high point on the city wall or on a tower or pillar nearby. Few remains have been found of such installations. According to Hirschfeld, remains of a *castellum* have been found on the northern gateway of Caesarea.[150] Similar types of installations have been found in cities such as Neapolis, in an area called Ras el-Ain, in which there was a large Roman-period structure with a conduit system that channeled water into a number of fountains in the city.[151]

Most of the water from the various distribution systems ended up at the fountains or *nymphaea*. Two of the most elaborate fountain structures built during the Roman period were in the Decapolis in Philadelphia and Gerasa. The *nymphaeum* of Philadelphia was located near Wadi Amman and near the main streets of the city. The two-story limestone *nymphaeum* had an imposing central wall with a large apse. This "baroque" building with its arches, columns, niches, and gables must have made quite an impressive sight in Philadelphia. The individual fountains were on the second floor, which one reached after going up a wide set of stairs.[152]

The *nymphaeum* of Gerasa, built in 190 C.E., was located almost in the center of the city and is considered the most magnificent of all the urban structures in that city. The three-story building is a 24-m long facade built in the form of a large central apse with smaller ones and niches along the sides.[153]

Archeological excavations at Beit Shean have also uncovered a *nymphaeum,* located between the temple and the central monument and *basilica.* This *nymphaeum,* like the one in Gerasa, was in the forms of an apse-shaped facade and was a number of stories high. A Greek inscription identifies the building as a *nymphaeum* built by Flavius Artemidorus, apparently in the fourth century C.E. The inscription, though, undoubtedly refers to the reconstruction or renewal of the building, which was originally built at the end of the second century C.E.[154] Other Roman-period urban fountains have been found in cities such as Abila, Hippos, and Pella, all in the Decapolis, and a medallion from a mid-third-century fountain in Ascalon has also been discovered, although the exact location of the fountain is not known. The medallion was a bust of Pan, which was attached to the fountain so that water could spurt from its mouth.[155]

Remains of water systems have also been found in other cities. In Sepphoris, for instance, two aqueducts brought water to a pool at the northern entrance of the city and to an underground reservoir at the southern end. The residents of the acropolis, though, were probably dependent on underground cisterns for their basic supply of water.[156] An ancient reservoir of Tiberias was discovered at the southern part of the city. An aqueduct from the area of the Yavneel Valley, some 15 km to the south fed into this reservoir, which could conceivably have contained enough water to supply the fountains of the city.[157] An underground reservoir was discovered in the survey of Hippos. This reservoir supplied water to the *nymphaeum* of that city.[158] A complex water system of aqueducts and channels was found under the *decumanus maximus* of Gadara. The details are not yet clear, but apparently the structure connected to the system was not a *nymphaeum.*[159] In the Early Roman period an underground water system was built at the site of a destroyed small Hellenistic temple in Acco. By the third century, though, its channels were no longer in use.[160] In Antipatris water passed through a complex system of drain pipes on the roofs of large houses and into an underground reservoir.[161] In most cities, in fact, drainage pipes or channels have been uncovered under main streets. Sewage pipes or channels have also been discovered in a number of cities.[162]

Notes

1. See Y. Tsafrir, *Ereẓ-Yisrael me-Ḥurban Bayit Sheni ve-Ad ha-Kibush ha-Muslemi,* vol. 2, *Ha-Mimẓ ha-Archeologi ve-ha- Amanuti* (Archeology and Art) (Jerusalem, 1985), p. 84.

2. See chapter 4 and Y. Dagan, M. Fisher, and Y. Tsafrir, "An Inscribed Lintel from Bet Guvrin," *IEJ* 35 (1985): 28–34, on an inn located near the city of Eleutheropolis on the main road from Aelia Capitolina to Ascalon. The inn dates to the mid-fourth century C.E. and technically is beyond the scope of our study.

3. See J. Geiger, "Local Patriotism in the Greek Cities of the Land of Israel," in *Yavan ve-Roma be-Ereẓ-Yisrael: Kovetz Meḥkarim,* ed. A. Kasher, G. Fuks, and U. Rappaport (Jerusalem, 1989), pp. 261–69, and E. J. Owens, *The City in the Greek and Roman World* (London and New York, 1991), pp. 121–22.

4. See P. Veyne, ed., *A History of Private Life,* vol. 1, *From Pagan Rome to Byzantium* (Cambridge and London, 1987).

5. We have not limited our discussion just to those cities which were *poleis* or *coloniae,* but obviously there was much more "city building" in these types of settlements than in what would be today defined as a "town." It is also sometimes difficult to determine exactly what constitutes "city building." Certain types of buildings or institutions (e.g., cemeteries, amphitheaters, and various types of industries) were by their nature usually built outside the city walls. We have, of course, made reference to such building when necessary, even if technically they may have been "outside" the city. Also, for purposes of comparison we have at times made reference to Roman-period cities that were outside the administrative boundaries of Palestine (in its various forms and fashions). These cities, for the most part, were located in the Decapolis and belonged to Provincia

Arabia. Many of the physical elements uncovered and excavated in these cities undoubtedly existed in the cities of Palestine. It should also be pointed out that our study is in no way meant to be complete. For the sake of convenience, we have also sought to simplify our references in the notes and we will often make do with a citation to a major reference work or handbook that in turn will provide full bibliographic detail.

6. See J. B. Ward-Perkins, *Roman Imperial Architecture* (Harmondsworth, 1981), figure 261.

7. See M. Dothan, *Ha-Encyclopedia ha-Ḥadashah le-Ḥafirot Archiologiot be-Ereẓ-Yisrael* (*EHHA*), vol. 1 (Jerusalem, 1992), pp. 95–96. On Hellenistic city planning in the Land of Israel, see R. Arav, *Hellenistic Palestine: Settlement Patterns and City Planning 337–31* B.C.E., B.A.R. International Series, 485 (Oxford, 1989).

8. See A. Segal, "Gerasa—An Archaeological-Historical Review," *Qadmoniot* 19 (1986): 12–22 and the bibliography cited ad loc.

9. Owens, *City,* p. 145.

10. The city, for instance, had no main streets that could be classified as a *cardo maximus* or *decumanus.* See G. Forster, *EHHA,* vol. 1, p. 211, and Y. Tsafrir and G. Foerster, "Mi-Scythopolis le-Beisan: Shinuyim be-Tefisat ha-Iyyur shel Beit Shean be-Tekufah ha-Bizantit ve-ha-Aravit," *Cathedra* 64 (1992): 3. The large amount of water in and around the city, however, also had quite a positive impact on the history of that city.

11. See the plan of the city in Tsafrir, *Ereẓ-Yisrael,* p. 84.

12. Tsafrir, *Ereẓ-Yisrael,* p. 85.

13. Ibid., p. 87. See also our discussion below.

14. Ibid., p. 66.

15. Ibid., p. 74.

16. See R. J. Bull et al., "The Joint Expedition to Caesarea Maritima: Tenth Season 1982," BASOR, Suppl. 27 (1991): 69 ff.

17. Segal, "Gerasa," pp. 12–22.

18. Y. Hirschfeld, "Ir Mishar Homiyah," in *Ashkelon,* vol. 1, ed. N. Arbel (Ashkelon, 1990), p. 157.

19. See M. Kochavi, *Aphek—Antipatris: Ḥameshet Alaphim Shenot Historiah* (Tel Aviv, 1989), p. 103.

20. Y. Hirschfeld, *EHHA,* vol. 2, p. 564.

21. It should be remembered that our discussion is based upon archeological remains. It is conceivable and indeed quite likely that cities in which a *cardo* has been discovered also had a *decumanus* and vice versa even if the archeologist's spade has not yet proven this to be the case. We also do not cite major streets depicted, for instance, in the Madaba Map, unless there is corroborative archeological evidence.

22. T. Weber, "Gadara of the Decapolis: Preliminary Report on the 1990 Season at Umm Qeis," *Annual of the Department of Antiquities of Jordan* 35 (1991): 224.

23. W. H. Mare, *EHHA,* vol. 1, pp. 10–12.

24. C. Epstein, *EHHA,* vol. 3, pp. 1102–1104.

25. Y. Magen, *EHHA,* vol. 4, p. 1533.

26. Owens, *City,* p. 149. See also W. Liebernam, *Staedteverwaltung im Roemischen Kaiserreiche* (Leipzig, 1900), p. 140.

27. Owens, *City,* pp. 149 ff.

28. Tsafrir, *Ereẓ-Yisrael,* p. 129.

29. P. Grimal, *Roman Cities,* trans. and ed. M. Woloch (Wisconsin, 1983), p. 78.

30. Tsafrir, *Ereẓ-Yisrael,* p. 84.

31. See J. J. Schwartz, *Lod (Lydda), Israel: From its Origins through the Byzantine Period, 5600* B.C.E.*–640* C.E.*,* B.A.R. International Series 571 (Oxford, 1991), pp. 140–41.

32. A. Segal, *EHHA,* vol. 1, p. 369; Tsafrir, *Ereẓ-Yisrael,* p. 131. On the more regular plans of the city walls of Bostra and Philippopolis in the Transjordan, see Tsafrir, pp. 131–32. On the city wall of Abila see W. H. Mare, *EHHA,* vol. 1, p. 11.

33. N. Avigad, *EHHA,* vol. 4, p. 1500.

34. Y. Magen, *EHHA,* vol. 4, p. 1533.

35. B. Z. Kedar and W. G. Mook, "Radiocarbon Dating of Mortar from the City Wall of Ascalon," *IEJ* 28 (1978): 175–76.

36. For a convenient presentation of sources and archeological remains in Tiberias see the guide put out recently by the Antiquities Authority written by Y. Hirschfeld, *Atarei Atikot be-Teveriah: Madrich* (Jerusalem, 1993).

37. Ibid., p. 10.

38. See Y. Hirschfeld and R. Reich, "The Plan of the City of Tiberias during the Roman-Byzantine Period," in *Tiveriah: me-Yisudah ve-ad ha-Kibush ha-Muslemi,* ed. Y. Hirschfeld (Jerusalem, 1988), p. 114. A free-standing Roman-period gate was constructed on a step on the southeastern slope of Tel Iṣṭba at Beit Shean and as was the case in Tiberias, was connected to the city wall only in the Byzantine period. See R. Bar-Natan and G. Mazor, "Merkaz ha-Ir (Darom) ve-Eizor Tel Iṣṭba," *Ḥadashot Archiologiot* (*HA*) 98 (1992): 43.

39. Tsafrir, *Ereẓ-Yisrael,* pp. 130–31.

40. This wall is most likely the חומת מגדל שרושן mentioned in the *baraita* of the "Boundaries of Israel." See Y. Sussmann, "Baraita d'Teḥumei Ereẓ-Yisrael," *Tarbiẓ* 45 (1976): 228.

41. See R. J. Bull et al., "The Joint Expedition to Caesarea Maritima: Ninth Season, 1980," *BASOR* Suppl. 24 (1986): 45.

42. E. Stern, *EHHA,* vol. 2, p. 406.

43. D. Bahat, *Atlas Karta ha-Gadol le-Toldot Yerushalayim* (Jerusalem, 1989), p. 57; Tsafrir, *Ereẓ-Yisrael,* p. 128.

44. See note 32.

45. See D. Barag, "King Herod's Royal Castle at Samaria–Sebaste," *PEQ* 125 (1993): 3–18.

46. Tsafrir, *Ereẓ-Yisrael,* pp. 131–32.

47. Z. Weiss, *EHHA,* vol. 4, p. 1332.

48. See Owens, *City,* pp. 153–54, and Tsafrir, *Ereẓ-Yisrael,* p. 89.

49. See Tsafrir, *Ereẓ-Yisrael,* pp. 89–92. Tsafrir's work was published in 1985. Tsafrir's own excavations in Beit Shean, for instance, have added much new information to what he published earlier.

50. See note 7.

51. N. Avigad, *EHHA,* vol. 4, p. 1501; Tsafrir, *Ereẓ-Yisrael,* pp. 89–90.

52. L. Stager, *EHHA,* vol. 1, p. 106.

53. See E. Stern, *EHHA,* vol. 2, p. 401, on a portico uncovered in Roman-period Area G, which perhaps surrounded the forum. On the basilica see E. Stern and I. Sharon, "Tel Dor, 1992: Preliminary Report," *IEJ* 43 (1993):

129–30. One suggested reconstruction for a building discovered in Area B2 is a roofed apsidal structure. The building, though, was smaller than the average main-size basilica, which was undoubtedly elsewhere (perhaps in Area G). In any case, numerous public unidentified buildings have been uncovered in Area B2.

54. See Z. Maoz, *HA* 99 (1993): 1–2, on a building with an apse from level III (third to fourth centuries C.E.) in Area B, which was perhaps a basilica, and on a series of arches of a building in Area C that may have been the forum. See also idem, *HA* 96 (1991): 1–2.

55. See Bahat, *Atlas,* p. 56.

56. A. Segal, *EHHA,* vol. 1, pp. 369–71.

57. M. Kochavi, *EHHA,* vol. 1, p. 65. The forum dates to the Late Roman period. On the relationship of this area to the earlier markets and shops see our discussion below on shops and markets.

58. See R. H. Smith and A. W. McNicoll, "The 1982 and 1983 Seasons at Pella of the Decapolis," *BASOR* Suppl. 24 (1986): 100–107, on the Early Roman "civic complex" and the "forumlike" area.

59. G. Foerster and Y. Tsafrir, "Merkaz Ha-Ir (Ẓafon)," *HA* 98 (1992): 3–4.

60. Y. Hirschfeld, *EHHA,* vol. 2, pp. 564–65. We refer to the first stage of construction of the building. The second stage of the building was Byzantine (sixth century).

61. Tsafrir, *Ereẓ-Yisrael,* p. 92.

62. G. Foerster, *EHHA,* vol. 1, p. 216; Foerster and Tsafrir, "Merkaz," p. 20.

63. R. J. Bull et al., "The Joint Expedition to Caesarea Maritima: Ninth Season, 1980," *BASOR* Suppl. 24 (1986): 37.

64. Unidentified remains in the area of the forum are often identified as stores or shops. See Z. Maoz, *HA* 96 (1991): 1–2, on the archways of shops in the forum area of Banias. It is important to remember that our discussion pertains only to the Roman period. Thus, for instance, the market of Tiberias, dated to the sixth century C.E. is beyond the purview of our discussion. See Y. Hirschfeld, *EHHA,* vol. 2, p. 564.

65. See Kochavi, *Aphek—Antipatris,* p. 101. The latest coin found in the commercial quarter dates to 67 C.E.

66. Ibid., pp. 109–11. The craters in front of the stores were also eliminated. See below in our discussion on streets.

67. See R. Ben Natan and G. Mazor, "Merkaz ha-Ir (Darom) ve-Eizor Tel Itstaba," *HA* 98 (1992): 38. On possible stores discovered along Valley (הגיא) Street see Y. Tsafrir and G. Foerster, "Mif'al Ḥafirot Beit Shean—1988–1989," *HA* 95 (1990): 34.

68. Tsafrir, *Ereẓ-Yisrael,* p. 86. Cf. Schwartz, *Lod,* p. 143.

69. See Tsafrir, *Ereẓ-Yisrael,* pp. 69–70.

70. Kochavi, *Aphek—Antipatris,* p. 113.

71. Owens, *City,* p. 167. Domitian, for instance, forbade shopkeepers from displaying goods in the street and restricting passage.

72. Tsafrir, *Ereẓ-Yisrael,* p. 93; Owens, *City,* p. 155.

73. It is somewhat ironic that in spite of the many temples which undoubtedly still lie underground somewhere in Caesarea, it was a Mithraeum, the only one found so far in Israel, that has been excavated there. See R. J. Bull and K. G. Holum, *EHHA,* vol. 4, pp. 1383–84.

74. A. Mazar, *EHHA*, vol. 1, p. 208; G. Foerster, *EHHA*, vol. 1, p. 216; and Forster and Tsafrir, "Merkaz Ha-Ir," p. 8.

75. Foerster and Tsafrir, "Merkaz Ha-Ir," p. 7. Likewise, the colossal statue of Zeus found in Gaza at the end of the nineteenth century came from a temple of Zeus. See A. Ovadiah, *EHHA*, vol. 3, pp. 1161–65.

76. Z. Maoz, "Mikdash Pan—1990," *HA* 97 (1991): 2; idem, "Banias: Mikdash Pan—1991–1992," *HA* 100 (1993): 2–6. See also Appendix 1 this volume.

77. E. Netzer, "The Augusteum at Samaria-Sebaste—A New Outlook," *Ereẓ-Yisrael* 19 (1987): 97–105.

78. See Barag, "King Herod's Royal Castle," pp. 3–18.

79. Tsafrir, *Ereẓ-Yisrael*, p. 100.

80. E. Stern and I. Sharon, "Tel Dor, 1992: Prelimenary Report," *IEJ* 43 (1993): 132–34.

81. Y. Magen, *EHHA*, vol. 1, pp. 353–57.

82. A. Segal, *EHHA*, vol. 1, pp. 369–72; Tsafrir, *Ereẓ-Yisrael*, pp. 95–96.

83. At present we are preparing a study on "Leisure Time Activities in Ancient Jewish Society" in which we shall address such issues of private leisure and recreation.

84. The literature on leisure time activities in the Roman world is voluminous. To cite just one example, see J. P. V. D. Balsdon, *Life and Leisure in Ancient Rome* (London, 1969).

85. To the best of our knowledge, there are no archeological remains of taverns or brothels from Roman-period cities of the Land of Israel. This is, of course, not to say that they did not exist, since they are well attested to in literary sources (see chapter 1), it is just difficult to identify them. It is possible that certain types of buildings or structures that have been discovered and identified could have also served as brothels or the like. This may have been the case, for instance, in the Byzantine-period bathhouse in Ascalon (see L. Stager, *EHHA*, vol. 1, p. 107) or in the Roman-period bathhouse to the west of the Temple Mount in Aelia Capitolina and used by Roman soldiers (see our discussion below on bathhouses).

86. Tsafrir, *Ereẓ-Yisrael*, p. 105.

87. Owens, *City*, pp. 151–54.

88. There were, of course, Roman-style bathhouses at other types of sites and settlements. See for instance, V. Tzaferis and T. Shai, "Ḥafirot be-Kefar a-Ramah," *Qadmoniot* 9 (1976): 83–85, on the bathhouse in A-Ramah in the Galilee, apparently a Jewish settlement from the Mishnah period. There were also bathhouses or units of bathhouses in private houses in Jerusalem in the Late Second Temple period. See R. Reich, "The Caldarium and Jewish Society in the early Roman Period (the Second Temple Period)," in *Yavan Ve-Roma Be-Ereẓ-Yisrael*, ed. A. Kasher et al. (Jerusalem, 1989), pp. 207–11. See also M. Gichon, "Merḥaẓaot Romiyim Be-Ereẓ-Yisrael," *Qadmoniot* 11 (1978): 37–53. We do not include in our discussion the medicinal hot baths at Ḥamat Gader. Ḥamat Gader, or Emmatha, was not a city but rather a village in the vicinity of Gadara (Onomasticon, ed. Klostermann, p. 22, line 26). In any case, the activities at these thermae were somewhat different from those at regular city bathhouses. The fourth-century Church Father Epiphanius, for instance, mentions that men and women bathed together at festivals at Ḥamat Gader, something that was not generally done in Roman-period city bathhouses. The baths were constructed originally during the second century C.E., but halls were added during

the rest of the Roman period and the Byzantine period. They were rebuilt in the Early Moslem period after an earlier period of destruction. See Y. Hirschfeld and G. Solar, "Ha-Merḥaẓaot ha-Romiyim shel Ḥamat Gader," *Qadmoniot* 13 (1980): 66–79; idem, *EHHA*, vol. 2, pp. 508–14 and idem, *The Roman Baths of Ḥamat Gader: Final Report* (Jerusalem, 1997).

89. Tsafrir, *Ereẓ-Yisrael*, p. 106. This, of course, can be said only regarding those bathhouses excavated in their entirety.

90. See M. Gichon, *EHHA*, vol. 1, pp. 39–41.

91. Tsafrir, *Ereẓ-Yisrael*, p. 107. The issue of oiling, however, and where exactly it took place is far from clear. See Sperber's discussion in chapter 6. In any case, the dating of this room is not clear.

92. On these traditions, see M. Hirschman, "Sipurei Bet Ha-Merḥaẓ be-Tiveriah," in *Tiveriah: me-Yisudah ve-ad ha-Kibush ha-Muslemi*, ed. Y. Hirschfeld (Jerusalem, 1988), pp. 119–22.

93. See R. Telgam, "Riẓpot Pesifas be-Tiveriah," in *Tiveriah*, pp. 125–31.

94. Such a pool is rather unusual in Roman-Byzantine bathhouses, and attempts have therefore been made to connect this pool with laws of ritual purity. See Hirschfeld, *EHHA*, vol. 2, p. 564.

95. The bathhouse is near the theater and Palladius Street and is indeed the largest bathhouse so far uncovered in archeological excavations. The bathhouse basically dates to the Byzantine period, although there is a slight possibility that part of it was originally built in the Late Roman period. See G. Foerster, *EHHA*, vol. 1, p. 215–16.

96. E. Stern, *EHHA*, vol. 2, pp. 401–2.

97. Z. Goldman, *EHHA*, vol. 3, p. 1232. Rabbinic sources mention the "bathhouse of Aphrodite."

98. Y. Hirschfeld, *Tiveriah*, p. 37.

99. Two have been found in this city. One in the western part and one in the eastern section, which has not been excavated at all. See A. Segal, *EHHA*, vol. 1, pp. 371–72.

100. R. H. Smith, *EHHA*, vol. 4, p. 1314.

101. Tsafrir, *Ereẓ-Yisrael*, p. 107.

102. Much of our discussion on theaters is based on the excellent concise study of A. Segal, "Theaters in the Land of Israel in the Roman-Byzantine Period," in *Yavan ve-Roma Be-Ereẓ-Yisrael*, ed. A. Kasher et al. (Jerusalem, 1989), pp. 230–49. Segal lists eleven theaters in the west and seventeen in the east. Needless to say, even if not all these theaters were in "cities," we will restrict our comments to a few representative examples.

103. Ibid., pp. 230–232.

104. Tsafrir, *Ereẓ-Yisrael*, p. 115 and detailed bibliography cited there.

105. Segal, "Theaters," p. 234, n. 14 and bibliography cited there.

106. Tsafrir, *Ereẓ-Yisrael*, pp. 117–18.

107. Z. Weiss, *EHHA*, vol. 4, pp. 1332–33.

108. Segal, "Theaters," p. 242.

109. Tsafrir, *Ereẓ-Yisrael*, p. 119 and bibliography at n. 98.

110. N. Avigad, *EHHA*, vol. 4, p. 1501.

111. Y. Magen, *EHHA*, vol. 4, pp. 1533–34.

112. Y. Hirschfeld, "Tiberias, 1990–1991," *HA* 97 (1991): 32–35.

113. M. Kochavi, *Aphek—Antipatris*, pp. 103–109.

114. Segal, "Theaters," p. 242.

115. R. Bar-Natan and G. Mazor, "Merkaz Ha-Ir (Darom)," p. 40.

116. Tsafrir, *Erez̤-Yisrael,* p. 121.

117. G. Forster, *EHHA,* vol. 1, pp. 214–15; Tsafrir, *Erez̤-Yisrael,* pp. 121–23.

118. Y. Magen, *EHHA,* vol. 4, p. 1535.

119. A. Kloner, *EHHA,* vol. 1, pp. 168–69. The plan of the city is not clear and therefore, it is impossible to determine the location of the amphitheater vis-à-vis other urban institutions.

120. Y. Porath, "Herod's 'Amphitheatre' at Caesarea, "*Qadmoniot* 29 (1996): 93–99.

121. See Y. Dan, "Ha-Kirkas ve-Si'otav (ha-Keḥulim ve-Ha-Yeruqim) be-Erez̤-Yisrael be-Tequfah ha-Byzantit," *Cathedra* 4 (1977): 133–46.

122. J. H. Humphrey, "Prolegomena to the Study of the Hippodrome at Caesarea Maritima," *BASOR* 213 (1974): 2–45; "A Summary of the 1974 Excavations in the Caesarea Hippodrome," *BASOR* 218 (1975): 1–24; Porath, "Herod's 'Amphitheatre.'" Josephus describes the entire amphitheater-hippodrome complex as "amphitheater."

123. Y. Magen, *EHHA,* vol. 4, pp. 1534–35.

124. See A. A. Ostrasz, "The Excavation and Restoration of the Hippodrome at Jerash: A Synopsis," *ADAJ* 35 (1991): 237–50. Large amounts of potsherds were discovered at the site as well as skeletal remains.

125. Y. Tsafrir and G. Foerster, "Mif'al Ḥafirot Beit Shean—1988–1989," *HA* 95 (1990): 35. On the linen industry in Beit Shean, see M. Stern, *Greek and Latin Authors on Jews and Judaism* (Jerusalem, 1980), p. 498.

126. Z. Goldman, *EHHA,* vol. 3, p. 1232.

127. A. Ovadiah, *EHHA,* vol. 3, p. 1164.

128. The Herodian harbor at Caesarea has aroused much interest at both popular and academic levels. See A. Raban, *EHHA,* vol. 4, pp. 1385–91, and the voluminous bibliography ad loc. p. 1385. Our discussion here is based for the most part on Raban. On harbors in general see D. Sperber, *Nautica Talmudica* (Ramat-Gan and Leiden, 1986), pp. 77–85.

129. See the list of ancient harbors and anchorages along the Mediterranean Sea as well as along the shores of the Sea of Galilee in A. Raban, *EHHA,* vol. 1, pp. 76–77.

130. See K. Ravch and S. A. Kingsley, "The Status of Dor in Late Antiquity: A Maritime Prospective," *BA* 54 (1991): 198–207.

131. A. Raban, *EHHA,* vol. 2, pp. 407–10.

132. A. Raban, *EHHA,* vol. 3, pp. 1237–40. There were, of course, quays and the like between Acco and Dor (*EHHA,* vol. 1, pp. 76–77).

133. I. Roll and E. Ayalon, *Apollonia ve-Darom ha-Sharon* (Tel Aviv, 1989), pp. 50–51.

134. See F. Vito, "Nemalah shel Yamniya," in *Yavneh-Yam ve-Sevivatah,* ed. M. Fischer (Palmahim, 1991), pp. 75–79. The earliest Roman-period coin found in the excavations of the city dates from the third century. See also E. Galili and Y. Sharvit, "Ma'agan Yavneh-Yam—Mimz̤aei Ha-Seker Ha-Tat Yami," in *Yavneh-Yam,* pp. 111–21. Underwater excavations have not revealed remains of the harbor. They have uncovered a few Roman-period coins and artifacts: nails, nets, weights, and the like.

135. Storehouses have been discovered at the southwest section of the city near where the southern wall reaches the coast. These probably were part of the

harbor complex. Although they have been dated to the Hellenistic period, they most likely continued to exist into the Roman-Byzantine period. See Y. Hirschfeld, "Ir Mishar Homiyah," in *Ashkelon,* vol. 1, ed. N. Arbel (Ascalon, 1990), p. 157. Cf. also Sperber, *Nautica Talmudica,* pp. 77–80. Talmudic tradition tells us that the port of Ascalon must have had boathouses equipped with stone slips onto which seagoing ships were dragged for the winter season. Unfortunately, archeological findings have not yet provided corroborative evidence.

136. See Hirschfeld, *Tiveriah,* pp. 22–24.

137. G. Foerster, *EHHA,* vol. 1, pp. 211–13.

138. On basalt stones in the Galilee and in other areas of the Land of Israel (particularly the Golan and Bashan) see E. Orni and E. Efrat, *Ha-Geografia shel Arẓenu*[6] (Tel Aviv, 1980), pp. 14–15. The *cardo* of Tiberias, for instance, was constructed of the same basalt laid out in the same diagonal pattern (see Hirschfeld, *Tiveriah,* p. 18). Many of the Roman-period buildings in Beit Shean were also constructed of this same stone.

139. This refers to the "open street" and not to the entire street complex including stylobate and stores. In terms of comparison, the width of the open part of the colonnaded street in Bostra, for instance, was 7.90 m (Tsafrir, *Ereẓ-Yisrael,* p. 81). Roman law established a width of 2.90 m or more for urban streets to allow for hanging balconies. In spite of attempts at planning, streets often became cluttered and congested.

140. Cf. D. Sperber, *Tarbut Ḥomrit be-Ereẓ-Yisrael be-Yemei ha-Talmud* (Jerusalem, 1993), pp. 25–28.

141. The width of the stoa is 7.10 m, while that of the row of shops is 7.20 m.

142. G. Foerster, *EHHA,* vol. 1, p. 213; Foerster and Tsafrir, "Merkaz Ha-Ir (Ẓafon)," pp. 18–22 (and particularly illustrations 33 to 34 on page 19; on the date of construction, see page 18).

143. Tsafrir, *Ereẓ-Yisrael,* p. 64; Bahat, *Atlas Karta ha-Gadol,* p. 55.

144. See Stern and Sharon, "Tel Dor: 1992," p. 129.

145. Kochavi, *Aphek—Antipatris,* p. 109.

146. Owens, *City,* p. 159 ff.

147. Tsafrir, *Ereẓ-Yisrael,* pp. 54–57. The aqueducts were often constructed with the help of or by Roman legions and related to "Imperial" aspects of water supply, which are, of course, beyond the scope of our discussion. On aqueducts in the Land of Israel see most recently D. Amit, Y. Hirschfeld, and J. Patrich, *Amot ha-Mayim ha-Kedumot be-Ereẓ-Yisrael: Qovetz Meḥqarim* (Jerusalem, 1989).

148. See chapter 9, Water Supply, Sewage, and Drainage, and the notes cited ad loc.

149. There are, of course, exceptions. The aqueduct of Hippos entered the city through the eastern gate and continued under the *cardo* bringing water to the *nymphaeum* of that city. It could be argued, though, that by this point it was really no longer technically an aqueduct.

150. Hirschfeld, "Amot Ha-Mayim Be-Olam Ha-Yevani-Romi," in *Amot Ha-Mayim,* pp. 20, 27, n. 126 and the bibliography cited ad loc.

151. Y. Magen, *EHHA,* vol. 4, p. 1533.

152. Hirschfeld, "Amot Ha-Mayim," p. 22; A. Segal, *EHHA,* vol. 4, p. 1448.

153. A. Segal, *EHHA,* vol. 4, p. 371; Tsafrir, *Ereẓ-Yisrael,* p. 77.

154. G. Foerster, *EHHA,* vol. 4, pp. 216–18. The *nymphaeum* was not the

only ornamental water structure in Beit Shean. Southwest of the basilica was a stoa surrounding a stepped ornamental pool also dating to the second century C.E.

155. Hirschfeld, "Amot Ha-Mayim," p. 22. On the bust of Pan, see Tsafrir, *Ereẓ-Yisrael,* p. 196.

156. Z. Weiss, *EHHA,* vol. 4, p. 1334.

157. Hirschfeld, *Atarei,* p. 28.

158. C. Epstein, *EHHA,* vol. 3, p. 1102.

159. T. Weber, "Gadara of the Decapolis: Prelimenary Report of the 1990 Season at Umm Qeis," *ADAJ* 35 (1991): 222–35.

160. Z. Goldman, *EHHA,* vol. 3, p. 1232.

161. Kochavi, *Aphek—Antipatris,* p. 111.

162. Such channels have been discovered, for instance, under Palladius Street in Beit Shean (G. Foerster, *EHHA,* vol. 1, p. 213) or in Dor (E. Stern, *EHHA,* vol. 2, p. 401), and most recently in Banias (Z. Maoz, "Banias, Miqdash Pan—1991–1992" *HA* 100 [1993]: 5). On Ashkelon see L. Stager, "Ḥafirot Ashkelon," in *Ashkelon,* vol. 1, ed. N. Arbel (Ashkelon, 1990), p. 64. It is not always easy to distinguish between drainage and sewage.

Appendix 1

Unidentified "Public" Buildings

Our preceding discussion was based on the archeological remains discovered in Roman-period cities in the Land of Israel. Unfortunately, not everything discovered has been successfully identified. It is likely, therefore, that absolutely none of the subjects discussed above has been described in anything approaching a complete manner. Undoubtedly, much still awaits the spade of the archeologist and the resultant study and thought that accompanies excavation. It is likely that even as I write this, new identifications are being postulated and perhaps new finds are being discovered. Below is a list of some of the "unidentified" major urban finds. It is our fond hope that this list will soon become exhausted or outdated.

Antipatris: Public building in the southeastern corner of the forum.[1]

Banias: Area B, a large rectangular monumental building with an apse constructed on a podium.[2]

Bethsaida: Public building in Area A.[3]

Beit Shean: "Central Monument" located near the *nyphaeum* and adjacent to the basilica;[4] "Antonius Antoninus Monument" located on Valley Street;[5] large round structure on Palladius Street;[6] large colonnaded building on Palladius Street;[7] and monumental basalt building southwest of colonnaded street.[8]

Dor: Public buildings to the east and west of gate in Area B;[9] unidentified building in Area E;[10] large public building on slope of the tel and to the east of Area C (this is proof that the Roman city extended beyond the tel);[11] large public building southwest of the city;[12] small section of hewn-stone building in Area F;[13] large hewn-stone building in Area B1;[14] and Roman public buildings in Area B2.[15]

Tiberias: Public building near Tiberias Purification Plant;[16] Area C, foot of Mt. Berenike monumental public building, perhaps theater (?).[17]

Susita (Hippus): Assorted public buildings.[18]

Gaza: Assorted public buildings.[19]

Sepphoris: Building with Nilotic mosaic motifs;[20] large building with Dionysiac mosaic panels.[21]

Caesarea: Field G, Phase 7b (Middle Roman), Area 8.[22]

Notes

1. Kochavi, *Aphek—Antipatris*, p. 113.
2. Z. Maoz, *EHHA*, I, p. 122. This first-century building might have been

a *nymphaeum* or temple. The building underwent changes in the third century but remained a "public" building. See also V. Tzaferis, "Banias—1989," *HA*, 94 (1989): 3; and V. Tzaferis and R. Avner, "Banias—1990" *HA* 96 (1991): 1–2. By 1991 the latter building was being described as a basilica-like building with an apse facing eastward. See also *HA* 99 (1993): 1–2. The building has now been tentatively identified as a Temple of Hadrian from the Middle Roman period. See most recently V. Tzaferis and S. Yisraeli, "Banias—1991," *HA*, 100 (1993): 4. Early publications on Banias left the series of arches of the structure in Area C unidentified, but most recent publications see this as part of the shops connected with the forum. See our discussion above.

3. R. Arav, "Beth Saidah 1990–1991," *HA* 99 (1993): 8–9.

4. G. Foerster, *EHHA*, vol. 1, p. 218; G. Foerster and Y. Tsafrir, "Merkaz, Ha-Ir (Ẓafon)," *HA* 98 (1992): 3–4.

5. Y. Tsafrir and G. Foerster, "Mifal Ḥafirot Beit Shean—1988–1989," *HA* 95 (1990): 34.

6. G. Foerster and Y. Tsafrir, "Merkaz Ha-Ir (Ẓafon)," *HA* 98 (1992): 13.

7. Ibid.

8. Ibid., p. 23.

9. E. Stern, *EHHA*, vol. 2, p. 401; E. Stern, A. Gilboa, and I. Sharon, "Tel Dor, 1991: Preliminary Report," *IEJ* 42 (1992): 40; Stern and Sharon, "Tel Dor, 1992: Preliminary Report," *IEJ* 43 (1993): 129.

10. Ibid.

11. Ibid., p. 402.

12. E. Stein, J. Barag, and I. Sharon, "Tel Dor 1988," *HA* 94 (1989): 26–27.

13. E. Stein and A. Gilboa, "Tel Dor 1989," *HA* 95 (1990): 27.

14. Ibid.

15. Stern and Sharon, *IEJ*, 43 (1993), p. 128.

16. Y. Hirschfeld, "Tiberias," *HA* 95 (1990): 19. According to Hirschfeld, the building was constructed at the end of the second century C.E. or the beginning of the third century. Hirschfeld has cautiously suggested that the building may have been the "Great Academy" of Tiberias. There is, as yet, no proof for this suggestion.

17. Hirchfeld, "Tiberias," 1990–1991," *HA* 97 (1991): 32–35. The size of the stones and the quality of the stonework point to construction in the second to third centuries C.E. Josephus makes no mention of a theater in Tiberias.

18. C. Epstein, *EHHA*, vol. 3, p. 1102 ff.

19. A. Ovadiah, *EHHA*, vol. 3, pp. 1161–65.

20. Z. Weiss and E. Netzer, "Ẓippori—1990–1991," *HA* 99 (1993): 13–14. The building is dated to the second century. It is not certain that the building is "public."

21. Z. Weiss, *EHHA*, vol. 4, p. 1331 ff. The purpose of this building is not clear. Perhaps it was the residence of the ruler or of a rich (Jewish ?) resident. In either case, it is beyond the scope of our study.

22. R. Bull et al., "The Joint Expedition to Caesarea Maritima: Ninth Season, 1980," *BASOR* Suppl. 24 (1986): 37 ff.

Appendix 2

Urban Synagogues

Roman-period cities in the Land of Israel were pagan both in spirit and population. The Hellenistic-Roman ethnic background of the urban pagans may have been somewhat questionable, and the residents of these cities may have basically derived from Semitic stock, but the "official" religious milieu was certainly Hellenistic-Roman. Thus, most of the religious structures in these cities were temples.

This does not mean, however, that there were not Jews or Christians in the cities of the Land of Israel. During most of the Roman period, Christianity was not recognized, and Christians suffered persecution. They were in no position to construct churches or other religious buildings in cities. This changed, of course, during the Byzantine period, but this is beyond the scope of our study.

The situation of the Jews was different. There were, of course, Jews in most Roman-period urban centers in the Land of Israel and, therefore, there were also synagogues in these cities.[1] Many of these synagogues are referred to in the various literary sources of the time. Unfortunately, but not surprising, there are not many remains of urban synagogues from the Roman period. A large percentage of the urban synagogue remains date to the Byzantine period, possibly as a result of generally favorable economic conditions and in spite of a possibly hostile religious environment. Since synagogues are not really city structures by nature, except perhaps in the more Jewish cities of Tiberias and Sepphoris, we have placed the discussion of Roman-period synagogues in an appendix.

The study of Roman-period synagogues can further our understanding of the relationship between urban Jews and their non-Jewish neighbors. Unfortunately, there are only a few cities in which it has been possible to determine the exact location of the synagogue. In the majority of the cities, the remains are fragmentary and have not been discovered in situ.

The synagogue at Caesarea belongs to this first category of remains. The synagogue was built in the northern part of the city near the area of Straton's Tower, somewhat removed from the center of activity of Roman-period Caesarea. Although some scholars feel that the location of the synagogue indicates that the northern area was the Jewish quarter, it is impossible to prove this, and there is no way of knowing if such a quarter indeed ever existed in Caesarea.[2]

The synagogue was originally built in the fourth century and measured 18 × 9 m, was entered from the east, and had a southern orientation. It was destroyed in the middle of the fourth century and rebuilt some hundred years later with changes and additions made as late as the sixth and seventh centuries.[3]

In spite of its present wretched state of preservation, numerous remains were found at this synagogue, although not all can be dated to the earlier one. The Greek inscription found on the mosaic floor mentioning, for example, an *archisynagogus* named Berullos, a *frontistes* the son of Iutos (or Iustos), and the *triclinium* of the synagogue are from the later Byzantine-period synagogue. The same is true of the other Greek inscriptions found on columns and the like.[4]

However, according to M. Avi-Yonah, the ivory pieces bearing fragmentary inscriptions from the list of the twenty-four priestly courses came from this earlier Roman-period synagogue.[5] There has, of course, been much discussion over why inscriptions of the twenty-four priestly courses were put in synagogues. In the final analysis, it is not really definite that the inscription came from the early synagogue.[6] Nor is there any proof that this early synagogue should be identified with the Maradata synagogue or with any other synagogue mentioned in Talmudic literature.[7]

Remains of a second Roman-period synagogue have been found in a rather unexpected site. Christian tradition mentions a synagogue on Mt. Zion in the first part of the fourth century. According to some scholars, this synagogue is to be identified with what is today called King David's Tomb.[8] If this is correct, the location of the synagogue would indicate that the Jews of Aelia Capitolina lived far from the center of that city.[9]

There was also a synagogue in Gerasa located somewhat to the west of the temple of Artemis, near enough to be convenient to the major municipal institutions of the city but, then again, not too close. It is, of course, impossible to determine the relationship between the location of the synagogue and the Jewish community of this city, as was the case regarding the synagogue in Caesarea.

The synagogue of Gerasa had a mosaic floor depicting scenes from the Flood and Noah's Ark in the east and inscriptions in Hebrew (Aramaic?) and Greek in the west. The eastern part of the floor has been dated to the fourth or fifth century, making it likely that the synagogue functioned in the Roman period. The western part belongs to the sixth century, about the time at which the synagogue apparently ceased to exist; in the sixth century C.E. around the year 530/1 C.E. a church was built on top of it, an important statement regarding the history of Jews and Christians in Byzantine-period Gerasa but beyond the scope of our discussion.[10]

Although we have mentioned a number of "Jewish cities," such as Tiberias or Sepphoris, these cities have not yielded much in the way of Roman-period synagogue remains. In Tiberias, for example, remains of a synagogue have been found west of the Plaza Hotel in the area of the

Crusader City. Unfortunately for our purposes, the synagogue is clearly from the Late Byzantine period.[11]

In Sepphoris fragments of a synagogue mosaic floor with an Aramaic inscription were published in 1909, and a synagogue lintel with a Greek inscription was found at the end of the nineteenth century. The Greek inscription mentions a "*scholasticos,*" a "*comes,*" and *archisynagogi* from Sidon and Tyre but apparently also dates to the fifth century, making the synagogue Byzantine and not Roman. It is not certain whether the Aramaic inscription came from this Byzantine synagogue or from an earlier one.[12] For the present, therefore, Talmudic tradition is the best source of information regarding the synagogues of Sepphoris and Tiberias.

Far more Roman-period synagogue remains have been found in Ḥamat Tiberias, the suburb of Tiberias to the south. Although the "urban" status of this settlement might be somewhat questionable, we include it in our brief discussion here as part of "Greater Tiberias."[13]

Two synagogues have been uncovered by archeologists at Ḥamat Tiberias.[14] The first is located to the south of the walls of Tiberias and in the northern section of Ḥamat. This synagogue, a square basilica with a central nave and two aisles, served the Jewish community of Ḥamat from the third to the eighth centuries. In the original synagogue one entered from the south, and the floor was constructed from basalt stones. In the fourth century the southern entrance was blocked, and three entrances were built in the north. The plain basalt floor was replaced by a colorful mosaic. A chancel screen was constructed in the south in front of *bema* and ark. Among the more important finds in the synagogue were a "Seat of Moses" and remains of a seven-branched menorah.[15]

The second synagogue is located in the the southern section of Ḥamat. This synagogue also had a long history, undergoing several periods of construction and renovation, some in the Roman period and some in the Byzantine period and afterward.[16]

The original synagogue, constructed in the mid-third century, is a basilica with "broadhouse" elements. It was divided into four halls by three rows of columns. The largest hall served as the central nave while the other ones functioned as aisles. Of particular interest is the second eastern aisle, which some scholars felt may have been for women worshippers. The entrance to this synagogue was either in the south or in the east. If the latter is true, then this early synagogue in Ḥamat conformed to Talmudic tradition regarding the building of synagogue entrances in the east.[17]

This synagogue was destroyed either at the end of the third century C.E. or at the beginning of the fourth century. A new synagogue was built, with minor alterations made on the original plan. The most important addition, however, was the mosaic floor, the most important part of which was in the nave and divided into a number of panels. One contained a Torah shrine (*'Aron Kodesh*) flanked by common symbols such as *menorot* and *lulab.* There was nothing very unusual about this. However, another panel contained a zodaic circle with Helios riding his chariot. This has led to endless speculation regarding the nature of the Judaism of those who prayed at or built this synagogue.[18]

There are also synagogue inscriptions in three different languages. The seasons and legends of the zodiac circle are in Hebrew. An Aramaic inscription blesses the donors. The Greek inscriptions are the longest and mention the "founders" of the synagogue, not all of whom may have been Jewish, although some like Severus, "the pupil of the illustrious Patriarchs" who "completed (the construction)," certainly was. These inscriptions have provided scholars with much material for discussion and study regarding the history of synagogues, Judaism, and Jewish-pagan relationships.[19]

The rest of the Roman-period urban synagogue remains are far more fragmentary and problematic.[20] We believe there was a synagogue in Roman-period Ascalon, assuming the fragments of the chancel screen and inscription found in 1878 can be dated to the third century. The other and more prominent synagogue remains from Ascalon, an inscription in Hebrew mentioning part of the twenty-four priestly courses and Greek dedicatory inscriptions, are clearly Byzantine.[21]

The same situation exists regarding the synagogue remains of Gaza. There apparently was at least one Roman-period synagogue in this city. Inscribed on a column located today in the major mosque of Gaza is a Hebrew-Greek inscription with Jewish motifs that mention Ḥananiah the son of Jacob. The inscription has been dated to the second or third centuries and comes from a Roman-period synagogue somewhere in Gaza. The other synagogue remains from the coastal city of Maiumas Gaza are Byzantine and beyond the scope of our study.[22]

Notes

1. The literature on synagogues is voluminous. See the articles of M. Avi-Yonah ("Synagogues: The Study of Synagogues Up to the 70s") and L. I. Levine ("Synagogues: The Study of Synagogues from the '70s and Afterwards") in *EHHA,* vol. 1, pp. 257–61 and the bibliography cited ad loc.

2. See L. I. Levine, *Roman Caesarea: An Archaeological-Topographical Study* (Jerusalem, 1975), pp. 40–45.

3. Ibid., p. 40 ff. M. Avi-Yonah dated the synagogue to the third century (*EHHA,* vol. 4, p. 1378). On the subject of entering the synagogue from the east see T. Megillah 4.22

4. See L. Roth-Gerson, *Ha-Ketovot ha-Yevaniyot me-Batei ha-Keneset be-Ereẓ-Yisrael* (Jerusalem, 1987), pp. 111–24, for the use of *archisynagogus* and *frontistes.*

5. M. Avi-Yonah, *EHHA,* vol. 4, p. 1378.

6. See J. Naveh, *Al Psifas va-Even* (Jerusalem, 1978), pp. 87–88, n. 51 and the bibliography cited ad loc.

7. Levine, *Roman Caesarea,* p. 44.

8. See J. Schwartz, *Ha-Yishuv ha-Yehudi be-Yehudah Aḥarei Milḥemet Bar-*

Kochva ve-Ad ha-Kibush ha-Aravi (Jerusalem, 1986), p. 187. On the Jewish community in Jerusalem at that time see pp. 183–91.

9. The feeling among scholars today is that most of the urban settlement of Aelia Capitolina was located in the northern areas of the present Old City of Jerusalem in what is today called the Christian and Moslem Quarters. Only the Tenth Legion was encamped in the southern part of the city. See Bahat, *Atlas Karta,* p. 52, and contra Tsafrir, *Ereẓ-Yisrael,* p. 60.

10. A. Segal, *EHHA,* vol. 1, p. 375. Cf. Roth-Garson, *Ha-Ketovot,* pp. 46–50, and Naveh, *Al Psifas,* p. 86, n. 50.

11. Y. Hirschfeld, *EHHA,* vol. 2, p. 566. It makes no difference to our study whether the synagogue is dated to the sixth or the seventh century C.E.

12. Z. Weiss, *EHHA,* vol. 4, pp. 1335. A synagogue has been found in the northern section of Sepphoris with numerous dedication inscriptions and magnificent mosaic floors. Unfortunately this synagogue too dates to the Byzantine period. See Z. Weiss and E. Netzer, "The Hebrew University Excavations at Sepphoris," *Qadmoniot* 30 (1997): 15–21. Cf. Roth-Garson, *Ha-Ketovot,* pp. 105–9, particularly on the use of titles in the Greek inscription, and Naveh, *Psifas,* p. 51–52, n. 29.

13. See S. Lieberman, *Tosefta Ki-fshuṭah,* vol. 3 (New York, 1962), pp. 386–87 and the sources cited there regarding the halachic-municipal relationship between Tiberias and Ḥamat.

14. For a convenient summary see Z. Weiss, "Batei Kenesset 'Atiqim be-Teveriah u-be-Ḥamat," in *Tiveriah me-Yisudah ve-ad ha-Kibush ha-Muslemi,* ed. Y. Hirschfeld (Jerusalem, 1988), pp. 34–48 and the bibliography cited ad loc., and M. Dothan, *EHHA,* vol. 2, pp. 514–19 and the bibliography cited ad loc.

15. The "Seat of Moses" (*Cathedra de-Moshe*) was a special seat usually for the head of the community. The menorah may have been placed near or on the side of the ark. It is not known whether it was purely decorative or served some other function. See the bibliography cited above regarding other sites in which similar remains have been discovered.

16. See the literature cited above in note 13 and in particular see M. Dothan, *Hammath Tiberias—Early Synagogues and the Hellenistic and Roman Remains, Final Excavation Report 1* (Jerusalem, 1983).

17. On the view that this synagogue was entered from the east, see Weiss, "Batei Kenesset," pp. 41–42 and the bibliography cited there.

18. See the literature cited in nn. 13, 16. On some of the problems inherent to these synagogue motifs, see N. Avigad, "Jewish Figurative Art, A Historical Review," chapter 7 in *Beth She'arim: Report on the Excavations during 1953–1958, III, Catacombs 12–23* (New Brunswick, 1976), pp. 275–87 and the literature cited ad loc.

19. See the discussion and bibliography of Roth-Garson, *Ha-Ketovot,* pp. 65–75.

20. Thus, for example, it is hard to know whether the inscribed synagogue column from Beit Guvrin came from a Roman- or Byzantine-period synagogue. See Schwartz, *Ha-Yishuv ha-Yehudi,* p. 88. The synagogue remains from Beit Shean seem to be Byzantine. See G. Foerster, *EHHA,* vol. 1, pp. 220–21.

21. See Schwartz, *Ha-Yishuv ha-Yehudi,* p. 138. The synagogue at Ashdod is also late (*Ha-Yishuv ha-Yehudi,* p. 145).

22. See Roth-Garson, *Ha-Ketovot,* pp. 91–104.

Index of Place Names

Abella. *See* Abila.
Abila, 136, 151, 155, 178, 188
Aelia Capitalina. *See* Jerusalem.
Aesernia, 16
Ailat. *See* Eilath.
Akko, 28, 67, 72, 78, 117, 165, 171, 175, 177, 179, 178, 185
Amastris (Bythnia), 141
Antipatris, 159, 160, 162, 169, 177, 179, 180, 182, 184, 186, 187
Apollonia, 175
A-Ramah, 183
Armon Ha-Naziv, 128
Ashdod, 117, 150, 154
Ashkalon. *See* Ashkelon.
Ashkelon, 23, 76, 78, 95, 100, 115, 117, 121, 123, 154, 159, 175, 178, 179, 180, 181, 183, 187, 193
Ascalon, Askelon. *See* Ashkelon.
Aspendos, 134
Azotus Paralius. *See* Ashdod.

Babylonia, 41, 42, 43, 44, 135
Baithos, 55
Banias, 100, 159, 162, 163, 182, 183, 187, 188, 189
Beirut, 95
Beit Guvrin, 101, 117, 154, 174, 179, 194
Beit Ilonim, 30
Beit Shean, 10, 20, 23, 24, 25, 30, 58, 72, 78, 79, 80, 82, 83, 88, 96, 97, 99, 100, 101, 111, 115, 116, 117, 121, 150, 159, 160, 161, 162, 163, 168, 169, 176, 177, 178, 180, 182, 185, 186, 187, 188, 189, 194
Beit Shearim, 102, 161
Bethsaida, 188, 189
Beth Shean, Beth Shean. *See* Beit Shean.
Bostra, 79, 80, 82, 85, 99, 101, 111, 181
Britain, 101, 123

Butna, 28
Bythnia, 14

Caesarea, 3, 69, 49, 50, 51, 65, 78, 79, 80, 84, 85, 87, 96, 99, 100, 101, 102, 119, 122, 123, 125, 126, 127, 132, 133, 135, 142, 143, 144, 153, 155, 160, 166, 171, 173, 175, 180, 181, 182, 185, 188, 189, 191, 193
Canatha, 79, 95
Casae, 26
Castella, 143
Cologne, 141
Corinth, 6
Coriovalum, 64

Damascus, 100
Decapolis, 97, 179
Diospolis. *See* Lod.
Dor, 157, 159, 163, 165, 168, 171, 175, 177, 188, 189

Egypt, 37, 38, 95
Eilat(h), 30, 131, 143
Elusa, 55
Elutheropolis, 78
Emmaus, 117, 177
Ephesus, 137
Eẓion Gever, 143

Fanum, 73
Florence, 109

Gadara, 78, 80, 94, 97, 121, 151, 178, 180, 183, 187
Gedera. *See* Gadara.
Gaul, 103
Gaza, 28, 78, 95, 99, 100, 117, 133, 146, 188, 193
Geder, 76

Gerasa, 23, 78, 79, 80, 81, 82, 85, 86, 95, 96, 97, 100, 101, 125, 134, 150, 151, 154, 159, 162, 164, 165, 168, 177, 178, 180, 191

Ḥaluẓa, 97
Ḥamat (Hammat) Gader, 82, 94, 134, 135, 142, 144, 183, 184, 194
Ḥamat Tiberias, 165, 175, 192, 194
Ḥebron, 30
Heerben, 64
Herculaneum, 24, 67, 71, 72, 143
Herodion, 126
Hippos (Hippus). *See* Susita.

Jabneh, Jamnia. *See* Yavne.
Jerash. *See* Gerasa.
Jericho, 78, 79, 85, 113, 128, 163
Jerusalem, 78, 79, 85, 96, 109, 115, 121, 123, 128, 134, 142, 146, 148, 151, 152, 154, 155, 159, 161, 166, 177, 179, 191, 194

Khorazim, 21, 112

Lod, 3, 6, 9, 20, 52, 154
Lydda. *See* Lod.

Madaba. *See* Medva.
Maiumas Gaza, 171, 193
Mamshit—Kurnub, 122
Medeba. *See* Medva.
Medva, 117, 123, 154, 180
Miletos, 134
Mt. Bernike, 124, 125, 155

Nablus. *See* Neapolis.
Naḥal Amal, 150, 159
Naḥal Ḥarod, 150
Naḥal Taninim, 135
Neapolis (=Shechem), 79, 80, 97, 99, 100, 101, 102, 117, 123, 151, 154, 163, 164, 168, 178
Nicomedia, 14
Nîmes, 145

Olympia, 99
Ostia, 6, 22, 53, 55, 115, 146, 147

Palmyra, 42, 46
Paneas, Panias. *See* Banias.
Pella, 159, 165, 178, 182
Petra, 103
Philadelphia, 78, 80, 82, 100, 101, 150, 154, 156, 158, 178
Philonopolis, 80, 82, 181

Pompeii, 16, 18, 22, 23, 32, 37, 56, 60, 61, 64, 68, 69, 73, 76, 92, 93, 94, 109, 110, 111, 115, 140, 143
Ptolomais. *See* Akko.

Reḥov, 71, 143
Rome, 3, 6, 10, 11, 12, 13, 16, 22, 23, 25, 26, 48, 86, 96, 102, 105, 108, 113, 115, 139, 141, 146, 147

Sachuta, 66, 71
Scythopolis. *See* Beit Shean.
Sebaste, 76, 82, 85, 151, 154, 155, 158, 159, 161, 163, 168, 169, 177, 181, 183
Sebatiya. *See* Sabaste.
Sepphoris, 3, 6, 20, 21, 23, 25, 60, 76, 77, 81, 82, 94, 136, 139, 146, 157, 166, 167, 168, 177, 178, 179, 188, 191, 192
Shiḥin, 13, 72
Shittim, 15
Shiqmona, 20
Shivta, 114, 126
Sidon, 134
Silcester, 101
Smyrna, 108, 115
Straton's Tower. *See* Caesarea.
Susia, 101, 103
Susita, 142, 144, 151, 155, 177, 178, 179, 186, 188
Syria, 101, 103

Tarichaeae, 78
Tel al-Ajjul, 147
Tel Aviv, 109
Tel Dor. *See* Dor.
Tel Istaba, 150, 182
Terebinthos, 30
Thamugadi. *See* Tingad.
Tiberias, 11, 12, 16, 20, 23, 24, 28, 46, 49, 54, 58, 63, 70, 75, 76, 108, 117, 118, 119, 120, 121, 123, 124, 125, 132, 136, 137, 1'42, 143, 154, 155, 156, 160, 168, 175, 177, 181, 188, 189, 191
Tingad, 147, 150
Tripoli (Lebanon), 136
Tyre, 28

Um Riham, 7, 19, 111
Um el Rasas, 123

Wadi Amman, 150
Wadi Kelt, 128, 178

Yavneel, 179
Yavneh, 131, 154, 175, 185

General Index

Acropolis, 155, 156, 158, 168
Aedile, 132
Agardemis, 132. See *Agoranomos*.
Agonothetes, 87–88, 96, 99
Agora, 158
Agoranomia, 38, 46
Agaranomos, 19, 27, 29, 32–47
Agrami, 38, 46
Agrippa, 95, 132, 134
Alley. *See* Streets.
Altar, 162, 163
Amara, 138, 147
Amphitheatre, 78, 79, 89–91, 95, 97, 101–102, 127, 152, 166, 169–70, 185
Angareia, 52
Annointing, 58–63, 184
Aphrodite, 67
Apodysterium, 59–60, 165
Apuleius, 18
Aqueducts, 132–33, 141–44, 146, 147, 177–78, 186
Arcade, 67
Arche, 76–79, 84
Archive, 76–77
Arena, 90, 94
Astynomi, 38, 39, 47
Ateles, 28
Athletics. *See* Sports.
Atrium, 148
Attics, 13
Ausonius, 62, 70
Awnings, 13
Axles, 115

Baal ha-shuk, 34, 37, 39, 42, 46
Bakers, 36, 37
Balconies, 108, 115
Balneator, 60
Basilica, 73–76, 80, 92, 93, 158–61, 171
Basket work, 11
Bathhouses, 3, 58–73, 80, 89, 125, 145, 165, 181–84, 189, 192
Bathra, 15, 109, 116
Beggars, 62
Boule, 111
Bouleuterion, 97, 158, 159
Bread, 36
Breakwater, 172, 175
Brothels, 15, 25, 183
Burgos, 125, 127

Calderium, 60, 65, 67, 165, 183
Capitals of columns, 21
Caravans, 17, 19
Carcares, 86, 94
Cardo, 151, 158, 161, 165, 169, 180, 186
Castellium, 130–32
Cataracts, 135–36
Cauponae, 16
Cavea, 82, 83, 85, 90, 97
Cella, 77
Cemeteries, 52, 56, 152
Cenacula, 137
Centonarii, 23
Ceramics, 72
Chariot, 89
Circuses, 78, 98, 127
Cisterns, 140
City council, 95, 97, 111
Clipeus, 67, 68
Cloaca, 137–39
Coins, 162
Caloacarius, 139–140
Collegia, 11–12, 21
Colliquia, 138
Colluviaria, 131
Colonnades, 11, 13, 20, 32, 188
Columnae, 21
Columns, 21
Confectionary store, 20

Council house, 73, 94
Court tribunal, 75, 76
Curia, 158
Custodia, 77

Decumanus, 151, 158, 168, 179, 180
Defense, 117–19, 151–57
Destrictarium, 69
Diatagna, 18, 25
Diatreta, 12
Digesta, 17, 26
Domitian, 182
Doors, 107–108, 114
Doorsteps, 107–108
Drainage. *See* Sewage.
Dromos, 12
Drunkenness, 51–53

Eating places, 30
Eirenarches, 55
Emporium, 15
Entertainments, 77–91, 94–102, 127, 164–65, 183
Epigrams, 12
Epikarsion 59
Ergastulum, 94
Euripus, 86

Fairs, 24, 31
Fasces, 18
Fascia, 15
"Fences" (of stolen goods), 50
Fire brigades, lack of, 13–14, 23
Fire, danger of, 13, 14, 22, 23
Fish shops, 18, 55
Flax traders, 11
Forica, 147
Fortification systems. *See* Walls.
Fortress, 155, 157
Forum, 9, 19, 58, 73, 76, 82, 158–59, 162, 181, 182, 189
Fountains, 23, 133–35, 199, 140, 142, 177
Friday which is not Friday, 29
Frigidarium, 60, 71, 165
Frontinus, 142

Gambling areas, 16
Gardens, 67, 113
Gatekeeper, 125
Gateways, 120, 121, 125, 154, 155, 181
Gladiators, 79, 89, 91, 96, 99–100, 102, 169
Glass vendors, 12
Gradum, 75
Granaries, 23, 32, 76
Guilds, 11, 12, 17, 21, 41–42, 56, 108

Ḥamarin, 52, 56
Ḥanut, 52
Ḥarbors, 73, 171, 176, 185
Ḥashban, 36, 37, 39, 42, 45
Ḥawkers, 21

Ḥenvani, 52
Ḥerod, 78, 89, 90, 96, 99, 102, 154, 168, 172, 181, 183,
Hippodrome, 78, 79, 85–89, 95, 98, 166, 170, 185
Hoarding, 35, 44
Horophylakeis, 55
Horea, 32
Hotels, 51, 53, 55
Hypocaustum, 67, 68

Idolatry, 15, 16, 133–34, 144
Import license, 39
Inns, 16, 17, 30
Insula, 107
Industry, 108, 152, 170–71, 185
Inscriptions, 118–19, 124, 126, 191–92, 193, 194
Itliz, 28

Josephus, 78, 90, 154, 163
Jugglers, 83

Kalendae, 27
Kaminion, 67
Kapeleion, 52, 56, 149
Kebar bread, 36, 37, 45
Koilia, 129
Kore, 169

Laconicum, 67, 68
Latrines, 137–38, 146–47
Leg irons, 94
Leges Sumptuarie, 49
Licensing laws, 49–50
Lighthouses, 92
Lighting, 13, 105, 113
Limen Inferium, 107
Linear systems, 103–104
Lintea, 60, 71
Litters, 113
Logistes, 33–34, 36, 37, 39, 42, 45
Loper, 51, 56
Low-life area, 12
Lucius Calidus Eroticus, 17

Macellum, 15, 24
Manipulation of prices, 44
Maps, 4
Markets, 3, 9–47, 58, 73, 80, 115, 158, 161, 165
Massage, 62, 63, 66, 72
Measuring systems, 103–104, 112
Meches, 28
Media Porticus, 75
Mesostulon, 75
Mikveh, 131
Millers, 37
Mime, 84, 98
Mithraeum, 182
Mondays and Thursdays, 27, 29

Money-changer, 27
Mosaics, 188, 191–92, 194
Muḥtasib, 45, 49
Muleteers, 52, 56
Multistory buildings, 10, 11, 13, 20, 23

Notice boards, 18
Nuktostratogoi, 50, 54–55
Nymphaeum, 133–35, 178–79, 186

Odeion, Odeon, 79, 82, 95, 97, 169
Officium, 27
Oiling. *See* Annointing.
Olearius, 62, 69
Opsonion, 42, 43
Orchestra, 82, 83, 97, 166

Pagan festivals, 27, 30
Palatium, 140
Palter, 36
Pandokeion, 17, 55, 56
Paneguris Ateles, 28
Pankration, 88, 89
Pantokokos, 84
Parables, 42–43
Pausanius, 142
Paving, 20, 106–107, 110, 177
Peddlers, 21, 22
Pegma, 127
Pentathlon, 89
Peor, 15
Persona, 144
Phortegoi, 15
Phulake, 55, 77
Pier, 175
Pilki, 55
Piping, 128–38, 177, 179
Platea, 9, 11, 21, 22, 25, 36, 104, 125
Pliny, 14
Podium, 83, 90, 97, 162–63
Police, 13–14, 50–52, 54–55
Polycarp, 14
Porters, 15, 104–105, 108, 109, 116
Potters, 11, 24
Praefectus Vigilum, 13
Praetor, 77
Praetorium, 140
Price control, 34–35, 43, 44
Prisons, 55, 73, 77, 94, 149
Prosodos, 106
Prostitutes, 15, 16, 17
Publication of edicts, 18, 25
Pubs, 3, 15, 48–57
Pule, 120
Pulophulax, 125

Quays, 171, 185
Quttus, 69

Ramparts, 121–22
Rav Shuk, 42, 46
Refuse, 9, 10
Resh Korei, 41
Roads. *See* Streets.
Road breadths, 22
Robbery, 18, 25
Roofs, 13, 22, 113
Rufilus, 56
Ruts in streets, 20, 106, 107, 108, 113, 114

Saccarrii, 15
Sacculum, 15
Saltuarii, 50, 54
Sandals, 113
Santer, 50, 54
Saturnalia, 27
Scaena, 82, 84, 166, 168
Seat of Moses, 194
Security, 117–19, 151–57
Semita, 21, 104
Sewage, 136–42, 147–48, 177, 179, 186–87
Shops, 15, 18, 19, 20, 21, 22, 24, 35, 46, 158, 161, 182, 186, 189
Shutters, 21
Sitonae, 36, 41–45
Solen, 145
Sports, 87–89, 98, 99, 100, 101
Stadium, 85–89, 93–95, 100, 126, 127, 169
Stalls, 12
Statuary, 67, 147
Stepping stones, 108, 110
Stoa, 11, 12, 20, 21, 30, 73, 75, 112, 158
Storage areas, 13
Stores. *See* Shops.
Storehouses. *See* Warehouses.
Strata, 21, 25, 91, 103, 106, 107
Strateion, 12
Street criers, 22
Street lighting, 13, 22
Streets, 3, 7, 10, 13, 20, 23, 46, 103–16, 125, 161, 162, 170, 176–77, 182, 186, 188
Strigil, 60, 61, 63, 69
Strosis, 107, 114
Suburbs, 153
Sudatio, 62, 68
Sudatorium, 62, 165
Swindling, 18, 25, 35, 56
Synagogues, 91–92, 190–94

Tabernae, 24
Taverns, 15, 16, 17, 24, 51, 53, 54, 56, 179, 183
Taxes, 28, 30, 110–11, 116, 122
Temples, 76, 114, 162, 163, 182
Tepidarium, 60, 62, 165
Tessarae, 60, 63
Tetrapylon, 125–26, 145, 162
Thalame, 130–31
Theater, 73, 76, 78, 79–85, 93, 95, 97, 98, 142, 166–69, 184, 189

Thermosarius, 69
Thresholds, 107, 114
Toilets. *See* Latrines.
Town planning, 6
Towers, 121, 154–55
Traffic, 9, 104–106
Transport, 105, 108, 113
Trapezites, 27
Treasury, 73
Triclinium, 148

Unctores, 60, 62, 69
Unctorium, 60, 165
Upper stories, 10–11, 13, 20, 122, 161
Urban planning, 150–51, 161, 176, 180
Urban security, 151–57

Venter, 131
Via Secundaria, 103
Vigiles, 13, 23
Villages, 7, 19
Vitruvius, 128, 132
Vomitoria, 82, 83, 85

Walls, 117–27, 151–57, 181
Warehouses, 172, 175, 185
Water, 11, 12, 15, 22, 23, 93–94, 128–48, 177–79, 186
Weights and measures, 32, 33, 40
Wheels, 115
Wine, 15, 24, 35–36, 48–49, 51–53, 56
Wrestling, 88, 98, 100